# Risk Inequality and Welfare States

The transformation of night-watchman states into welfare states is one of the most notable societal developments in recent history. In 1880, not a single country had a nationally compulsory social policy program. A few decades later, every single one of today's rich democracies had adopted programs covering all or almost all of the main risks people face: old age, sickness, accident, and unemployment. These programs rapidly expanded in terms of range, reach, and resources. Today, all rich democracies cover all main risks for a vast majority of citizens with binding public or mandatory private programs. Three aspects of this remarkable transformation are particularly fascinating: the trend (the transformation to insurance states happened in all rich democracies); differences across countries (the generosity of social policy varies greatly across countries); and the dynamics of the process. This book offers a theory that not only explains this remarkable transition but also explains cross-national differences and the role of crises for social policy development.

Since receiving his master's degree in Germany and his PhD from Duke University, Philipp Rehm has worked at Oxford University, the European University Institute, and Ohio State University. His work on risk and welfare states is published in leading journals, such as the *American Political Science Review* and *World Politics*.

# Cambridge Studies in Comparative Politics

## General Editors

Kathleen Thelen   *Massachusetts Institute of Technology*
Erik Wibbels   *Duke University*

## Associate Editors

Robert H. Bates   *Harvard University*
Gary Cox   *Stanford University*
Thad Dunning   *University of California, Berkeley*
Anna Grzymala-Busse   *University of Michigan, Ann Arbor*
Stephen Hanson   *The College of William and Mary*
Torben Iversen   *Harvard University*
Stathis Kalyvas   *Yale University*
Margaret Levi   *Stanford University*
Peter Lange   *Duke University*
Helen Milner   *Princeton University*
Frances Rosenbluth   *Yale University*
Susan Stokes   *Yale University*

## Other Books in the Series

(*continued after index*)

# Risk Inequality and Welfare States

## Social Policy Preferences, Development, and Dynamics

PHILIPP REHM

*Ohio State University*

CAMBRIDGE
UNIVERSITY PRESS

# CAMBRIDGE
## UNIVERSITY PRESS

32 Avenue of the Americas, New York NY 10013–2473, USA

Cambridge University Press is part of the University of Cambridge.

It furthers the University's mission by disseminating knowledge in the pursuit of education, learning, and research at the highest international levels of excellence.

www.cambridge.org
Information on this title: www.cambridge.org/9781107518872

First published 2016

Printed in the United Kingdom by Clays, St Ives plc

A catalog record for this publication is available from the British Library.

Library of Congress Cataloging in Publication Data
Names: Rehm, Philipp Benjamin, author.
Risk inequality and welfare states : social policy preferences, development, and dynamics / Philipp Rehm.
New York NY : Cambridge University Press, 2017. | Includes bibliographical references and index.
LCCN 2015051002 | ISBN 9781107108165 (Hardback)
LCSH: Social policy. | Equality. | Welfare state.
LCC HN18.3 .R445 2017 | DDC 306–dc23 LC record available at http://lccn.loc.gov/2015051002

ISBN 978-1-107-10816-5 Hardback
ISBN 978-1-107-51887-2 Paperback

*For Lea and Inés*

# Contents

# Contents

# Figures

# Tables

# Acknowledgments

Many individuals and institutions have supported my work on this book, and I am very grateful for their help. I would like to thank the Ohio State University, the Mershon Center, the European University Institute, Yale's Institution for Social and Policy Studies, and the Rockefeller Foundation for institutional and/or financial support.

Many of my current and former students and colleagues at the Ohio State University provided comments on this project, including Sarah Brooks, Agnar Helgason, Marcus Kurtz, William Minozzi, Vittorio Merola, Tony Mughan, Irfan Nooruddin, Jeremy Wallace, Sara Watson, and Wei-Ting Yen. I appreciate their feedback. Over the years, I have also received helpful advice on the project from many scholars, including Ben Ansell, Stuart Craig, Pepper Culpepper, Ray Duch, Silja Häusermann, Achim Kemmerling, Philip Manow, Yotam Margolit, Kai Muehleck, Austin Nichols, Alexander Petring, Georg Picot, Jonas Pontusson, Ken Scheve, Hanna Schwander, Alex Street, Erik Wibbels, and Anne Wren. I am thankful for their input. I am also grateful to Lewis Bateman at Cambridge University Press and the anonymous readers of this manuscript. Johannes Lindvall, Lyle Scruggs, and Daniel Ziblatt were kind enough to share data with me.

I was very fortunate to receive continuous help and encouragement from Pablo Beramendi, Jacob Hacker, Torben Iversen, Herbert Kitschelt, David Rueda, Mark Schlesinger, and David Soskice. I am deeply grateful for their friendship and guidance throughout this project. Parts of this manuscript are derived from co-authored work with Jacob Hacker, Torben Iversen, and Mark Schlesinger. This manuscript owes much to them and their inspiring scholarship, but all errors are my responsibility. I am particularly indebted to Herbert, Jacob, and Torben – their close mentorship throughout the years has been wonderful.

I dedicate this book to my wife, Inés, and our daughter, Lea. They mean the world to me.

# Introduction

Nothing can be said to be certain except death and taxes.
— Benjamin Franklin

The transformation of night-watchman states into insurance states is one of the most notable societal developments in recent history. In 1880, not a single country had a nationally compulsory social policy program. A few decades later, every single one of today's rich democracies had adopted programs covering all or almost all of the main risks people face: old age, sickness, accident, and unemployment. These programs rapidly expanded in terms of range (number and types of risks covered), reach (number of people covered), and resources (money spent). Today, all rich democracies cover all main risks for a vast majority of citizens with binding public or mandatory private programs. Three main aspects of this transformation are particularly fascinating: the trend (the transformation to insurance states happened in all rich democracies), differences across countries (the generosity of social policy varies greatly across countries), and the dynamics of the process.

Concerning the *trend*, Figure 1.1 shows the development of social policy in terms of range, reach, and resources. What explains this meteoric rise in all the rich democracies? How can we understand their fundamental transformation from night-watchman states into insurance states? Regarding *differences* across countries, Figure 1.2 presents two measures of welfare state generosity: total social expenditure as a percentage of GDP and the average percentage of benefits in case of unemployment (replacement rates). Why does Sweden spend almost twice as much

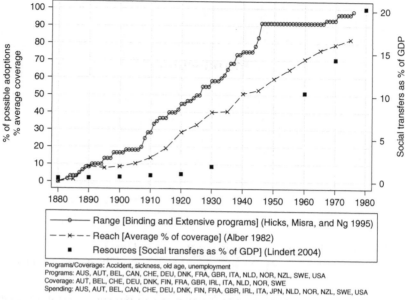

FIGURE I.I: Welfare state expansion.

*Note*: Ghent unemployment programs are coded as binding (Hicks 1999, 53)

of its national wealth on social policy as the United States? Why is the
benefit for an unemployed worker in Switzerland almost 80 percent of her
previous wage, while it is less than 50 percent in Ireland? Why does
welfare state generosity vary across countries? With respect to *dynamics*,
why and when did social policy emerge? What conditions led to
expansion? What conditions led to retrenchment? What explains the
timing of social policy milestones?

### EXISTING APPROACHES

The large welfare state literature offers a variety of explanations for social
policy provision in general, and the questions of trend, differences, and
dynamics in particular.[1] Let me distinguish three broad approaches to

---

[1] Numerous detailed reviews exist (Cousins 2005; Myles and Quadagno 2002; Quadagno
1987; Van Kersbergen and Becker 2002; Van Kersbergen and Manow 2008). It is
important to keep in mind that different explanations have been developed at different
times to explain different phenomena, and different perspectives are not necessarily
mutually exclusive. It is therefore not surprising that some accounts of social policy are

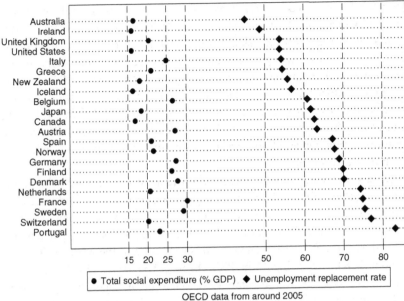

FIGURE I.2: Welfare state divergence.

*Source:* OECD (http:/dx.doi.org/10.1787/182506528237)

making sense of the enormous scale and cross-national diversity of social insurance provision: functionalist, antagonistic, and cross-class approaches.[2]

*Functionalist approaches* understand social policy development largely as a response to changing societal conditions. One example is the "logic of industrialism" argument (Rimlinger 1971), where the disappearance of traditional welfare provision by the family and the emergence of

more successful at explaining some facts, while they are less so at explaining others. Lumping together the dazzling variety of existing explanations into a few "approaches" does injustice to any specific account. But identifying broad commonalities of different existing explanations even at the expense of caricaturizing them is still useful for focusing on their strengths and weaknesses.

[2] Readers may wonder why (historical) institutional accounts are absent from the following categorization of approaches. This is for two reasons. First, institutionalist arguments are typically complementary to the main theories of welfare state politics. Second, many institutionalist – especially historical institutionalist – arguments have little ambition with respect to explaining general developments; rather, they are interested in understanding specific historical instances.

industrial capitalism created new risks – such as industrial accidents, unemployment, or lack of income due to sickness or old age – and demands to address these risks. Another example is the "logic of modernization" argument, which understands welfare states as a response to the economic and social disorder that modernization created (Alber 1982; Flora and Alber 1981).[3] The main strength of functionalist approaches is their ability to account for common trends. But they fail at explaining deviations from the trend line. If welfare states are a reaction to the common experience of industrialization and modernization, why are welfare states so different?

*Antagonistic approaches*, which are the most prominent in the literature, highlight the redistributive aspect of social policy and focus on different societal groups with antagonistic social policy goals, such as labor versus capital, or poor versus rich. Two theories are particularly prominent: the Power Resources Theory (PRT) and the Meltzer–Richard model (MR). According to the PRT (Esping-Andersen 1985; Korpi 1983; Stephens 1979), the welfare state is the outcome of a class struggle: where labor was strong (strong social democratic parties and/or strong unions), welfare states expanded rapidly. According to the MR model, redistribution is to be expected in democracies, because the poor outnumber the rich (Meltzer and Richard 1981). More precisely, the MR model predicts a positive relationship between income inequality and redistribution: more unequal societies will redistribute more. The main strength of antagonistic approaches is their ability to account for dynamics: social policy changes if the balance of power between antagonistic groups in a society shifts. They are less successful in making sense of the breathtaking expansion of social insurance. If social policy is so contested, why is it so common? And why does the weaker side always win?[4] Some versions of the antagonistic approach also have difficulties explaining cross-national variation. In fact, the key theoretical insight of the MR model – that welfare states will be larger in more unequal societies – is not well supported by the data. This puzzling non-finding is called the "Robin-Hood paradox" (Lind 2005; Lindert 2004; Pecoraro 2014).

---

[3] Another functionalist explanation is the "logic of economic growth" (Wilensky 1975), or Wagner's law: the richer countries become, the more social policy they will provide. De Swaan's work probably also can be interpreted as a functionalist account (Swaan 1988).
[4] Power Resources Theory also has little to say about *why* the left becomes dominant in some countries. For an exception see Pontusson (1990).

*Cross-class approaches* analyze welfare states from an insurance perspective (Dryzek and Goodin 1986; Ewald 1993). From this point of view, social insurance is not zero-sum and can garner support not only from the poor, or workers (as in antagonistic approaches), but also from other (risk) groups within a society. Different authors have highlighted different ways in which countries end up with generous social policies, but they share the assumption that groups exposed to risks turn to the state for security. These may be employers that benefit from socializing risk (Mares 2003; Swenson 2002), individuals or firms that want generous social policies in order to encourage investment in specific skills (Estevez-Abé, Iversen, and Soskice 2001; Iversen 2005; Iversen and Soskice 2001), or groups that are particularly vulnerable to the vagaries of markets because of their country's insertion into international markets (Cameron 1978; Katzenstein 1985; Rodrik 1998) due to globalization (Garrett 1998) or deindustrialization (Iversen 2001; Iversen and Cusack 2000). The main strength of cross-class approaches is their ability to explain cross-national differences – perhaps not surprisingly, because they emerged as a reaction to antagonistic approaches. But they have little to offer in terms of dynamics, especially accounts based on the Varieties of Capitalism scholarship. If social policy is part of a complex system of institutions in equilibrium, why does it change? And why do all rich democracies – even those with economies that heavily rely on general (not specific) skills – boast social insurance systems that cover all main risks?

## OPEN QUESTIONS

Existing accounts clearly help us understand many important aspects of welfare state politics. But they are less successful in accounting for others. First, the *universality* of social insurance goes hand in hand with its enormous popularity. In all rich democracies today, the vast majority of citizens – including many rich citizens – largely agrees that governments have the responsibility to insure the main risks citizens face. Table 1.1 shows that across the 20 or so rich democracies for which data are available, the typical (median) percentage of respondents who reply it "definitely should be" or "probably should be" the government's responsibility to engage in social policy is as follows: (i) Provide a decent standard of living for the old: 96.1 percent; (ii) Provide health care for sick: 98 percent; (iii) Provide a decent standard of living for unemployed: 67.8 percent; (iv) Reduce income differences between rich and poor: 69.9

TABLE 1.1: *Popularity of social policy*

| | Percentage of respondents who reply it "definitely should be" or "probably should be" the government's responsibility to … | | | | |
| --- | --- | --- | --- | --- | --- |
| | Provide decent standard of living for the old | Provide health care for sick | Provide decent standard of living for unemployed | Provide decent housing for those who can't afford it | Reduce income differences between rich and poor |
| Portugal (PRT) | 98.7 | 98.7 | 91.9 | 94.8 | 93.5 |
| Spain (ESP) | 99.5 | 97.7 | 92.8 | 95.8 | 86.3 |
| Ireland (IRL) | 99.6 | 99.6 | 79.6 | 96.2 | 79.1 |
| France (FRA) | 92.6 | 92.0 | 67.8 | 86.0 | 78.0 |
| Finland (FIN) | 96.7 | 98.9 | 85.3 | 86.9 | 77.0 |
| Italy (ITA) | 98.0 | 98.7 | 75.7 | 88.3 | 75.6 |
| Norway (NOR) | 98.6 | 99.2 | 88.5 | 81.5 | 74.1 |
| Netherlands (NLD) | 96.0 | 99.1 | 66.8 | 82.2 | 71.8 |
| Switzerland (CHE) | 89.9 | 88.4 | 67.1 | 64.0 | 70.3 |
| Germany (DEU) | 94.0 | 95.9 | 69.1 | 75.8 | 69.9 |
| Sweden (SWE) | 97.0 | 93.6 | 83.4 | 79.4 | 67.7 |
| United Kingdom (GBR) | 97.2 | 98.8 | 54.8 | 85.7 | 67.4 |
| Canada (CAN) | 95.4 | 96.3 | 61.7 | 83.3 | 66.3 |
| Japan (JPN) | 88.5 | 86.8 | 56.5 | 37.9 | 66.0 |
| Australia (AUS) | 94.9 | 98.4 | 57.3 | 79.9 | 60.6 |
| Denmark (DNK) | 97.5 | 99.1 | 80.8 | 82.3 | 55.3 |
| Austria (AUT) | 96.1 | 93.3 | 59.0 | | 53.8 |
| United States (USA) | 90.2 | 90.7 | 50.9 | 75.6 | 51.1 |
| New Zealand (NZL) | 95.3 | 98.0 | 49.2 | 71.5 | 50.2 |
| Range | 88.5–99.6 | 86.8–99.6 | 49.2–92.8 | 37.9–96.2 | 50.2–93.5 |
| Average | 96.1 | 98 | 67.8 | 82.2 | 69.9 |

*Note:* Question wording: On the whole, do you think it should or should not be the government's responsibility to … .
*Source:* Based on ISSP 2006 (ISSP 1996 for Italy, ISSP 1985 for Austria).

percent.[5] Why is social insurance so popular? Why is the basis of social policies often "highly consensual" (Swaan 1988, 225)? The universality of welfare state expansion and the popularity of social insurance are difficult to square with existing theories of social policy development.

Second, what is the role of popular support for social policy? While it is enormously popular, support for social policy varies greatly across countries. Moreover, there is a noticeably close correlation between demand for social policy and its supply (Brooks and Manza 2007). This suggests that popular support can potentially account for the *diversity* of social policy generosity. But what drives the popularity of the welfare state? Existing literature has little to say on the topic.

Third, most theories in the social sciences are better at explaining equilibrium outcomes rather than dynamic processes, and theories of social policy development are no exception.[6] One aspect of social policy *dynamics* is particularly poorly understood: the role of economic and societal crises in the development of the welfare state. In some cases, crises have played an instrumental part in social policy emergence and expansion – the impact of the Great Depression on the Social Security Act is a good example. But in other cases, crises have led to welfare state backlash and retrenchment. Why? Existing explanations have little, if anything, to say about the role of crises in social policy development.

## THE ARGUMENT

In this book, I develop a theoretical perspective centered on risk that speaks to these omitted or poorly understood topics.[7] I offer a theoretical framework that rests on micro-level foundations which are empirically

---

[5] These numbers are based on ISSP 2006 (ISSP 1996 for Italy, ISSP 1985 for Austria). Countries are AUS, AUT, CAN, CHE, DEU, DNK, ESP, FIN, FRA, GBR, IRL, ITA, JPN, NLD, NOR, NZL, PRT, SWE, and USA. The question's wording is "On the whole, do you think it should or should not be the government's responsibility to . . . ." See Table 1.1 for country-specific results.

[6] Explaining dynamic processes is a particular challenge for institutional theories (Thelen 2010).

[7] For now, risk is the actual or perceived probability of experiencing a bad event that can be covered by social insurance. In recent years, risk has played an increasingly important role in the welfare state literature. See, for example: Anderson and Pontusson 2007; Baldwin 1990; Brooks 2009; Dryzek and Goodin 1986; Ewald 1991; Goodin 1990; Hacker 2008; Iversen 2005; Iversen and Soskice 2001; Mares 2003; Mughan 2007; Mughan, Bean, and McAllister 2003; Mughan and Lacy 2002; Rueda 2007; Scheve and Slaughter 2001; Swenson 2002.

plausible. In particular, I derive and show that an individual's relative position in the risk distribution is a powerful predictor of his or her social policy preferences. Because risk and risk perceptions are critical correlates of social policy preferences, and because most citizens are risk-averse, social insurance enjoys broad support. In my framework, risk is the critical factor at the micro-level. Consequently, the distribution of risk – the *risk pool* or *risk inequality* – is crucial for understanding macro-level outcomes. I suggest that three aspects of risk distributions are important for understanding social policy dynamics and outcomes.

First, the *average level* of risk indicates how common a problem is – not all risks lead to social questions. But, historically, some risks became prevalent enough to put social insurance firmly on the agenda. For example, industrial accidents and unemployment are concepts that make little sense in agricultural societies, but they became social problems in industrializing societies. Likewise, the processes of modernization and urbanization led to the erosion of traditional family structures, which undermined family solutions for managing the risks of old age and sickness, turning these risks into social ones. These developments fueled the expansion of the social policy agenda: because citizens seek security – they are risk-averse – they look for ways to insure their risks. Early attempts to find private solutions were not viable (Swaan 1988), and eventually large numbers of citizens turned to their governments for solutions. Sooner or later governments reacted to the social questions generated by industrialization and modernization with social policy answers – it took only about half a century to transform night-watchman states into insurance states. Risk, I argue, was a key factor in this transformation.

Second, the *shape* of risk distributions indicates whether a majority (and the median) has above- or below-average risk. If the distribution is top-heavy (median > mean), a majority benefits from socializing risk, that is, from social insurance (in which contributions are not scaled to risk). In this scenario we can expect social policy adoption and expansion. In contrast, if the distribution is bottom-heavy, social policy still has fairly widespread support (because individuals are risk-averse), but the birth and growth of generous programs are unlikely. This is the "normal" shape of risk distributions. This specifies the conditions under which social policy "milestones" – adoption or decisive expansion – are more likely.

Third, the *spread* of (bottom-heavy) risk distribution indicates how commonly shared risk is, which influences how similar social policy preferences are, with implications for polarization, aggregate support, and generosity of social policy. In particular, more homogeneous risk distributions (lower risk inequality) lead to less contestation around social policy issues and – given the general popularity of social insurance – more support for generous benefits. Ultimately, lower risk inequality leads to comparatively more generous social insurance systems, because democracy follows majority rule. This explains differences across space, domains, and time in terms of social policy generosity.

Because risk pools can change over time, my framework is well suited to explain dynamics. All of the three characteristics of risk distributions discussed previously – mean, standard deviation, and skew – can change. Average risk can increase or decrease; risk inequality can rise or fall; and risk distributions can "flip" from being bottom-heavy to being top-heavy, or vice versa. Change can occur slowly or quickly. Slow changes are typically due to structural change, and they primarily affect the level and inequality of risk. Industrialization and modernization, for example, generated or made commonplace the risks of accident, sickness, old age, and unemployment, as mentioned earlier. The pattern of polarized job growth that many advanced industrialized economies experience today – only low- and high-risk jobs grow and the middle is much reduced – will likely increase risk inequality, which can be expected to undermine broad support for risk pooling. Quick changes, or shocks, are often due to exceptional circumstances, such as a depression or a war. They can have important consequences for welfare state politics because they have the potential to change levels and inequality abruptly, or perhaps even lead to a "risk flip," which can profoundly affect patterns of support and reshuffle welfare state coalitions.

Finally, my framework provides an intuitive interpretation of crises and their potential impact on social policy: crises are shocks to risk pools, and different shocks result in different kinds of crises. I distinguish three types of crises. First are crises that affect the weakest first and most, resulting in an increase in risk inequality by increasing average risk without affecting the majority much.[8] In this scenario, for which recessions are a good example, support for social policy wanes and retrenchment is more likely to occur. Second are crises that affect a majority of citizens, thereby decreasing risk inequality and perhaps eventually even leading to a "risk flip," that is, a situation where bottom-heavy risk distributions become top-heavy. In this scenario, for which depressions are a good example, we would expect the adoption and/or expansion of

---

[8] This is a median preserving spread of a bottom-heavy (right-skewed) risk distribution.

social policy. Third are crises that are so pervasive or systemic that risk is replaced with uncertainty: people do not know what the future will hold. In this scenario, for which wars or other national emergencies are examples, citizens are behind the "veil of ignorance" and can more easily agree on setting up and/or expanding welfare states. This sheds theoretical light on the role of crises in social policy development and explains why some crises lead to the adoption or expansion of social insurance, while others lead to retrenchment.

## PLAN OF THE BOOK

The next chapter develops my framework in more detail and lays out some of its observable implications. As I hope is clear at this point, risk distributions play an important role in my account. Because risk pools have not received much attention so far, the next chapter also investigates them empirically.

Chapters 3 and 4 deal with the micro-level. Chapter 3 explores the individual-level determinants of social policy preferences. Theoretically, someone's relative position in the risk pool should correlate well with his or her demand for social protection. Empirically, this proposition is strongly supported. Chapter 4 explores the largely uncharted topic of perceptions regarding social policy risks. I find that subjective risk perceptions are surprisingly accurate – citizens seem to have a fairly good sense of where they are in the risk distribution. Furthermore, I develop an account of how people form these subjective risk perceptions. I show that risks are correlated over time and within social networks (and across domains). This provides useful information to individuals, and I show that individuals indeed rely on this information to form their risk perceptions.

I then turn to the macro-level. Chapter 5 develops and tests my explanation for social policy difference, which links more homogeneous risk pools (lower risk inequality) with more generous social policy outcomes. Unlike in the MR model, where higher (income) inequality is expected to lead to *more* generous social policy, my argument suggests that higher (risk) inequality leads to *less* generous social policy. My hypothesis is supported by various tests, which I present in the chapter.[9]

---

[9] Some of these tests directly address the possibility that risk pools are a function of existing welfare states (a reasonable proposition); still, I find empirical support for my framework.

Chapters 6–8 deal with social policy dynamics. Chapter 6 treats German unification as an exogenous shock to risk pools: overnight, West and East Germany were reunified under the umbrella of the West German welfare state, a development which I show led to a sharp rise in risk inequality. For this situation, my account predicts plummeting social policy support in West Germany, and likely retrenchment – and both of these phenomena can be observed empirically. This explains the puzzling fact that one of the most significant examples of retrenchment in Western Europe occurred on the watch of a left government (Schröder's SPD-led red-green coalition).

Chapter 7 looks at cases of social policy adoption. I offer an explanation for the varying speed of unemployment insurance (UI) adoption in US states during the Great Depression. I furthermore explore the determinants of relatively recent social insurance adoptions in various Asian countries. I find that risk pool dynamics help us make sense of what happened in these cases. Chapter 8 details how my risk pool perspective helps us understand the role of crises in social policy development, and it empirically analyzes the role of crises for social policy development between 1870 and 1950 (and even 2000). I find that "social policy milestones" were much more likely to occur in close proximity to peaks in suicide rates, which is my measure of deep societal crises in that chapter. The final chapter reviews and concludes my research.

My argument is simple. Individuals strive for security. Risk drives social policy preferences and popularity. Different risk pools explain cross-national differences. And changes in risk pools drive domestic changes in social policy. Ultimately, I argue that *because* nothing is certain except death, there are taxes.

# 2

# Theoretical Framework

In rich democracies, about one-fifth of government expenditure goes to the main state prerogatives – general public services (including debt service), defense, public order, and safety. About one-half goes toward social policy narrowly defined – social protection and health. And more than three-fifths (almost two-thirds) is allocated to social policy more broadly defined – social protection, health, and education (OECD 2011, tables 5.1 and 5.3).[1] In other words, government expenditures on welfare functions dwarf those on night-watchman functions. In all rich democracies, governments force their citizens to be part of mandatory social insurance systems covering all main risks. Taxing their citizens and spending huge amounts of money on social policy are the main activities of governments today.

It is inconceivable that, in democracies, the single most prominent government activity – social policy – can be performed without widespread support by citizens. Yet, the potential importance of public opinion for social policy making has largely been neglected. Clem Brooks and Jeff Manza, who have perhaps most systematically addressed this shortcoming, argue that existing accounts are "reaching for, but not grasping,

---

[1] Data are averages for rich OECD countries and refer to 2008. The remaining categories of the structure of general government expenditures (by COFOG function) are economic affairs, environment protection, housing and community amenities, and recreation, culture and religion. The data are derived from tables 5.1 and 5.3 (http://dx.doi.org/10.1787/888932391792 and http://dx.doi.org/10.1787/888932391830) in OECD's Government at a Glance 2011. Expressed as percentage of GDP, the average numbers are 9.1 percent for general public services, defense, and public order and safety; 22.3 percent for social protection and health; and 28 percent for social protection, health, and education.

public opinion": "Analysts within multiple theoretical traditions have anticipated the possibility that mass opinion is a factor relevant to shaping social policymaking, and perhaps in accounting for differences between countries. But none of these scholars has taken the next steps of explicitly theorizing and attempting to measure its policy impact" (Brooks and Manza 2007, 25–26). Analyzing the potential policy impact of public opinion – as in the seminal work by Clem Brooks and Jeff Manza – is a step in the right direction, but it begs the important question: why does popular support for social policy differ across space and time? We have to turn to the individual level to explore this topic.

Despite its shared focus on democracies, the welfare state literature has, for the longest time, paid very little attention to citizen preferences. Only recently have scholars investigated the topic, but existing studies typically exclusively concentrate on the micro-level. A joint perspective of micro-level determinants of social policy preferences and the latter's impact on social policy making has yet to be conducted. It is such a perspective that I develop in this chapter. To this end, the following section briefly reviews the literature on social policy preferences. Because how we think about the determinants of social policy preferences depends on what social policy does, the next section explores that question. The chapter then sketches a simple formal model and lays out its micro- and macro-level implications, many of which will be tested in later chapters.

## 2.1 DETERMINANTS OF SOCIAL POLICY PREFERENCES

To make sense of the macro-level development of social policy – the common trend of massive expansion, cross-national differences, and dynamics – we need to understand its micro-level underpinnings. Only recently have questions about the determinants of social policy preferences – including attitudes toward redistribution – entered the mainstream political economy literature. Today, quite a wide range of explanations exist (for recent reviews, see [Alesina and Giuliano 2011; Rehm 2009]). Existing accounts can be classified into material and predispositional approaches.

*Predispositional accounts,* which are prominent in the political psychology literature, focus on values, beliefs, and norms as key explanatory variables of social policy and redistribution preferences. People are assumed to care about inequality per se – for example, because they are altruistic, have certain conceptions of fairness or social justice, or adhere to a certain ideology or religion (Alesina and Angeletos 2005; Bénabou and Tirole 2006; Fong 2001; Kangas 1997, 2003; Kangas et al. 1995; Rueda 2013; Scheve and Stasavage 2006, 2012; Sears and Funk 1991; Shayo 2009).

Predispositional variables have an impressive empirical record – they are among the strongest predictors of social policy and redistribution attitudes. This is hardly surprising, however, since *explanans* (say: altruism) and *explanandum* (say: attitudes toward redistribution) are very close to each other and arguably just different measures of the same latent attitude.[2] For example, one of the most prolific contributors to the scholarship on redistributional attitudes, Alberto Alesina, uses respondents' left-right self-placement "as a proxy for favoring redistribution and government intervention" (Alesina and Angeletos 2005, 963) in one article as a dependent variable. In another contribution, Alesina regresses redistribution attitudes on a set of right-hand-side variables that include left-right self-placement (Alesina and Giuliano 2011), leading to endogeneity bias.

The larger issue at stake is how much we can learn from "explaining" attitudes with other attitudes (Hamermesh 1989, 2004). To be sure, exploring the relationships among different attitudinal variables can be interesting and useful, and I will do so in the next two chapters myself. But it is hardly surprising that citizens with liberal/progressive/left ideology are more supportive of social policy and redistribution than citizens who are conservative – after all, this is how we define left and right. A more profound explanation should answer the question of *why* some citizens end up with progressive attitudes while others do not. Where do values, beliefs, and norms originate? Scholars in the predisposition paradigm typically point to socialization as a critical factor in shaping worldviews. But to the extent that anything more specific can be said about the genesis of political preferences – besides waving one's hands and blaming the parents – scholars often point to material factors. For example, it is conceivable that values about social justice are shaped by an individual's experience with misfortune (Giuliano and Spilimbergo 2009), or that conceptions of fairness are shaped by wars (Scheve and Stasavage 2010, 2012). In that sense, material and predispositional approaches share common ground.

*Material approaches* have a strong footing in sociology and economics. All three classical sociologists – Karl Marx, Max Weber, and Emile Durkheim – suggest that people's political behavior is influenced by their

---

[2] Even firm adherents of predispositional approaches acknowledge this possibility (Sears and Funk 1991, 69).

position in the economy. Marx, who focused on property relationships, expressed this most explicitly by saying that "being determines consciousness." But economic factors also play an important role in Weber's work (market relationships and their impact on life chances in particular) and Durkheim's opus (sites of production). In terms of these sociological giants, the variables that one may suspect to correlate with social policy and redistribution attitudes are employment status, class, income, education, and occupation.

Material approaches have thrived in the political economy literature. A standard view in economics is that individuals weigh costs versus benefits to calculate their preferred policies. Utility is derived from consumption, which depends on current income. Income, therefore, is predicted to be an important determinant of redistribution attitudes (Meltzer and Richard 1981); the expectation is, of course, that those who are net beneficiaries of a policy will support it, while those who are not will not. More recently, the literature has extended this basic idea to incorporate the effect of (upward and downward) mobility on redistributional preferences (Alesina and Glaeser 2004; Alesina and La Ferrara 2005; Barber, Beramendi, and Wibbels 2013; Bénabou and Ok 2001; Iversen and Soskice 2001; Moene and Wallerstein 2001; Piketty 1995; Rehm 2009). The reasoning goes that besides someone's current position in the income distribution, the prospect of upward mobility, or the risk of downward mobility, should shape social policy attitudes as well.[3] An influential and original version of the argument has been developed within the Varieties of Capitalism framework. That argument suggests that workers who have specific skills (skills that are difficult to transport from one employer to another) demand generous social policy as a safety net in case matters do not work out.

Some scholars in the material paradigm have suggested that individuals not only care about how much income they have (in relative or absolute terms), but where they are in the income distribution relative to particular other members of society (Lupu and Pontusson 2011). In these accounts, people have other-regarding preferences, not in the sense of caring for others (as in some predispositional accounts), but in the sense of caring about their own position relative to others. According to these accounts, preferences could be shaped by group loyalty (Luttmer 2001), concerns about relative status (Corneo and Gruner 2000; Wilensky 1975), or race

---

[3] A recent important contribution highlights the relevance of wealth holdings for social policy preferences, a much understudied topic (Ansell 2014).

or ethnicity (Alesina, Glaeser, and Sacerdote 2001). Material approaches have also been employed to argue that people have preferences about income distributions themselves, not just their position in the system. Inequality may enter utility indirectly because it may have societal consequences that, in turn, affect an individual's utility. For example, high inequality may be costly for the rich because of increased crime (Rueda and Stegmueller 2013, 2014) or lower productivity due to worse education systems. It may also benefit the rich, according to some arguments, by providing incentive effects (Alesina and Giuliano 2011).

In terms of the empirical performance of material approaches, conventional wisdom has it that the record is – at best – mixed. In fact, the proposition that self-interest[4] meaningfully shapes attitudes is explicitly rejected by prominent contributions (Citrin and Green 1990; Coughlin 1990; Lau and Heldman 2009; Mutz 1993, 1998; Mutz and Mondak 1997; Schlozman and Verba 1979; Sears and Funk 1990a, 1990b, 1991); some have even refuted it as a "myth" (Miller and Ratner 1996).[5] In a similar vein, scholars regularly find that sociotropic accounts outperform egotropic accounts. For example, Diana Mutz concludes that "consistent with previous research ... perception of collective-level experiences matter more to political attitudes than people's personal experiences" (Mutz 1998, 22). One exception to this finding, however, are risk perceptions where egotropic motives perform well: "In forming judgments about personal risk, people are more influenced by personal experience and experiences conveyed through social networks than through media

---

[4] A prominent definition of self-interest reads (Sears and Funk 1991, 16): "We define an individual's self-interest in a particular attitudinal position in terms of (1) its short to medium-term impact on the (2) material well-being of the (3) individual's own personal life (or that of his or her immediate family)" (see also Chong, Citrin, and Conley 2001, 542; Citrin and Green 1990).

[5] However, even the most vocal critics of egocentric interest approaches note important qualifications to the general negative findings. David Sears and Carolyn Funk, whose studies are particularly often referenced for the finding of limited effects of economic self-interest on political attitudes, report a set of findings in which "virtually every indicator of self-interest had a statistically significant effect on virtually every relevant dependent variable" (Sears and Funk 1991, 49). More generally, economic self-interest "has significant political effects when the issue or candidate has unusually clear and important personal consequences for the respondent" (Sears and Funk 1990b, 257). Other systematic investigations have found the same: "people are more likely to recognize their own self-interest, and to act upon it, when their stakes in the policy are clear or when they have been primed to think about the personal costs and benefits of the policy" (Chong, Citrin, and Conley 2001, 541); this conclusion is confirmed over and over (Baslevent and Kirmanoglu 2011; Chong, Citrin, and Conley 2001; Erikson and Stoker 2011; Hudson and Jones 1994; Pitlik et al. 2011).

reports" (Mutz 1998, 74). Similarly, it has been established that "feared negative outcomes" appear to be "more salient than desired positive outcomes," especially under uncertainty (Sears and Funk 1991, 61).

The great attraction of material approaches is that they shed light on non-attitudinal factors – such as income or mobility – that potentially shape political attitudes. This also allows scholars to make macro-predictions. For example, the Meltzer-Richard (MR) model predicts that redistribution increases when income inequality increases (a prediction that has little support in the data). Besides their determinism, the weakness of material approaches is their meager empirical record. One area, however, where even vocal critics of material approaches admit their usefulness are risk and risk perceptions. Risk and risk perceptions, of course, closely relate to the welfare state. It seems promising, therefore, to focus on material factors in order to explain attitudes toward the welfare state. From a material self-interest perspective, support for social policy should be predictably related to an individual's expected net benefits. To understand the determinants of expected net benefits – and ultimately social policy preferences – we therefore need to establish what social policy does.

## 2.2 WHAT DO WELFARE STATES DO?

What do welfare states do? They insure (redistribution across the life course) and they redistribute (redistribution across income classes).[6] Or, put differently: they mitigate risks and redistribute incomes. Arguably, the insurance (or income maintenance) function is more central than the redistribution function, for several reasons. First, insurance is what distinguishes "welfare state" policies from previous social policy efforts, namely, "poor laws" (Briggs 1961; Flora and Alber 1981) and "social insurance"' plays a prominent role in the (early) history of the welfare state: "Judging from their form ... the original initiatives of the welfare state seem to serve essentially an insurance (i.e., risk-sharing) function" (Goodin and Dryzek 1987, 44). Second, social insurance is still the lion's share of social policy, at least outside Australia and New Zealand (Alber 2010). Third, if welfare states mainly concerned redistribution, they would be spectacularly ineffective: rich democracies spend on average around 20 percent of GDP on social policy, yet the reduction in inequality

---

[6] On the different dimensions of the welfare state (security-insecurity vs. equality-inequality), see also (Flora and Heidenheimer 1981, 25–28; Goodin 1988, 1990).

due to government intervention is rather modest. Moreover, the most straightforward way to reduce income inequality is a negative income tax (Friedman 1962; Overbye 1995), but this policy is not being used in most rich democracies.[7] In sum, one should not "confuse the redistribution of individual income through time or the sharing of risk, which are obvious motives for social insurance measures, with the redistribution of income between classes. But since most social insurance programs are financed by payroll taxes or the equivalent, the redistribution of income between classes is not at all obvious and it seems much more reasonable to assume that the primary motive of welfare expenditures is risk-sharing" (Pryor 1968, 136).[8]

Despite the importance of the insurance function, much of the literature conceptualizes the welfare state as a tool for redistribution.[9] There is no question that social insurance is also redistributive and leads to the reduction of inequality. But one can think of this as a side effect of insurance. In social insurance, benefits are tied to risk, while premiums are decoupled from it. A major redistributive impact, therefore, is simply

---

[7] The exceptions are the earned income tax credit (EITC) in the United States and the working tax credit (WTC) in the United Kingdom. But neither of these policy instruments is particularly important in the grand scheme of things.

[8] See also Robert Goodin (1990), who observes: "Conventional moral wisdom has long held that the welfare state is justified principally as a device to benefit the poor. ... Given that understanding of the welfare state, we would be hard pressed to explain why welfare programs should sometimes actually – and, indeed, intentionally – pay more to the better off. Yet that is precisely what is done through earnings-related benefits built into many social welfare programs. The more you earn, the more you will receive when you cease to earn, in the form of old age pensions, unemployment benefits, sickness and disability benefits, maternity benefits, and so on down the list" (p. 530–31). This puzzle, Goodin argues, can be resolved when understanding the welfare state as providing insurance: "At least in part, the function of the welfare state is to underwrite, and in that way to help stabilize, people's market-based earnings expectations. Its job is, first, to smooth out the peaks and troughs in their earnings patterns, bringing their short-term rewards more into line with their long-term average earnings. And when through some unanticipatable event their long-term earnings expectation suffers a sharp and irreversible decline, the role of the welfare state is, second, to ease the transition from the old, higher expectation to the new, lower one" (p. 539). Moreover: "The point of social insurance more generally is, according to Beveridge (par. 12) (see W. H. Beveridge, *Social Insurance and Allied Services*, Cmd. 6404 [London: HMSO, 1942]) to make "provision against interruption and loss of earning power" – or, in the words of Pechman, Aaron, and Taussig (p. 55), to "protect individuals against catastrophic losses of income (Joseph A. Pechman, Henry J. Aaron, and Michael K. Taussig, *Social Security: Perspectives for Reform* [Washington, DC: Brookings Institution, 1968], pp. 246–47)" (FN 22).

[9] For example, "in the power resources approach, attention is focused on distributive conflict and on the nature and distribution of assets" (Korpi 2004).

due to the unequal experience of risk. Social policy is mainly redistributive across risk groups (Baldwin 1990), not income groups, and the redistributive outcome can be thought of as a consequence of the overlap between the two (Rehm, Hacker, and Schlesinger 2012).[10]

Taken together, therefore, welfare states do insure (they reduce risk) and they do redistribute (they reduce inequality). Or put differently: social insurance insures against income losses and redistributes between the lucky and the unlucky (it "reapportions risks," as Baldwin [1990] eloquently put it). This happens to have redistributive consequences as well – either by design or as a side effect of a negative correlation between income and risk.

## 2.3 THEORY: *HOMO INSECURITAS*

Given the two effects of social policy – insurance and redistribution – it is natural to focus on two characteristics of individuals to understand their attitudes toward social insurance: risk (the probability of experiencing a bad event that is covered by social insurance) and income. Because the role of income is well understood, I focus in the following simple model of social policy preference formation on risk.[11] In the simple model that focuses on the impact of risk on preferences for social benefit generosity, the key insight will be that demand for insurance is a function of one's *relative* (not absolute) position in the risk distribution.

### 2.3.1 The Model

In the following, I sketch a simple, fairly generic, model that explains demand for social insurance by the degree of risk exposure, building on the social insurance literature.[12] For concreteness, we can think of the risk

---

[10] For example, if contributions are proportional to income, and if risk is concentrated at the bottom of the income scale (as tends to be the case), social insurance will redistribute from the rich to the poor. But in principle, it is possible to construct a social insurance scheme that is close to actuarially fair and leads to no redistribution (ex ante).

[11] In the model, I will also abstract from the reality that different social policies are differently regressive in different countries. This should have an impact on the strength of the relationship between income and social policy attitudes (Beramendi and Rehm 2016), but should not change the expected relationship as long as social policies are progressive, as they are, once taxes and benefits are taken into account.

[12] Including, but certainly not limited to (Baldwin 1990; Barr 2001, 2004; Dryzek and Goodin 1986; Goodin and Dryzek 1987; Iversen and Soskice 2001; Mares 2003; Overbye 1995; Sinn 1995, 1996; Swenson 2002).

in terms of being unemployed, and several models along these lines exist (Atkinson 1990; Di Tella and MacCulloch 2002; Iversen and Soskice 2001; Moene and Wallerstein 2001; Neugart 2005a; Overbye 1995; Saint-Paul 1996, 2000; Wright 1986). For simplicity, I will assume that all individuals have the same exogenous income – I will return to this point; suffice to say that the qualitative results are the same if income is agent specific (Rehm 2008). I will further assume that individuals are risk-averse and face an agent-specific probability of losing their income in the future.

With these assumptions in mind, consider the following model.[13] Individuals either have an exogenously given income $y$ (e.g., from working) or collect a benefit $b$ if they lose their source of income (e.g., while they are unable to work). The probability of the bad event is $p$, and it is agent specific. The benefit is financed by a proportional tax rate ($t$) on incomes of the employed, and handed out as a flat rate benefit $b$ to those not in employment; budgets need to be balanced. An individual's utility over consumption is

$$U(c_i) = (1-p_i)(1-t)y + p_i b$$

Note that the only agent-specific parameter is the probability of needing the benefit ($p$) – income ($y$) is assumed to be the same for everybody. Balanced budgets imply (bars over letters are expected averages, that is, $E(p_i) = \bar{p}$)

$$b = ty\frac{(1-\bar{p})}{\bar{p}}$$

To model risk aversion, I employ the exponential utility function $U(c) = -e^{-ac}$, with $\alpha$ as a measure of risk aversion, $\alpha > 0$. An individual's expected utility is then given by

$$U(c_i) = -(1-p_i)e^{-a(1-t)y} - p_i e^{\frac{aty(1-\bar{p})}{\bar{p}}}$$

Solving the first order conditions for $t$ leads to the following expression for the optimal tax rate (I am ignoring $y$, since it is a constant)

$$t^* \text{ is proportional to } \frac{\bar{p}}{\alpha}\left(\alpha + \ln\left(\frac{p_i}{\bar{p}}\frac{1-\bar{p}}{1-p_i}\right)\right)$$

---

[13] I am most grateful to William Minozzi for input on the model.

The comparative statics (the analysis of changes of an endogenous variable resulting from changes of exogenous variables) reveal that the preferred tax rate increases in $p_i$ (more risk-exposed individuals prefer higher benefits). It decreases with the overall level of risk for low-risk individuals (a standard result in the literature, see Atkinson 1990; Di Tella and MacCulloch 2002; Wright 1986), but it increases with the overall level of risk for high-risk agents.[14] If one allows for agent-specific income, the comparative statics would reveal that demand for social insurance declines with income, as long as social insurance is redistributive (Iversen and Soskice 2001; Rehm 2008).

### 2.3.2 The Model's Micro-Level Implications

The model's key micro-level implication is intuitive: demand for social insurance increases with risk exposure. The reason for this relationship is that individuals are risk-averse and an individual's risk exposure shapes expected net benefits from a social insurance program.[15] In the preceding model, someone who faces zero unemployment risk will always be a net benefit loser. Someone who has a high risk of unemployment will receive more in benefits than paid in taxes and therefore be a net benefit winner.

More specifically, the model shows that demand for insurance depends (among other things) on one's relative position in the risk

---

[14] The comparative statics are $\frac{\partial t^*}{\partial p_i} = \frac{\bar{p}}{\alpha p_i(1-p_i)} > 0$ and $\frac{\partial t^*}{\partial \bar{p}} \begin{cases} < 0 \, for \, low \, p_i \\ > 0 \, for \, high \end{cases}$, where "low" and

"high" values of $p_i$ depend on risk aversion $(\alpha)$ and aggregate risk $(\bar{p})$. In particular: $\frac{\partial t^*}{\partial \bar{p}} < 0$ iff $p_i < \cfrac{1}{\left(1 + \left(\left(\frac{\bar{p}}{1-\bar{p}}\right)e^{\left(\frac{1}{1-\bar{p}}-\alpha\right)}\right)^{-1}\right)}$ The intuition is that, on the one hand, an increase in

aggregate risk $(\bar{p})$ makes insurance more expensive (because fewer individuals pay taxes that finance the benefit, and the benefit is distributed among more recipients) – a price effect. On the other hand, an increase in $\bar{p}$ makes it more likely that a given individual will need the benefit – an insurance effect. These two effects work against each other (and, once one adds risk aversion, that trade-off changes), and how matters work out depends on where an individual is in the risk distribution. Roughly speaking, if $p_i$ is (much) lower than $\bar{p}$, the price effect will dominate the insurance effect, and the preferred tax rate will decline with aggregate risk. For "reasonable" levels of risk aversion $(\alpha < 1.5$ or so), demand for insurance will decrease for below-average agents.

[15] If income were agent specific, the model would also yield that demand for social insurance declines in income, as in the classic Meltzer-Richard model (Meltzer and Richard 1981). The reason is that the rich pay more in taxes than they receive in benefits, while the reverse is true for the poor.

distribution (roughly proportional to $p_i/\overline{p}$). Individuals who have relatively high risk benefit from socialized risk pools, while individuals with relatively low risk are subsidizing others.[16] Citizens at the tails of the risk distribution are either net beneficiaries (bad risks, or unlucky citizens) or contributors (good risks, or lucky citizens) of social insurance, while citizens in the middle of the risk distribution can expect to break roughly even. Finally, the model shows that – under reasonable assumptions – demand for insurance declines in the aggregate level of risk. However, the model also shows that this is not unconditionally true (though reasonable parameters yield that result). Chapter 3 will test whether social policy preferences are, indeed, a function of risk exposure.

The model predicts a correlation between someone's relative position in the risk distribution (roughly $p_i/\overline{p}$) and his or her demand for social insurance. This focuses attention on the fascinating topic of risk perceptions. How accurate are citizens' risk perceptions? How do people arrive at assessments of the future? Chapter 4 explores this largely uncharted terrain. I discover that risk perceptions are surprisingly accurate in relative terms: respondents have a good sense where they are in the risk distribution. In some areas – most importantly the risk of job loss – respondents also have a good assessment of their absolute risk: respondents' subjective risk perceptions and objective risk exposure match quite closely.

But how do citizens know their position in the risk distribution? Briefly put, risks are correlated in three ways: over time, across domains, and within networks (Hacker, Rehm, and Schlesinger 2013). This allows citizens to assess their risk exposure on the basis of their own past experiences, their present experiences in different domains, and the past and present experiences of their close networks. By its very nature, risk is about the future. And, as is often quipped: prediction is very difficult, especially about the future. To assess their own risk, people have to consider the experience of others. As a result, self- and other-regarding motives are fused in my approach, although the model's utility function does not include other-regarding preferences directly.

---

[16] This dynamic was clearly understood by contemporary analysts when mandatory unemployment insurance systems were adopted; see Chapter 7 for some examples (Andersson 1938, 171).

### 2.3.3 The Model's Macro-Level Implications

If risk determines social policy preferences, the distribution of risk – the shape of the risk pool, or the degree of risk inequality – influences aggregate social policy preferences. There are three magnitudes of interests with respect to risk distributions. A risk pool's location (mean) indicates how common risk is. A risk pool's spread (standard deviation) indicates how commonly shared a risk is and it influences how homogeneous societal preferences are. And a risk pool's shape (skew) governs whether a majority benefits from social insurance or not.[17]

In terms of *shape*, risk pools can be either top- or bottom-heavy. A top-heavy (left-skewed) risk distribution means that a majority of citizen faces high risk, while a minority faces low risk. Here, the majority is very supportive of social policy – these are fertile times for social policy emergence or expansion. A bottom-heavy (right-skewed) risk distribution means that a majority of citizens faces low risk, while a minority faces high risk. Hence, the majority (and the median voter) essentially subsidizes a minority of higher-risk citizens.[18] Support for social insurance will be lower in this scenario and the emergence and expansion of social policy should be unlikely. Moreover, benefit levels will be relatively lower than in the top-heavy risk pool case.[19] I show in the Appendix to this chapter that risk distributions are normally bottom-heavy.

The *spread* of risk pools indicates how similarly risk is distributed within a society, a factor that influences the similarity of social policy preferences. It could be that citizens face very different probabilities of experiencing a bad event. In this scenario of high risk inequality (or a heterogeneous risk pool), reaching agreement is difficult, and social policy

---

[17] The mean (location), standard deviation (spread), and skew (shape) are the first, second, and third moments of a distribution. As discussed, the role of absolute risk levels (summarized by the mean, i.e., the first moment) is somewhat ambiguous, and most empirical models that follow will control for the level of risk explicitly.

[18] Randy Stone makes a similar point with respect to the underprovision of public goods in international environmental agreements (Stone 2009).

[19] If we adopted a utilitarian model of utility maximization, the socially optimal insurance level would be the one that maximized the sum of all utilities, which is the same as maximizing the average utility – the utility of the mean risk citizen. From this perspective, social insurance will be underprovided in the bottom-heavy scenario – the median voter's preferred benefit is lower than the mean citizen's preferred benefit, that is, the socially optimal level.

will typically[20] be more contested. Alternatively, it could be that citizens are fairly equally likely to experience a bad event: that is, risk inequality is low. In this scenario of a homogeneous risk pool we would expect attitudes toward social insurance to be fairly similar. The similarity of social policy preferences is relevant because it is closely related to the degree of opposition to the welfare state. Since social insurance is generally popular,[21] the only way to generate dissimilar preferences is by increasing opposition, thereby lowering support. Therefore, *ceteris paribus*, lower risk inequality should lead to more similar social policy preferences and higher social policy support, which should influence social policy making. Cross-national (or over-time) differences in social policy effort, I argue, can be explained by differences in risk inequality. I test this hypothesis in Chapter 5.

In my framework, *changes* in the distribution of risk can lead to changes in social policy outcomes. These changes can be incremental (e.g., due to technological change, or changes in returns to skills) or sudden (e.g., because of exogenous shocks, such as a recession). Since risk pools are characterized by their level, spread, and shape, three kinds of changes are of interest. The first kind of change is an increase or decrease in risk levels; as mentioned earlier, levels are historically relevant, but their effect is somewhat ambiguous once a risk is recognized as a social problem. The second – and rare – kind of change is a transformation of the risk distribution's shape. A change from a bottom- to a top-heavy risk distribution shape can be called a "risk flip." Risk flips in terms of objective risk are rare[22] and require extraordinary circumstances, such as national emergencies (a topic to which I will return in a moment). I argue in Chapter 7 that the Great Depression in America probably led to a risk flip and I show that states with "more flipped" risk distributions adopted unemployment insurance (UI) faster.

The third – and more common – kind of change is a change in the spread of the (bottom-heavy) risk distribution. Risk inequality can go up or down. If risk inequality decreases, social policy popularity should increase, as should – eventually – social policy generosity. In contrast, if risk inequality increases, social policy support should plummet, and welfare state backlash – and even retrenchment – is more likely. I show

---

[20] Typical means that these are the expected effects of risk inequality (risk pool homogeneity/heterogeneity) in the case of right-skewed risk distributions.

[21] See table 1.1.  [22] They may be, however, more common in terms of risk perceptions.

in Chapter 6 that German unification led to a dramatic increase in risk inequality. I argue that this led to declining support for generous social policy, and eventually resulted in harsh labor market reforms (the Hartz reforms). In Chapter 7, I show that all recent cases of social insurance adoption only occurred after a significant decrease in risk inequality (an increase in risk homogeneity).[23]

My framework also provides an interpretation of crises and their potential impact on social policy. In Chapter 8, I argue that crises are shocks to risk pools, and different shocks signify different types of crises. In particular, crises are of three kinds.[24] The first type of crisis affects the weakest first and most, resulting in an increase in risk inequality by increasing average risk without affecting the majority much.[25] In this scenario, of which recessions are a good example, social policy support wanes and retrenchment is more likely to occur. The second type of crisis affects a majority of citizens, thereby decreasing risk inequality and perhaps eventually even causing a "risk flip," that is, a situation in which bottom-heavy risk distributions become top-heavy. In this scenario, of which depressions are a good example, we would expect adoption and/or expansion of social policy. In the third type of crisis, the shock is so pervasive or systemic that risk – where the future is not known, but the probability distribution of possible futures is known – is replaced by uncertainty – where the probability distribution is unknown (Knight 1921). People simply do not know what the future will hold. In this scenario, of which wars or other national emergencies are good examples, citizens are behind the "veil of ignorance" (Rawls 1971) and can more easily agree on setting up and/or expanding welfare states. This is how my framework explains why national emergencies – wars, depressions, hyperinflation, epidemics, and the like – played an instrumental role in the history of the welfare state (Alber 1982, 58, 154; Castles 2010).

To summarize, I link different risk distributions to different social policy outcomes. Risk distributions differ in terms of mean (location),

---

[23] In all recent cases of unemployment insurance adoption (South Korea, Taiwan, Thailand, and Turkey, all in the 1990s or 2000s), risk pools became markedly more homogeneous before social insurance adoption (Vietnam also adopted unemployment insurance recently, but I do not have data for this case), while no such pattern is observable in arguably similar cases (Hong Kong, Philippines, Singapore).

[24] In the following, I will concentrate on crises that are "shocks." But a crisis can also be slowly evolving. For example, technological change is a factor that likely shapes risk pools.

[25] This is a median preserving spread of a right-skewed risk distribution.

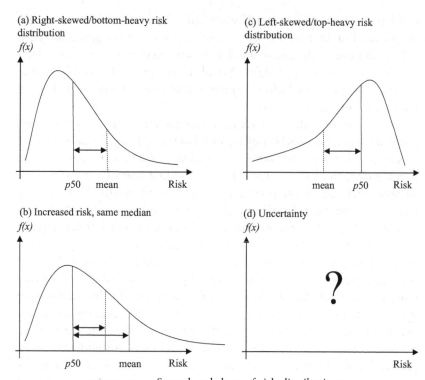

FIGURE 2.1: Spread and skew of risk distributions.

standard deviation (spread), and skew (shape, or lopsidedness), with predictable consequences for social policy:

- If risk distributions are top-heavy (left-skewed, i.e., median risk > mean risk), popular support for social policy will be high and social insurance adoption or expansion is likely. This is situation (c) in Figure 2.1. Top-heavy risk distributions are probably rare and likely coincide with crises (such as economic depressions).
- If risk distributions are bottom-heavy (right-skewed, i.e., median risk < mean risk) – and they normally are – social policy will be comparatively less popular. This is situation (a) in Figure 2.1.
- If risk distributions are bottom-heavy, higher risk inequality leads to lower support for social insurance and – ultimately – less generous social policy. Lower risk inequality is conducive to the opposite outcomes: higher support and more generous benefits. See situation (a) compared to situation (b) in Figure 2.1.

- If risk distributions are unknown, risk (known probabilities) is replaced with uncertainty (unknown probabilities). These situations – which may resemble the situation during a war – should be particularly favorable for social insurance enactment. See situation (d) in Figure 2.1.
- Risk distributions can change and one natural interpretation of "crises" is that they are shocks to risk pools. Depending on the type of change – increasing or decreasing risk inequality; flipping of the risk distribution – we can expect different types of social policy change due to crises (adoption; expansion; retrenchment).

### 2.3.4 The Joint Distribution of Income and Risk

The discussion so far has almost exclusively focused on risk and largely ignored income as a determinant of social policy attitudes. Previously I have argued that the primary task of welfare states is to provide insurance – hence my focus on risk. But welfare states also redistribute resources from the rich to the poor, and demand for social insurance should – and empirically does – decrease in income. In the micro-level analysis to come, I will therefore take income into account by controlling for it in most models.

Matters are more complicated at the macro-level because income and risk can work in the same or opposite direction. If income and risk were cross-cutting traits – the poor have low risk; the rich have high risk – the effect of risk might be offset by the effect of income. If income and risk were reinforcing traits – the poor are doubly disadvantaged because they are also risk exposed; the rich are doubly advantaged because they face low risk – the effect of risk is reinforced by the effect of income. In most instances, income and risk are negatively correlated: they are reinforcing traits. With respect to unemployment risk, a negative relationship with income is to be expected because education influences both variables (higher education is associated with higher incomes and lower incidence of unemployment). The socioeconomic gradient of risk in many other domains is also unsurprising (loss of housing, workplace accidents, etc.). In principle, however, income and risk can be positively correlated.[26]

---

[26] For example, rich people tend to be more exposed to the adversities of longevity (because they tend to live longer); rich people also tend to be more exposed to the adverse effects of stock market crashes on wealth holdings.

But for the risk factors discussed in this book, the correlations with income are negative.[27] To be sure, the degree of overlap between prosperity and good fortune can vary across countries, time, and social policy domains, and this provides theoretical leverage. For example, income and unemployment risk became increasingly correlated over time in the United States, a correlation that likely has contributed to increasing attitudinal sorting (Rehm 2011a). Moreover, in cross-national comparison, income and unemployment risk are particularly reinforcing traits in the United States, a circumstance that may explain why social policy is particularly contested and unpopular in America (Rehm, Hacker, and Schlesinger 2012). The analysis that follows focuses on risk and risk inequality, but whenever appropriate and possible, I take into account income inequality when examining the effect of risk pools on social policy outcomes.

### 2.3.5  Political Model

My theoretical framework links individual level social policy attitudes to social policy outcomes, via aggregate public opinion: majority popular demand for social policy leads to its supply. Of course, the policy making process is much more complicated than this view implies: parties aggregate and translate citizen preferences or not; interest groups try to influence politics in their favor; different political systems have different institutions with different decision-making rules; electoral systems differ and shape how votes are translated into seats; and so on. Therefore, using such a simplified political model requires some explanation. I discuss theoretical justifications first and then turn to empirical justifications.

*Theoretically*, we have excellent reasons to expect that public opinion influences policy making. The claim that democracies follow majority rule should not be contested – it is true almost by assumption. In all (rich) democracies, substantive legislation cannot pass without a majority – or even supermajority – in the legislature(s).[28] Likewise, the conjecture that public policy reflects citizen preferences should not be very controversial,

---

[27] Each of the risk indicators discussed previously – and displayed in Figure 2.4, Figure 2.5, and Figure 2.6 below – is negatively correlated with income: the poor are also the unlucky. Data availability limits the ability to establish the relationship between income and risk for every country, but the correlation between income and unemployment risk is negative in the countries for which data exist. This implies that the risk profiles of the top half of the income distribution are fairly similar, while they are very diverse for the bottom half. I am grateful to Torben Iversen for pointing this out to me.

[28] Though some of the "core laws" in social policy development are actually decrees.

at least when it comes to important, visible, and durable policies such as those underpinning welfare states. In fact, congruence between citizen preferences and policy output is a core part of many definitions of democracy.[29] Furthermore, as argued previously, all major theories of social policy making are compatible with the possibility that citizen preferences decisively shape social policy, and that democracies follow majority rule. For example, the dominant welfare state perspective – the Power Resources Theory – asserts that welfare state politics is a struggle between classes with different preferences (preferences matter), and that the stronger side is able to shape outcomes (majority politics).

In democracies, representation can occur through two main mechanisms: either indirectly through elections – "where the public selects like-minded politicians who then deliver its wants in policy" – or directly "where sitting politicians respond to what the public wants" (Wlezien 2004, 2). Both of these mechanisms assume that citizens know what they want – an assumption that appears to be at odds with a plethora of studies showing just how "unmotivated, ill-informed, and inattentive" voters are (Erikson, MacKuen, and Stimson 2002, xvii). How can this ignorance at the micro-level be the basis for a meaningful macro-level public opinion, "the global preferences of the ... electorate" (Stimson, Mackuen, and Erikson 1995, 543)? Erikson, MacKuen and Stimson have solved this riddle by arguing that public opinion at the aggregate level provides a meaningful signal because "those that act as if at random cancel out [and] those who act always the same produce no variance. [Consequently] the aggregate 'signal' arises almost wholly from those who are orderly in their behavior," which can lead to "extraordinary sophistication of the collective electorate" (Erikson, MacKuen, and Stimson 2002, 6, 7).

*Empirically*, links between public opinion and policy making are well established in the United States (Erikson, MacKuen, and Stimson 2002; Stimson, Mackuen, and Erikson 1995; Wlezien 2004) and "politicians' responsiveness to public preferences reflects the public importance of different policy domains" (Wlezien 2004, 1).[30] Given the significance of social policy in rich democracies, it is perhaps therefore not surprising

---

[29] According to John May, for example, democracy can be defined as "necessary correspondence between acts of governance and the wishes with respect to those acts of the persons who are affected" (May 1978, 1).

[30] Wlezien (2004, 1) observes that "[m]uch research shows that politicians represent public preferences in public policy" and provides ample citation to bolster this claim.

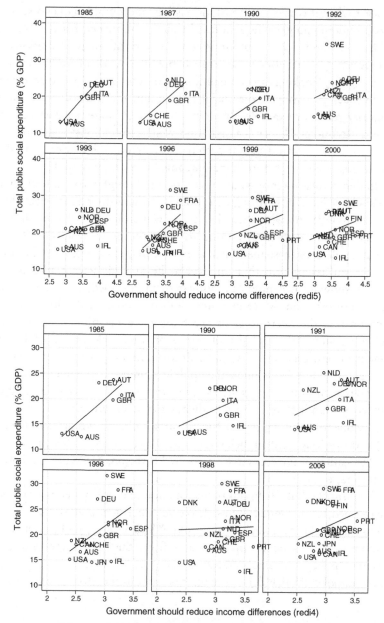

FIGURE 2.2: Mean support for redistribution and total public social expenditure.
*Note*: Top panel: ISSP item: "What is your opinion of the following statement: It is the responsibility of the government to reduce the differences in income between people with high incomes and those with low incomes"? 1 Disagree strongly; 2 Disagree; 3 Neither agree nor disagree; 4 Agree; 5 Agree strongly.
*Note*: Bottom panel: ISSP item: "On the whole, do you think it should be or should not be the government's responsibility to: Reduce income differences between the rich and poor?"
1 Definitely should not be; 2 Probably should not be; 3 Probably should be; 4 Definitely should be.

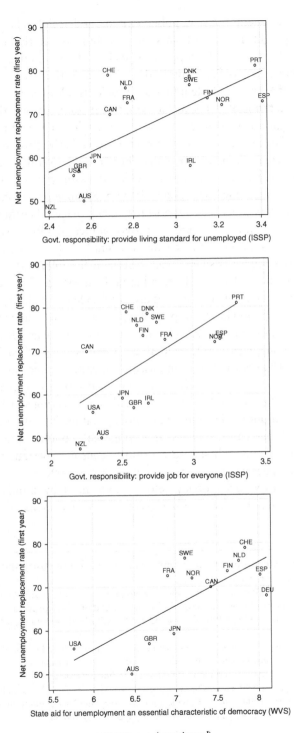

FIGURE 2.3 (*continued*)

that the relationship between public opinion and social policy making is particularly tight. In fact, scholars have established a fairly high positive correlation between public support for social policies and their provision. This relationship has been amply documented in terms of levels in the work by Jeff Manza and Clem Brooks (Brooks and Manza 2006a, 2006b, 2007) and in terms of changes in a more recent contribution (Abou-Chadi and Immergut 2014). Figures 2.2 and 2.3 provide a flavor of this kind of evidence. The two panels of Figure 2.2 show fairly close correlations between average support for redistribution and overall social policy expenditure. Figure 2.3 shows that we find the same positive correlations if we analyze a specific social policy domain: all three panels show a clear positive correlation between support for unemployment benefit generosity (measured in various ways) and the provision thereof. Obviously, "correlation is not causation – but it sure is a hint" (Tufte 2003, 4). And of course, this evidence is suggestive, at best. In the following, I will offer more systematic evidence and will address the question of causality.

Surely, there are policy areas that are not decided by majority rule, or in which public opinion has no impact. But for a government activity as vital, visible, and important as social policy making, it seems plausible that public opinion plays a role, and that decisions are backed by (large) majorities. Theoretically and empirically, therefore, there are excellent reasons to rely on a relatively simple political model that posits a link between social policy preferences and social policy making in democracies.

But what about public opinion and policy making in non-democracies? Napoleon Bonaparte is quoted as saying that "public opinion is the thermometer a monarch should constantly consult" (Bertaut 1916, 31). Even non-democratic rulers cannot ignore citizen preferences altogether. Were Bismarck's social policy reforms influenced by public opinion? Perhaps – arguably, Bismarck's legislation was a response to workers'

←───────────────────────────────────────

FIGURE 2.3: Mean support for unemployment benefit generosity and net unemployment replacement rates.

*Note*: Top panel: ISSP item: "On the whole, do you think it should or should not be the government's responsibility to ... Provide decent standard of living for the unemployed?" 1 Definitely should not be; 2 Probably should not be; 3 Probably should be; 4 Definitely should be.

*Note*: Middle panel: ISSP item: "On the whole, do you think it should or should not be the government's responsibility to ... Provide a job for everyone?" 1 Definitely should not be; 2 Probably should not be; 3Probably should be; 4 Definitely should be.

*Note*: Bottom panel: ISSP item: "On the whole, do you think it should or should not be the government's responsibility to ... Provide a job for everyone?" 1 Definitely should not be; 2 Probably should not be; 3 Probably should be; 4 Definitely should be.

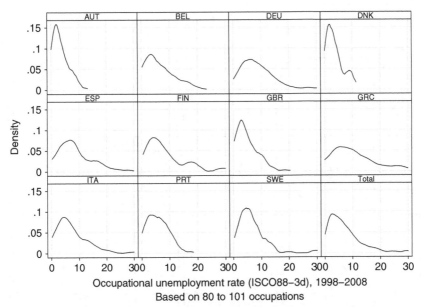

FIGURE 2.4: Empirical risk distributions – occupational unemployment risk.
*Note*: Occupational unemployment rates are top-coded at 30 percent.
*Source*: Based on EU-LFS data.

demands. But, surely, the link between public opinion and policy making in non-democracies – if it exists – can be expected to be less clear than in democracies. In the analyses that follow, therefore, I will restrict the sample to democracies or control for type of governance.

## 2.4 APPENDIX: SHAPE OF RISK DISTRIBUTIONS

In this Appendix, I explore risk distributions empirically. Throughout the book, occupational unemployment rates will play an important role as a measure of objective risk (they are explained in more detail in Chapter 3). Figure 2.4 displays the distribution of detailed occupational unemployment rates, based on 80 to 101 occupations in each country.[31] In all

---

[31] Shown are kernel densities. The underlying occupational classification is ISCO88-3d, and the data source is the European Labor Force Survey (EU-LFS). The risk distributions displayed in the figure are not strictly comparable with each other because they rely on different numbers of occupations (as a result of availability of data). In the following I will rely on less detailed classifications, which have the advantage of higher comparability, lower noisiness, and wider country-year coverage.

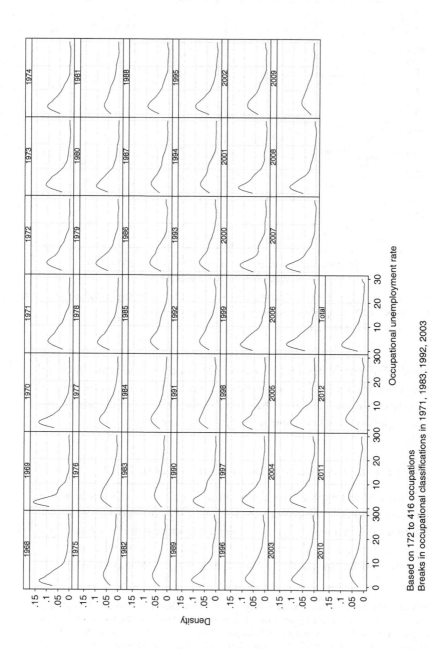

Based on 172 to 416 occupations
Breaks in occupational classifications in 1971, 1983, 1992, 2003

FIGURE 2.5: Empirical risk distributions – occupational unemployment risk in the United States over time.
*Source:* Based on March CPS files.

countries, the unemployment risk distribution is bottom-heavy (skewed to the right: i.e., the mean unemployment rate is higher than the median unemployment rate). In a similar vein, Figure 2.5 displays the unemployment risk distributions in the United States for each year since 1968 and shows that they are right-skewed as well.[32] The figure also shows that risk distributions change over time. Note, for example, the risk distributions in 1975, 1982, 1983, and 2000–01, which are much less skewed (more normally distributed) than the risk distribution in other years. Needless to say, these are recession or post-recession years (although not all recessions are characterized by this pattern).[33]

One aspect of risk that occupational unemployment rates do not indicate is the duration of unemployment. For some countries, it is possible to calculate the duration of unemployment for relatively detailed occupational groups; that allows the construction of a measure that takes into account both the unemployment rate as well as the duration of unemployment.[34] Because unemployment rates and unemployment duration are positively correlated, it is unsurprising that the resulting distributions of risk are, once again, skewed to the right (not shown).

In the following, I will also rely on subjective risk perceptions to measure risk. In particular, I will rely on the *Survey of Economic Risk Perceptions and Insecurity* (SERPI) which asked respondents to assess "out of 100 people, how many like you" will experience bad event X within the next 12 months. Figure 2.6 displays the distributions of these risk measures, which cover various (social policy) domains, ranging from job loss to home loss. Once again, these distributions are bottom-heavy.

It can be concluded, then, that risk distributions with higher means than medians – bottom-heavy or right-skewed distributions – seem to be the norm, at least for unemployment risk. But Figure 2.6 suggests that right-skewed distributions of risk or at least risk perceptions in various social policy domains – employment, health (accident, sickness), wealth, and family – are normally also right-skewed.

---

[32] The underlying occupational classification changes several times over the decades (1971, 1983, 1992, 2003), and the data source is the Current Population Survey (March annual supplements).

[33] In the United States, official recession years since 1960 are 1960, 1961, 1969, 1970, 1973, 1975, 1980, 1981, 1982, 1990, 1991, 2001, 2007, 2008, and 2009.

[34] Such a measure is fairly arbitrary because there is no obvious way to combine these two variables. But the product of unemployment rate times (weighted) unemployment duration seems to be an obvious choice (where the weight is not obvious).

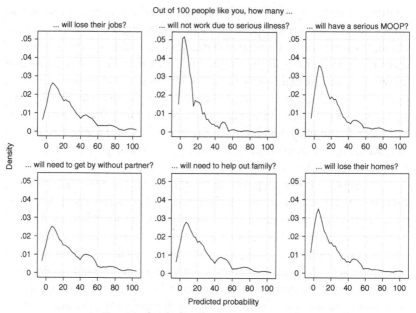

FIGURE 2.6: Empirical risk distributions – various domains (SERPI).
*Source*: SERPI.

While typically right-skewed, risk pools do differ in terms of their homogeneity – how evenly risk is distributed – across countries, domains, and time. Moreover, risk pools can in principle be top-heavy (left-skewed) as well: that is, a majority of citizens faces or perceives high risk – earlier I have called this extraordinary phenomenon a "risk flip" and suggested that it can occur in times of emergencies, such as during wars, depressions, systemic crises (banking crises, stock market crashes, hyperinflations), or epidemics.[35] During these hard times, a majority of citizens may objectively face above-average risk (or even uncertainty). But it may take less than (objective) emergencies for "risk flips" to occur, especially when it comes to (subjective) risk perceptions.

---

[35] It has been argued that public good provision was initiated because a majority (including the rich) was scared of cholera (Swaan 1988) – a good example of a left-skewed risk distribution. In a similar vein, Rimlinger has argued that the "problem of relief in the preindustrial society ... was primarily a police and sanitation problem. It was not a question of social rights" (Rimlinger 1971, 335).

# 3

## Preference Formation

Given the ubiquity of risk management by welfare states one might expect that empirical investigations of the role of risk exposure on social policy attitudes have a long tradition in the field. Yet, while the relationship between risk and social policy at the macro-level has prominently figured in the literature for decades, the first empirical contribution exploring the link between risk and social policy preferences at the micro-level appeared only in 2001 (Iversen and Soskice 2001).[1] This trailblazing study by Torben Iversen and David Soskice focuses on the relationship between social policy attitudes and one particular risk: asset specificity, that is, the degree to which skills are portable across employers. However, the portability of skills is only one of several aspects that contribute to one's risk exposure in the labor market.[2] For example, David Rueda's important work singles out job protection, which varies between labor market insiders and outsiders, and argues that their interests "are fundamentally different" (Rueda 2005, 62). A measure that is broader than "asset specificity," therefore, seems to be desirable.

---

[1] Insofar as class is a tracer of risk, the work by Stefan Svallfors could be counted as a starting point from a sociological perspective (Svallfors 1995). The literatures on trade and immigration preferences started to pay closer empirical attention to micro-level mechanisms at around the same time (Mayda and Rodrik 2005; Scheve and Slaughter 2001).

[2] For now I focus on labor market risks; later, I will broaden this focus to include risks in other domains as well.

## 3.1 THE MEASUREMENT OF RISK EXPOSURE

How can we measure risk exposure in order to test a central micro-level implication of my theoretical framework, namely, that risk exposure correlates with social policy attitudes? Individuals face numerous risks that are – or could be – covered by social insurance programs, ranging from "old risks" (accidents at the workplace, old age, sickness, and unemployment) to "new risks" (lack of skills, single parenthood, domestic care, etc.) (Armingeon and Bonoli 2006; Taylor-Gooby 2005). Ideally, we would want to have – objective and subjective – measures of risk exposure in these different domains (labor market, family, health, retirement) as well as an overall measure of an individual's degree of risk exposure in all realms of life. While one survey (discussed and employed later) moves into that direction, existing domain-specific and overall risk exposure measures are not available cross-nationally, and they are purely subjective. Because my goal is not only to evaluate the impact of risk exposure on social policy attitudes (this chapter) but also to compare and contrast risk distributions across countries and over time (in later chapters), cross-national availability and an objective measure are crucial for my purposes.

I propose that an individual's probability of losing his or her job ("job insecurity" or "threat of unemployment") is a good objective proxy for risk exposure. I also propose that the probability of job loss can be measured by occupational unemployment rates. While certainly not the only risk that people face, involuntary job loss can have particularly dramatic, negative material and psychological consequences (De Witte 1999, 2005; Hayes and Nutman 1981, chap. 4).[3] Because gainful employment is the most important income source for those in the labor market (and those who depend on people in the labor market), losing one's job jeopardizes one's livelihood. Moreover, most formal treatments, including the one sketched previously in Chapter 2, model risk exposure as the probability of job loss. Measuring risk exposure by the probability of job loss, therefore, seems to be an approach that not only is true to the model, but also picks up something important. Furthermore and contra Baldwin, I consider unemployment risk and unemployment insurance (UI)

---

[3] Unemployment can have many negative psychological effects, since work performs many important functions for individuals in work-oriented societies: work is a source of income; is a form of activity; it structures time; is a source of creativity and mastery; is a source of identity; and gives people a sense of purpose (Hayes and Nutman 1981, chap. 4).

a particularly promising area for studying the politics of social solidarity: because the incidence of risk is more unequally distributed than most risks (old age and health, in particular), and because unemployment risk was historically regarded as an uninsurable risk (mainly because of moral hazard problems), the emergence of mandatory UI systems in virtually all rich democracies is all the more puzzling (Baldwin 1990, 96, 130).

I have suggested that *occupational unemployment rates* are a good proxy for the probability of job loss (Rehm 2005, 2009), and hence a good indicator of risk exposure. Occupational unemployment rates are calculated exactly as national unemployment rates are, except that the calculations are performed for detailed occupations. These unemployment rates can then be assigned to respondents in a survey based on their occupation. As an example, let us say we calculate from labor force surveys (or a similar data source) that the unemployment rate of bakers in the United States in 2000 was 8 percent, while it was 4 percent for teachers. In a public opinion survey of interest from 2000, we would then assign a risk exposure value of 8 percent for American respondents who are bakers, and 4 percent for respondents who are teachers.

My measure of risk exposure – occupational unemployment rates – has several characteristics that are, in my opinion, desirable. First, the measure is objective ("actual" risk), not subjective (perceived risk). In the following I will show that objective and subjective measures of risk exposure correlate well with each other, and that both correlate well with social policy attitudes. From this perspective, the choice between a subjective and an objective measure is inconsequential. However, objective measures have at least three advantages: they are (arguably) exogenous to attitudes, (arguably) unlike subjective measures.[4] As discussed in Chapter 2, it is not clear how much we learn from "explaining" attitudes with other attitudes. Another advantage of objective measures is that they allow us to add a risk exposure measure to existing surveys, even if they do not contain an item recording subjective risk exposure (at least as long as the survey includes a reasonably detailed measure of occupations). A final and perhaps most crucial advantage of objective risk exposure measures is that they are calculated from labor force surveys, which are widely available (across both time and space), at least much more widely available than public opinion surveys. This allows me to analyze the

---

[4] Unless people chose occupations on the basis of their risk preferences. I will address this point later.

distribution of risk cross-nationally, and over time – this is a central undertaking in the chapters to follow.

Second, I measure risk exposure at the group level (meso-level). This is almost a necessity when relying on objective unemployment risk measures since getting micro-level estimates of objective job loss probabilities is almost impossible.[5] But this is a small price to pay because measuring risk exposure at a group level, such as occupations, makes sense: risk exposure is the probability of a bad event,[6] and we cannot meaningfully establish probabilities without reference to a group.[7] I suggest that using a worker's occupation as a reference group and approximating the probability of job loss by the unemployment rate of his or her occupation provides a good measure of risk exposure.

Third, one could estimate unemployment rates for reference groups other than occupations – for example, for age cohorts, levels of education, regions, sectors of employment, or a combination thereof.[8] But I prefer to use occupations as the group level because someone's job is a particularly plausible locus of preference formation, theoretically and empirically (Kitschelt and Rehm 2014; Rehm 2009). But it is worth emphasizing that my measure of risk does not pick up someone's class location.

My occupational unemployment rates measure also has several characteristics that may be somewhat problematic. First, occupational unemployment rates by no means encompass all aspects of risk. They do not even capture all aspects of unemployment risk: the probability of job loss is just one important aspect of unemployment – the length of the unemployment spell is another important aspect. But because unemployment rates and unemployment duration are positively correlated, we

---

[5] One could use panel data to look at future employment history of respondents and predict present attitudes with unemployment experience in the future – something that works out empirically in the Swiss Household Panel survey.

[6] The literature on insiders and outsiders has relied on various measures of labor market attachment/vulnerabilities, but these are not probabilistic. In contrast, my risk exposure measure captures a probability; it is continuous and theoretically ranges from 0 to 100.

[7] A coin flip revealing tails does not mean that the probability of heads was 0. We know that the probability of heads was 0.5, but we can only approximate this empirically by looking at lots of tossed coins.

[8] In principle, occupational unemployment rates can be measured at detailed levels and they can be additionally broken down by other characteristics (gender, region, etc.). But there is a trade-off between how well occupational unemployment rates can be estimated from labor force data, and how many levels of detail (occupation, gender, etc.) they distinguish. Later, I will employ measures of risk exposure that distinguish nine broad occupations (ISCO88-1d level), but a more detailed breakdown of occupations (27 different categories, ISCO88-2d) yields comparable results.

would expect that this omission lowers the estimated impact of risk exposure, introducing a conservative bias.[9] The nature of the employment contract is another aspect that my measure does not directly consider; however, not only is it plausible that occupational unemployment rates are correlated with different types of contracts, but one could also control for employment contracts directly.

Second, one may wonder whether people select their occupations on the basis of their (risk) attitudes, in which case a correlation between attitudes and occupational unemployment rates would be due to selection. I find self-selection based on risk preferences implausible, for several reasons. To begin with, future occupational developments are shrouded in uncertainty – it seems implausible that people can predict the fate of certain occupations decades down the road. Moreover, occupational choice is highly complex and unlikely to be dominated by risk preferences. Finally, this objection vastly overestimates the luxury of choice people actually have when it comes to their careers – in contrast, it seems that the mismatch between one's preferred and actual job is rather large.[10]

---

[9] As noted, it is possible to calculate unemployment duration at the occupational level for some countries, and therefore one can take this additional information into account when constructing a measure of risk exposure. Such a measure is fairly arbitrary because there is no obvious way to combine these two variables (the product of unemployment rate times [weighted] unemployment duration seems to be an obvious choice, but the weighting is not obvious).

[10] Four more or less anecdotal pieces of evidence on this: first and most importantly, the International Social Survey Programme's (ISSP) module on Work Orientation III (ISSP Research Group 2005) contains the following survey item: "Suppose you were working and could choose between different kinds of jobs. Which of the following would you personally choose? I would choose (1) working in a private business vs. (2) working for the government or civil service." Restricting the sample to the employed working-age population (18–65) allows me to calculate the percentage of respondents who either are employed in the public sector but wish to be employed in the private sector or are employed in the private sector but wish to be employed in the public sector. That percentage of respondents employed in the "wrong" sector ranges from 17.8 percent to 47.2 percent, with an average of 26.6 percent across the 18 rich democracies in the sample (AUS 22.3%, BEL 17.8%, CAN 36.8%, CHE 19.8%, DEU 30.0%, DNK 18.3%, ESP 47.2%, FIN 25.3%, FRA 34.4%, GBR 21.9%, IRL 22.2%, JPN 34.5%, NLD 18.0%, NOR 18.3%, NZL 25.7%, PRT 35.9%, SWE 25.5%, USA 26.2%).

Second, a survey conducted by the University of Phoenix "finds that more than half (55 percent) of working adults are interested in changing careers, with nearly a quarter (24 percent) extremely or very interested in a career change. Only 14 percent of American workers are in their dream careers. … Among those working adults who are interested in changing careers, 95 percent identify barriers that are preventing them from doing so" (www.phoenix.edu/news/releases/2013/07/more-than-half-of-working-adults-are-inter ested-in-changing-careers-and-nearly-three-quarters-are-not-in-the-career-they-planned-reveals-university-of-phoenix-survey.html). Third, "70% of American workers are 'not

Third, one may also wonder whether someone's occupation is a tracer of socialization experiences (parental or otherwise). I do not find it implausible that occupations reflect socialization processes, but it is worth noting that my measure of risk exposure captures unemployment rates at the occupational level – which vary by year – and not occupations directly. However, to dispel any doubts, I will address this issue later and will show that occupational unemployment rates predict only specific but not all spending preferences (i.e., they do not simply reflect socialization).

In the following section, I will provide several tests of the proposition that risk exposure and income correlate with attitudes on social insurance.

### 3.2 RESULTS

#### 3.2.1 Objective Risk and Social Policy Attitudes

For a first, cross-national test of the micro-level predictions developed earlier, I employ the International Social Survey Program's Role of Government IV module, which was conducted around 2006 (ISSP Research Group 2006). One survey item closely relates to unemployment benefit preferences. It reads:

Please show whether you would like to see more or less government spending in each area. Remember that if you say "much more," it might require a tax increase to pay for it. Here: "More or less government spending for unemployment benefits."

The five answer categories are 1 spend much less; 2 spend less; 3 spend the same as now; 4 spend more; 5 spend much more.

Note that the item reminds respondents that insurance is not free, that is, that taxes may increase if more is spent on unemployment benefits. For the purposes of this analysis, this is ideal since the insurance-redistribution trade-off is exactly what drives the argument.[11]

---

engaged' or 'actively disengaged' and are emotionally disconnected from their work-places" (Gallup 2013, 12). Fourth, "only a mere six percent ... work in the exact occupation that they aspired to as children (when they were 11–15 years old)" (Polavieja and Platt 2014, 18).

[11] The reader may wonder whether the reference to the status quo built into the question poses a problem. It would if I were to use the variable as an explanatory variable. However, I employ this variable as a dependent variable and all individual level regressions contain country fixed effects, which take care of the potential problem that the

Besides income, the key explanatory variable is the *risk of unemployment*. As discussed, unemployment rates at the occupational level are a good proxy for an individual's unemployment risk. Occupational unemployment rates are calculated just as national unemployment rates are, except that the calculations are performed at the occupational level. These unemployment rates are assigned to respondents in the survey on the basis of their occupation.[12]

The ISSP survey reports *respondents' family incomes*. This variable is standardized and employed in the estimations.[13] With respect to the control variables, I largely follow the set employed in Iversen and Soskice (2001) and include the following variables: education (highest degree in three categories), age (in years), gender (dummy for female), and employment status (dummies for employed, unemployed, not employed, student, and retired). Because they are missing for too many country years, three other desirable control variables are left out (union membership, self-employment, and employment in the public sector), but this does not meaningfully alter the results. For robustness checks, I also estimate models that include skill specificity[14] and left-right party support (as in Iversen and Soskice 2001) as well as church attendance (Scheve and Stasavage 2006).[15] All estimations include country dummies.

country "means" differ. Second, no inferences are made to the country level on the basis of these individual level data. Third, robustness checks reveal that the findings with an alternative dependent variable are quite similar. It reads: "On the whole, do you think it should be or should not be the government's responsibility to: Provide a decent standard of living for the unemployed?" (Answer categories: 1 "definitely should not be"; 2 "probably should not be"; 3 "probably should be"; 4 "definitely should be"). The relevance of context for attitudinal preferences has been explored by Gingrich and Ansell (2012).

[12] I assign 2001–04 averages to the 2006 survey because they are shown in Figure 5.2. Assigning the values from the actual year in which the survey was fielded leads to the same findings. All respondents with non-missing values on their current or previous occupation (or – if missing – their spouse's occupation) are in the sample, even if they are not in the labor force (anymore). The results tend to be even stronger if the sample is restricted to currently employed respondents.

[13] I convert the variable into nine quantiles. The income variable differs across country-years and leaves much to be desired. But since the estimations later include country dummies, this is not very problematic.

[14] This is the variable "Absolute skill specificity (ISCO88-1d)" (www.people.fas.harvard.edu/~iversen/data/Measuring_skill-specificity.xls), divided by education.

[15] The specification of these robustness checks is problematic. First, skill level is in the denominator of the skill specificity index, and I therefore need to drop the education variable from these models (as in the Iversen-Soskice 2001 setup). But since education is an important determinant of unemployment risk, it is important to include the variable as a control. In other words, I can include either skill specificity or education, but not both.

The dependent variable is ordinal (with five answer categories). I therefore estimate ordered logit models. However, respondents can be easily grouped into those who want (more or much more) spending versus those who oppose higher spending. This dichotomization not only increases interpersonal comparability[16] but also simplifies the presentation of the explanatory variables' substantive effects. Therefore, the dependent variable is also recoded into a binary variable (a dummy equaling 1 if a respondent wants to see "more" or "much more" government spending on unemployment benefits, 0 for the other three answer categories). I estimate logit regressions with this variable and standard errors are clustered at the country-occupation level. For each version of the dependent variable, I estimate three models: unemployment replacement rate (URR) preferences are regressed on (1) income and a set of control variables; on (2) the occupational unemployment risk variable, income, and a set of control variables; and (3) the occupational unemployment risk variable, income, and a different set of control variables (adding skill specificity, left-right party support, and church attendance, but dropping education).

With respect to the control variables, the coefficients point in the expected directions; most of the time, they are also statistically significant at conventional levels. Support for generous unemployment benefits is higher among respondents with low education, women, the elderly, and the unemployed. Skill specificity and left-right ideology are statistically significant and correctly signed, while church attendance is not statistically significant. More relevant for my purpose are the results on the occupational unemployment rate and income variables. Rendering support for the prediction derived previously, support for unemployment benefits increases with the risk of unemployment and decreases with income. In all models, the two variables' coefficients are statistically significant and point in the conjectured direction (see Models 1 through 6 in Table 3.1). This provides support for the individual level predictions discussed in Chapter 2.[17]

---

Second, left-right party support not only reduces the sample size dramatically but is also likely to be endogenous to social policy preferences.

[16] Not all respondents will interpret the difference between "more" and "much more" in the same way. In contrast, it is arguably safe to assume that the distinction between "more" and "not more (or less)" is meaningful and comparable.

[17] The econometric analyses also clearly show a negative correlation between income and demand for insurance, which casts some doubts on the assumption regarding relative risk aversion (RRA) in Moene and Wallerstein (2001, 2003).

TABLE 3.1: *Attitudes toward unemployment benefit generosity*

|  | (1) | (2) | (3) | (4) | (5) | (6) |
|---|---|---|---|---|---|---|
|  | Dependent variable: "Please show whether you would like to see more or less government spending [for unemployment benefits]. Remember that if you say 'much more,' it might require a tax increase to pay for it." | | | | | |
|  | 1 "Spend much less"  2 "Spend less"  3 "Spend the same as now"  4 "Spend more"  5 "Spend much more" | | | Dummy for 4 "Spend more" or 5 "Spend much more" (vs. 1 "Spend much less," 2 "Spend less," or 3 "Spend the same as now") | | |
|  | Coefficients from ordered logit | | | Coefficients from logit | | |
| Occupational unemployment rate | −0.129** (0.011) | 0.032* (0.015) | 0.035* (0.016) |  | 0.041* (0.018) | 0.050* (0.020) |
| Family income in 9 quantiles | −0.071** (0.020) | −0.121** (0.010) | −0.100** (0.013) | −0.130** (0.013) | −0.119** (0.013) | −0.104** (0.017) |
| Education |  | −0.046* (0.023) |  | −0.159** (0.026) | −0.124** (0.030) |  |
| Female | 0.183** (0.047) | 0.189** (0.047) | 0.170** (0.053) | 0.081 (0.058) | 0.087 (0.059) | 0.125 (0.077) |
| Age in years | 0.014** (0.002) | 0.014** (0.002) | 0.016** (0.002) | 0.009** (0.003) | 0.009** (0.003) | 0.011** (0.003) |
| Full-time employed (vs. part-time) | −0.141* (0.055) | −0.129* (0.055) | −0.163* (0.073) | −0.139# (0.079) | −0.127 (0.079) | −0.184# (0.098) |
| Church attendance |  | −0.007 (0.019) | −0.007 (0.019) |  |  | −0.029 (0.028) |
| Skill specificity |  | 0.021** | 0.021** |  |  | 0.035** |

*(continued)*

TABLE 3.1: (continued)

|  | (1) | (2) | (3) | (4) | (5) | (6) |
|---|---|---|---|---|---|---|
|  | Dependent variable: "Please show whether you would like to see more or less government spending [for unemployment benefits]. Remember that if you say 'much more,' it might require a tax increase to pay for it." | | | | | |
|  | 1 "Spend much less" 2 "Spend less" 3 "Spend the same as now" 4 "Spend more" 5 "Spend much more" | | | Dummy for 4 "Spend more" or 5 "Spend much more" (vs. 1 "Spend much less," 2 "Spend less," or 3 "Spend the same as now") | | |
|  | Coefficients from ordered logit | | | Coefficients from logit | | |
| Party affiliation: left-right |  |  | (0.008) |  |  | (0.008) |
|  |  |  | −0.494** |  |  | −0.484** |
|  |  |  | (0.032) |  |  | (0.044) |
| Country dummies | Yes | Yes | Yes | Yes | Yes | Yes |
| Constant | Cut Points | Cut Points | Cut Points | 0.152 | −0.306 | 0.460 |
|  |  |  |  | (0.191) | (0.271) | (0.296) |
| No. of cases | 10218 | 10218 | 7061 | 10218 | 10218 | 7061 |
| Pseudo $R^2$ | 0.101 | 0.101 | 0.111 | 0.171 | 0.173 | 0.175 |
| Wald chi$^2$ | 1666.7 | 1589.5 | 1519.9 | 1375.6 | 1404.6 | 901.6 |
| Log likelihood | −12529 | −12518 | −8268 | −4841 | −4830 | −3110 |
| DF | 19 | 20 | 22 | 19 | 20 | 22 |

*Notes:* #$p < 0.1$, *$p < 0.05$, **$p < 0.01$. Coef./Std. err (clustered at the country-occupation level).
Models (1) to (3) display coefficients from ordered logit estimations. Models (4) to (6) display coefficients from logit estimations. Sample restricted to respondents employed full- or part-time.
Sample (models 1, 2, 4, 5): Australia (1,413), Canada (500), Denmark (770), Finland (542), Germany (601), Ireland (423), Netherlands (535), New Zealand (756), Norway (723), Portugal (605), Spain (1,023), Sweden (673), Switzerland (482), United States (856), United Kingdom (439).
*Source:* ISSP.

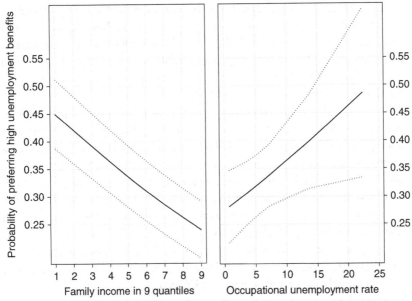

FIGURE 3.1: Income and risk as determinants of support for unemployment benefit generosity.

*Note*: "Please show whether you would like to see more or less government spending in each area. Remember that if you say 'much more,' it might require a tax increase to pay for it." Here: "More or less government spending for unemployment benefits" (ISSP 2006) ("spend much more" and "spend more" vs. "spend much less," "spend less," and "spend the same as now"). Based on logit regressions with a full set of controls. Standard errors clustered by country and occupation

To get a sense of the substantive effect of the key explanatory variables Figure 3.1 displays changes in predicted probabilities. These simulations are based on Model 5 in Table 3.1. They show how the predicted probability to prefer "more" or "much more" government spending for unemployment benefits changes as a result of simulated changes in income and occupational unemployment risk, respectively, while all other explanatory variables are held constant.[18] There is no rule about what amounts to a substantively important effect. But the simulations show that income and occupational unemployment risk are among the best predictors of attitudes toward unemployment benefits. Simulating a change from lowest to highest income decreases the probability of preferring "more" or "much more" spending on unemployment benefits by the

[18] The predicted probability to be in favor of generous benefits is 0.376 when continuous variables are set to their means, and dummy variables to their minimum.

government from about 0.45 to about 0.24, or by about 0.21 probability points. A change from lowest unemployment to highest unemployment risk increases the same probability from about 0.28 to about 0.49, that is, by about 0.20. This is roughly comparable to the change in predicted probability when simulating a change to unemployment, if one does not restrict the sample to the employed.[19]

In substantive terms, therefore, the simulations show that the risk of unemployment is almost as powerful in shaping preferences for unemployment benefits as actually being unemployed, and almost as important as income. In my opinion, these are large substantive effects. But they are derived from extreme simulations. Figure 3.1 displays values of the simulated variables on the horizontal axis, allowing the reader to assess less extreme simulations. For example, the occupational unemployment rate of elementary occupations (ISCO88-1d code 9) is about 4 percent in Switzerland, while it is about 18 percent in Finland. The respective simulated probabilities to prefer redistribution are about 0.30 (Switzerland) and about 0.44 (Finland).

From the respective coefficients' performances in terms of their statistical significance, their robustness across models, their substantive effects, and their (partial) non-effects for irrelevant domains (see later discussion), I conclude that occupational unemployment risk is a strong and important predictor of preferences for unemployment benefits; something similar can be concluded for income. As conjectured, people favor generous unemployment benefits if they are poor, or if they are exposed to a high risk of becoming unemployed. At the micro-level, then, the logic of preference formation outlined in Chapter 2 finds empirical support.

### 3.2.1.1 Validity of the Occupational Unemployment Risk Measure

Since the occupational unemployment risk measure plays an important role not only in this chapter but in the macro-level analyses later, I empirically explore two concerns: whether the measure predicts subjective risk well; and whether the measure picks up socialization, but not risk. I will address these questions in reverse order.

First, are occupational unemployment rates picking up unemployment risk, or something else? Since the measure is based on occupations, one may conjecture that it really just is a proxy for socialization or general

---

[19] When changing from the minimum to the maximum values, the results for changes in predicted probabilities for the other variables are education -0.14; female 0.02; age 0.16; full-time employed -0.03.

spending preferences. I do not find this particularly worrisome since occupational unemployment rates can be measured at extremely detailed levels, and since they differ over time (unlike, e.g., measures of class, which are typically also based on occupational information). But, fortunately, we can explore this possibility directly by regressing attitudes that are more or less (un)related to unemployment risk on my measure of unemployment risk. Ideally, the risk measure should predict labor market attitudes well, but not (as well) those attitudes toward policy domains that have little connection to unemployment risk (health insurance, outside the United States, or defense spending). The following Table 3.2 shows that this is, by and large, the case. It displays the regression coefficients for occupational unemployment rates as well as income from models that are equivalent to Models 2 and 5 in Table 3.1, except that the dependent variables are attitudes on spending in various policy domains.

Table 3.2 shows that the occupational unemployment rate measure performs best when predicting spending on unemployment benefits, as it should. It has some predictive power with respect to retirement spending and the environment, but little or none for the other domains (culture and arts; defense; law enforcement). Perhaps most remarkably, unemployment risk does not consistently predict preferences for health or education spending. If we allow for non-linearities, most of the significant effects of occupational unemployment rates on attitudes other than unemployment benefits are fairly non-linear, and the strongest, if any, effect occurs at the very bottom of the risk distribution (this likely picks up professionals). Finally, if we restrict the sample to respondents 60 years or older, occupational unemployment risk (based on respondents' previous occupations) does not predict attitudes toward unemployment benefit generosity (neither does it for the other spending domains, with the exception of retirement spending).

Second, do occupational unemployment rates predict subjective measures of job insecurity? I will discuss the relationship between objective and subjective measures of economic insecurity at length in the next chapter. Here, I simply want to explore the link between occupational unemployment rates and subjectively perceived probabilities to lose one's job. To this end, I employ the following item, which is included for many years in the American General Social Survey (Smith et al. 2011):

"Thinking about the next 12 months, how likely do you think it is that you will lose your job or be laid off?" The (recoded) answer categories are: 1 not likely, 2 not too likely, 3 fairly likely, 4 very likely.

TABLE 3.2: *Occupational unemployment rates as predictors of various social policy attitudes*

| More or less spending for: | Ordered logit (Spend much less; Spend less; Spend the same as now; Spend more; Spend much more) (Model 2 in Table 3.1) | | Logit (Spend more or Spend much more vs. other categories) (Model 5 in Table 3.1) | |
|---|---|---|---|---|
| | Occupational unemployment rates | Income | Occupational unemployment rates | Income |
| Unemployment benefits | 0.032* | −0.121** | 0.041* | −0.119** |
| | (0.015) | (0.010) | (0.018) | (0.013) |
| Retirement | 0.024 | −0.071** | 0.038* | −0.069** |
| | (0.015) | (0.012) | (0.015) | (0.013) |
| Environment | −0.029** | −0.003 | −0.032** | 0.001 |
| | (0.007) | (0.010) | (0.008) | (0.011) |
| Culture and arts | −0.022* | −0.020# | −0.014 | −0.046** |
| | (0.010) | (0.011) | (0.012) | (0.013) |
| Education | −0.020** | 0.012 | −0.015 | 0.014 |
| | (0.007) | (0.010) | (0.009) | (0.012) |
| Defense | 0.011 | 0.004 | 0.020* | −0.018 |
| | (0.009) | (0.010) | (0.010) | (0.014) |
| Law enforcement | 0.003 | 0.009 | 0.003 | 0.005 |
| | (0.008) | (0.011) | (0.009) | (0.012) |
| Health | 0.002 | −0.048** | 0.010 | −0.051** |
| | (0.011) | (0.011) | (0.017) | (0.014) |

*Notes:* #$p < 0.1$, *$p < 0.05$, **$p < 0.01$. Coefficients (standard errors, clustered by country-occupation level).
Models are equivalent to Models 2 and 5 in Table 3.1 (the same control variables are included, but not shown).
*Source:* ISSP.

I use this item as the dependent variable. The explanatory variables of interest are occupational unemployment rates, which I measure at two different levels of detail: at the ISCO88-1d level, distinguishing nine different occupations, and at the ISCO88-2d level, distinguishing 27 different occupations. The General Social Survey (GSS) does not code occupations as in the ISCO classification, but by means of concordances one can derive it from the existing classification (Meyer and Osborne 2005). Occupational unemployment rates are derived from the Current Population Survey (King et al. 2009). In terms of control variables, I largely follow the arrangement in McCarty, Poole, Rosenthal (McCarty, Poole, and Rosenthal 2006). I also restrict the sample to employed respondents, ages 22 to 65.

Table 3.3 displays the results from regressing subjective perceptions of job security onto occupational unemployment rates plus a set of control variables. The table has four models. Models 1 and 2 estimate ordered logit since the dependent variable has four categories. In Models 3 and 4, the dependent variable is a dummy equaling 1 for respondents who chose answer categories "fairly likely" or "very likely." These models are estimated with logit regressions. The results show a statistically significant correlation between my objective measure of unemployment risk and subjectively perceived job security, whether the occupational unemployment rates are measured at the ISCO88-1d level (Models 1 and 3) or at the ISCO88-2d level (Models 2 and 4).[20]

In substantive terms, the impact of occupational unemployment rates on perceived job security is fairly large (and comparable across the models). Simulations based on Model 4 in Table 3.3, for example, suggest that the probability of finding it "fairly likely" or "very likely" to lose one's job within the next 12 months increases from less than 7 percent for a respondent in an occupation with less than 1 percent unemployment rate to more than 23 percent for a respondent in an occupation with 20 percent or more unemployment. Figure 3.2 plots the predicted probabilities against values of occupational unemployment rates since this allows for a first – albeit crude – assessment of how closely risk assessments and risk realities match. Figure 3.2 suggests a fairly close match between objectively measured and subjectively perceived probabilities to lose one's job, at least for middling values. For example, about 12 percent of respondents in occupations with 10 percent unemployment rate consider it to be likely that they will lose their job. This is a first indication that risk assessments could be fairly accurate. The next chapter will offer more nuanced evidence on the same topic.

### 3.2.2 Subjective Risk and Social Policy Attitudes

In the main, the preceding analysis employed objective measures of risk exposure to predict social policy attitudes; the analysis was also restricted

---

[20] Subjective job insecurity is also a statistically significant predictor of spending preferences for unemployment benefits. In substantive terms, the probability of being in favor of "more" or "much more" government spending on unemployment benefits increases from 0.22 to 0.32 comparing a respondent who thinks it is "not likely" that he or she will lose his or her job within the next 12 months with one who thinks it is "very likely" (controlling for the same factors as in Table 3.3).

TABLE 3.3: *Occupational unemployment rates and perceptions of job security*

| | (1) | (2) | (3) | (4) |
|---|---|---|---|---|
| | Thinking about the next 12 months, how likely do you think it is that you will lose your job or be laid off? | | | |
| | 1 Not likely, 2 Not too likely, 3 Fairly likely, 4 Very likely | | Dummy for fairly likely/very likely | |
| | Ordered logit | | Logit | |
| Occupational unemployment rate, ISCO88-1d | 0.050* (0.021) | | 0.073** (0.022) | |
| Occupational unemployment rate, ISCO88-2d | | 0.054** (0.016) | | 0.077** (0.017) |
| Income (in 10K) | −0.079** (0.012) | −0.078** (0.010) | −0.119** (0.031) | −0.114** (0.021) |
| Age | −0.005* (0.002) | −0.004* (0.002) | −0.002 (0.003) | −0.002 (0.002) |
| Female | −0.023 (0.054) | −0.005 (0.072) | −0.166* (0.082) | −0.130 (0.094) |
| Working part-time | 0.336** (0.050) | 0.331** (0.066) | 0.513** (0.113) | 0.502** (0.113) |
| Some college | −0.006 (0.081) | 0.008 (0.085) | −0.407** (0.122) | −0.378* (0.148) |
| College or more | 0.035 (0.058) | 0.049 (0.065) | −0.285** (0.087) | −0.275** (0.099) |
| African American | 0.430** (0.042) | 0.425** (0.060) | 0.653** (0.097) | 0.655** (0.093) |
| South and not black | 0.040 (0.048) | 0.020 (0.041) | −0.002 (0.090) | −0.033 (0.087) |
| Frequent church attendance | −0.139** (0.050) | −0.142** (0.051) | −0.144* (0.065) | −0.145* (0.057) |
| Constant | Cut Points | Cut Points | −2.087** (0.203) | −2.144** (0.170) |
| No. of cases | 14083 | 13907 | 14083 | 13907 |
| Pseudo $R^2$ | 0.020 | 0.021 | 0.056 | 0.059 |
| Log likelihood | −12921 | −12715 | −4419 | −4332 |

*Notes*: Shown are coefficients above standard errors (clustered by occupations) in parentheses.
#$p < 0.1$, *$p < 0.05$, **$p < 0.01$.
*Source*: GSS.

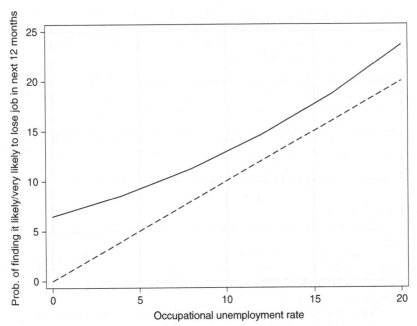

FIGURE 3.2: Occupational unemployment rates and perceptions of job security.
*Notes*: Simulations are based on Model 4 in Table 3.3.
The dashed line is the 45-degree line. The solid line shows the predicted probability of finding
it likely or very likely to lose one's job within the next 12 months.

to labor market related risks and attitudes. What happens if subjective
measures of risk exposure are used? And what is the relationship between
risk exposure and attitudes in other domains? In the following brief
analysis, I employ parts of a battery of questions in the *Survey of Economic Risk Perceptions and Insecurity* (SERPI) that asked respondents to
assess "out of 100 people, how many like you" will experience bad event
X within the next 12 months. This item was designed to address various
known issues when it comes to probability assessments in surveys –
something respondents are typically considered to do badly (Hacker,
Rehm, and Schlesinger 2013).

I will deal with these subjective probabilities in great detail in the next
chapter. Here, I simply want to explore whether they predict social policy
attitudes or not. I can explore this for a subset of subjective probabilities
and matched spending preferences. The mapping of items from risk
expectations to spending attitudes is shown in Table 3.4. In the following
analysis, I will regress a binary variable indicating whether a respondent

TABLE 3.4: *Mapping of risk expectations and spending attitudes (United States)*

| Risk expectations (for March 2009–March 2010) | Spending attitude (March 2009) |
|---|---|
| "People face certain risks that can affect their economic situation or other important aspects of their lives. We'd like you to indicate how likely each of the following risks might be, in terms of the chance that they'll affect the lives of people like you over the next year. Out of 100 people like you, how many … " | "Consider a list of existing federal programs. If you had a say in making up the federal budget this year, should federal spending be increased or decreased for … " [a] |
| … will lose their jobs during the next year?" | Unemployment Benefits |
| … will have a serious illness in their immediate family that creates major out-of-pocket medical expenses during the next year?" | Health insurance for working-age adults |
| … will lose a couple of months from work due to serious illness during the next year? | Health insurance for working-age adults |
|  | Health and financial benefits for the disabled |
| … will have been victims of violent crime during the next year?" | Dealing with crime |
| … will be directly harmed by a terrorist act during the next year?" | The war on terrorism |

*Note:* [a] This item has seven answer categories: Spend a great deal less; Spend a moderate amount less; Spend a little less; Spend about the same; Spend a little more; Spend a moderate amount more; Spend a great deal more.

wants to spend more on a particular program in the United States[21] on a subjective risk variable related to the same domain and a set of control variables (income, education, age, female, black, Hispanic, number of kids, married, ability to buffer, two measures of risk aversion). For example, the dependent variable in the second model equals 1 for respondents who would like to increase federal spending for "health

---

[21] The dummy equals 1 for the following answer categories: 5 Spend a little more; 6 Spend a moderate amount more; 7 Spend a great deal more. It equals 0 for the following answer categories: 1 Spend a great deal less; 2 Spend a moderate amount less; 3 Spend a little less; 4 Spend about the same. The exact question wording is displayed in Table 3.4.

insurance for working-age adults," and the matched risk variable records the answer to the following survey item: "Out of 100 people like you, how many will have a serious illness in their immediate family that creates major out-of-pocket medical expenses during the next year?"

Table 3.5 reports the results from logit estimations that explore the relationship between spending attitudes in a domain and subjective risk in the same domain. The table shows that in all cases/domains, risk expectations are a statistically significant predictor of attitudes toward spending by the federal government: respondents who have higher self-perceived risk favor more government spending. The substantive effects are quite large: the predicted probability to favor increased federal spending on unemployment benefits increases (fairly linearly) from 0.466 to 0.787, that is, by almost 70 percent (Model 1). Expecting high medical out-of-pocket expenditure versus not expecting them increases the probability of favoring increased spending on health insurance for the working age population from 0.521 to 0.769, that is, by almost 50 percent (Model 2). Higher self-perceived risk of losing a couple of months from work as a result of serious illness raises support for increased spending on health insurance (from 0.506 to 0.878 in the extreme, i.e., by almost 75 percent) (Model 3); it also increases the probability of supporting increased spending for health and financial benefits for the disabled by about 46 percent (from 0.555 to 0.813) (Model 4). Finally, higher subjective probabilities of being a victim of a violent crime or being directly harmed by a terrorist act are strongly associated with attitudes in favor of increased spending on dealing with crime and the war on terrorism, respectively (simulating the extremes, the increase with respect to spending on crime is more than 50 percent [0.495 to 0.764], and it is about 112 percent with respect to terrorism [0.258 to 0.549]). Subjective risk perceptions are closely associated with spending attitudes, across different (social) policy domains.

The performance of income as a predictor in these estimations is also interesting. In all but Model 4, income is *not* a significant predictor of spending preferences. A variable that taps into respondent's wealth (how long till in financial trouble? 1 Less than a week through 6 months or more) is typically significantly correlated with spending preferences, but the substantive effects are relatively modest. This mediocre performance of income as a predictor of social policy attitudes – at least in models that include subjective, domain-specific risk perceptions – offers an empirical justification for prioritizing risk over income as a source of social policy preferences.

TABLE 3.5: *Subjective risk perceptions and spending attitudes (United States)*

| Risk | (1) | (2) | (3) | (4) | (5) | (6) |
|---|---|---|---|---|---|---|
| | "If you had a say in making up the federal budget this year, should federal spending be increased or decreased for ..." | | | | | |
| | Unemployment benefits | Health insurance | Health insurance | Benefits for the disabled | Dealing with Crime | The war on terrorism |
| Job loss | 0.015** | | | | | |
| | (0.003) | | | | | |
| High medical out of pocket expenditures | | 0.012** | | | | |
| | | (0.003) | | | | |
| Unable to work due to injury | | | 0.020** | | | |
| | | | (0.005) | | | |
| Unable to work due to injury | | | | 0.013* | | |
| | | | | (0.005) | | |
| Victim of violent crime | | | | | 0.012** | |
| | | | | | (0.005) | |
| Victim of terrorism | | | | | | 0.013** |
| | | | | | | (0.005) |
| Income quintiles | -0.087 | 0.042 | 0.045 | -0.141** | 0.046 | -0.039 |
| | (0.055) | (0.056) | (0.055) | (0.054) | (0.056) | (0.061) |
| Education | 0.086 | -0.037 | -0.015 | -0.050 | -0.159 | -0.445** |
| | (0.109) | (0.113) | (0.112) | (0.109) | (0.106) | (0.125) |
| Age | 0.013* | -0.000 | -0.001 | 0.009# | 0.022** | 0.020** |
| | (0.005) | (0.005) | (0.005) | (0.005) | (0.005) | (0.006) |
| Female | 0.143 | 0.246# | 0.231# | 0.340** | 0.028 | -0.290# |
| | (0.129) | (0.129) | (0.131) | (0.130) | (0.129) | (0.152) |

| | 2014 | 2010 | 2003 | 2006 | 2016 | 2007 |
|---|---|---|---|---|---|---|
| Black | 1.196** | 1.017** | 0.896** | 1.015** | 0.967** | 0.114 |
| | (0.287) | (0.287) | (0.295) | (0.292) | (0.257) | (0.261) |
| Hispanic | 0.364 | 0.104 | 0.054 | -0.201 | 0.295 | -0.846# |
| | (0.324) | (0.302) | (0.303) | (0.308) | (0.311) | (0.465) |
| No. of kids | -0.042 | -0.074 | -0.090 | -0.093# | -0.046 | -0.052 |
| | (0.057) | (0.055) | (0.056) | (0.055) | (0.056) | (0.073) |
| Married | 0.176 | -0.263# | -0.244 | -0.036 | -0.086 | -0.070 |
| | (0.157) | (0.160) | (0.162) | (0.163) | (0.157) | (0.177) |
| How long till in financial trouble? | -0.114* | -0.153** | -0.143** | -0.094# | -0.117* | 0.039 |
| | (0.049) | (0.049) | (0.049) | (0.049) | (0.046) | (0.055) |
| Risk averse (job) | -0.009 | -0.052 | -0.048 | 0.025 | -0.021 | -0.055 |
| | (0.044) | (0.043) | (0.044) | (0.045) | (0.041) | (0.047) |
| Risk averse (general) | 0.333** | 0.297** | 0.279** | 0.287** | 0.303** | 0.081 |
| | (0.102) | (0.098) | (0.101) | (0.099) | (0.090) | (0.094) |
| Constant | -1.927** | -0.354 | -0.360 | -0.760 | -1.739** | -1.180# |
| | (0.634) | (0.618) | (0.626) | (0.628) | (0.583) | (0.668) |
| No. of cases | 2014 | 2010 | 2003 | 2006 | 2016 | 2007 |
| Pseudo $R^2$ | 0.081 | 0.064 | 0.068 | 0.076 | 0.059 | 0.061 |
| Wald chi² | 93.6 | 78.8 | 76.4 | 80.6 | 58.6 | 63.9 |
| Log likelihood | -1241 | -1252 | -1241 | -1215 | -1282 | -1093 |

Notes: Coefficients from logit estimations displayed above standard errors in parentheses.

#$p < 0.1$, *$p < 0.05$, **$p < 0.01$.

See Table 3.4 for exact wording of risk and spending variables.

Source: SERPI.

57

More importantly, the results in this chapter provide strong correlational support for the claim that welfare state preferences are importantly shaped in the way my theoretical framework suggests. In particular,
risk exposure turns out to be an important predictor of social policy
attitudes. This raises the intriguing question of how individuals figure
out their risk exposure. Chapter 4 will explore this question.

# 4

## Risk Perceptions

Every year, about 30 Americans die because they are struck by lightning. About 45,000 die as a result of lack of health insurance. Excluding the 9/11 atrocities, which killed 2,997 people and injured more than 6,000, fewer than 500 people died in the United States of terrorist attacks between 1970 and 2010. Every single month, millions of Americans lose their jobs.[1] Yet we know more about people's perception of the risk of being hit by lightning or being the victim of a terrorist attack than their perceptions of the risk of losing their health insurance or their job.

In fact, the rich literature on risk perceptions largely ignores risks covered by social policy programs, such as old age, ill health, accident, and unemployment. Because much of what governments do is the management of social policy risks, and because risk perceptions motivate political behavior, this is no small omission. Two questions are particularly relevant: How do citizens form risk perceptions? And are risk perceptions accurate? With respect to social policy risks, neither of these questions has been explored systematically in the existing literature. This chapter will address them, in reverse order.

The next section explores whether risk perceptions are accurate. Using the *Survey of Risk Perceptions and Insecurity* (SERPI), an original panel survey, I find that subjective risk perceptions are fairly realistic, at least in relative terms. I then analyze the correlates of risk perceptions and find

---

[1] *Sources*: (i) www.struckbylightning.org: 2012 statistics: 28 killed, 212 injured. See also www.cdc.gov/nchs/data/mortab/98gm3_10.pdf, table III (p. 52); (ii) (Wilper et al. 2009, 2294); (iii) www.start.umd.edu/start/announcements/BackgroundReport_10YearsSince9_11.pdf; (iv) www.bls.gov/cps/cps_flows.htm

that one of the best predictors of the subjective probability of experiencing a bad event at time $t$ is the actual occurrence of that bad event
at future time $t + 1$. Next, I turn to the question of how risk perceptions
are formed. Since people seem to have a good sense of whether they are
exposed to higher or lower risk, I analyze the characteristics of social
policy risks in order to explore how people can form reasonably accurate
risk perceptions. I find that social policy risks (in the United States) are
correlated in three ways: over time, across domains, and within networks.
I conclude by showing that respondents draw on the clustering of shocks
over time and within network as sources of information in order to form
their own risk perceptions.

## 4.1 ARE SOCIAL POLICY RISK PERCEPTIONS ACCURATE?

The rich and contentious literature on risk perception not only largely
ignores risks covered by social policy; it also does not agree on a definition
of risk and risk perceptions. In the risk literature, the concept of risk is used
"as an expected value, [as] a probability distribution, as uncertainty and
as an event" (Aven and Renn 2010, 2). In the previous chapters, risk was
loosely defined as the probability of experiencing a bad event. Despite not
being a universally accepted definition, this characterization of risk turns
out to be a widely shared understanding. For example, Graham and
Wiener (1997, 23) define risk "as the chance of an adverse outcome" and
Schaeffer (2008, 37) concludes that "there is generally an accepted assumption that ... the probability of something bad happening constitutes risk."

   In this chapter, I define and measure risk perceptions as subjective
probabilities that a bad event will happen. In collaboration with Jacob
Hacker and Mark Schlesinger, I have developed a new survey instrument,
the *Survey of Economic Risk Perceptions and Insecurity* (SERPI), which
addresses two difficulties with the measurement of risk perceptions defined
in this way. The first difficulty is that existing research has established that
risk perceptions vary greatly depending on the target. Typically, respondents have an optimism bias: they assign much higher probabilities to
occurrence of bad events to "people in general" and slightly higher probabilities to "their family" as compared to "themselves" (Knuth et al. 2013;
Mutz 1998; Sjöberg 2000). It is therefore important to be specific about
the target of risk perceptions. In this chapter, the target of risk perceptions
is the respondent herself, not society as a whole. Consequently, respondents are asked to give subjective probabilities that bad events will happen
to "people like them." The second difficulty in the measurement of risk

perceptions is that the concept of "probabilities" is difficult to comprehend for many respondents. To mitigate this problem, the SERPI made use of the fact that it was administered over the Internet by employing a new visual tool for helping respondents estimate the probability of risky outcomes. A pictograph of 100 green people was displayed beside the question; once a respondent typed an answer to the question "Out of 100 people like you, how many will experience bad event X," the respective number of people turned from green to red in the pictograph. This approach strongly mitigated the problem of response "clumping" at focal points (0 percent, 25 percent, 50 percent, and 100 percent).

This chapter relies on a series of risk perceptions from the SERPI that were asked in March 2009 (wave 15 of the 2008 ANES [American National Election Studies] Time Series Study). To elicit risk perceptions, the following questions were asked:

People face certain risks that can affect their economic situation or other important aspects of their lives. We'd like you to indicate how likely each of the following risks might be, in terms of the chance that they'll affect the lives of people like you over the next year:

- Out of 100 people like you, how many will lose their homes during the next year because they won't be able to pay their mortgages?
- Out of 100 people like you, how many will need to help out someone in their extended family with a substantial amount of money during the next year?
- Out of 100 people like you, how many will lose their jobs during the next year?
- Out of 100 people like you, how many will have a serious illness in their immediate family that creates major out-of-pocket medical expenses during the next year?
- Out of 100 people like you, how many will need to start getting by with less money because their spouse/partner is no longer there during the next year due to death, divorce, or some other circumstance?
- Out of 100 people like you, how many will lose a couple of months of work due to serious illness during the next year?
- Out of 100 people like you, how many will have been victims of violent crime during the next year?
- Out of 100 people like you, how many will be directly harmed by a terrorist act during the next year?

In order to assess whether risk perceptions are accurate, I compare them with realizations of risk in the future. This analysis requires panel data that ask about risk expectations at time $t$ and record risk experiences at $t + 1$. The SERPI not only includes the set of questions that capture subjective probabilities listed previously, which were asked in March

2009 (wave 15), but also contains items recording risks experienced since March 2009, which were asked 6 months later in September 2009 (wave 21 of the 2008 ANES Time Series Study). Therefore, subjective assessment of risk can be matched with objective risk. Table 4.1 displays the mapping of risk expectations with risk experience that is used in the following empirical investigations (crime is listed, but not systematically explored). The match of risk expectations and risk experiences is not perfect. Perhaps most problematically, the risk expectations item asks about the likelihood of bad events "over the next year," that is, roughly from March 2009 to March 2010. In contrast, the risk experiences item fielded in September 2009 asks about events "at any time since March 2009," therefore covering the 6 months between March 2009 and September 2009. As a simple and clearly imperfect fix, I multiplied the realized risk numbers by a factor of 2, converting them from 6 to 12 months.

Furthermore, the probabilistic nature of risk makes it impossible to study the accuracy of risk perceptions at the individual level. If we ask about the probability of a bad event, the experience of a single individual is not informative for the accurateness of this probability. The level of analysis must therefore be groups. To compare risk expectations with actual risk experiences in the future, I divide respondents into groups based on their subjective risk perceptions. These groups could be defined in various ways – I group respondents into quintiles (and, at times, also deciles), which are based on their expected risk. Table 4.2 provides summary statistics for each risk quintile in each domain. For example, the table shows that the middle quintile for the expected probability of losing one's job had a minimum estimate of 18, a median of 25, a mean of 24.1, and a maximum of 30.

To assess the accuracy of risk perceptions at the group level, I rely on a simple graphical approach: plotting the average subjective probability of a group (at time $t$) against the average risk experience in that group (occurring in the 6 months after $t$).[2] The top left panel of Figure 4.1 shows the results for the risk of job loss (the other domains shown in the same figure will be discussed later). The figure not only shows the scatterplot of average risk expectations and future risk experiences, but also indicates

---

[2] As mentioned previously, I multiply the risk experience rate by 2 to align the risk expectation period of 12 months with the risk experience period of 6 months. Therefore, interpreting the following findings in absolute terms is somewhat problematic and I will avoid that or alert the reader of the perils of doing so.

TABLE 4.1: *Risk expectations and risk realizations*

| Risk expectations (for March 2009–March 2010) | Label | Risk experiences (between March 2009 and September 2009) |
|---|---|---|
| "People face certain risks that can affect their economic situation or other important aspects of their lives. We'd like you to indicate how likely each of the following risks might be, in terms of the chance that they'll affect the lives of people like you over the next year. Out of 100 people like you, how many … " | | "At any time since March 2009, have you: … "[a] |
| … will lose their jobs during the next year?" | Loss of job | Been unemployed not by personal choice (Had other working adults in your household unemployed, not by personal choice)[b] |
| … will need to help out someone in their extended family with a substantial amount of money during the next year?" | Family help | Spent a substantial sum helping out your extended family |
| … will lose their homes during the next year because they won't be able to pay their mortgages?"; | Loss of home | Lost your home because you couldn't pay the mortgage Been evicted because you failed to pay the rent |
| … will have a serious illness in their immediate family that creates major out-of-pocket medical expenses during the next year?" | Major out-of-pocket expenses | Had major out-of-pocket medical expenses as the result of serious illness or injury (Had to pay a lot more for your health insurance than expected)[b] (Lost your health insurance)[b] |
| … will need to start getting by with less money because their spouse/partner is no longer there during the next year, due to death, divorce, or some other circumstance?" | Loss of spouse | Been divorced or separated from your spouse Had your spouse/partner pass away |
| … will lose a couple of months from work due to serious illness during the next year?" | Loss of hours at work | You or someone in your immediate family lost substantial time from work due to illness or injury |
| … will have been victims of violent crime during the next year?" … will be directly harmed by a terrorist act during the next year?" | Victim of crime | Been the victim of a violent crime NA |

*Notes:* [a] If there is more than one risk listed, the experience with either of them is taken [b] These could be added, with little difference for the overall patterns.
*Source:* SERPI.

TABLE 4.2: *Distribution of expected probabilities, by expected probabilities quintiles*

| Quintile | Min | Median | Mean | Max |
|---|---|---|---|---|
| | | Loss of job | | |
| I | 0 | 3 | 3.4 | 8 |
| 2 | 9 | 10 | 11.9 | 17 |
| 3 | 18 | 25 | 24.2 | 30 |
| 4 | 32 | 45 | 44.3 | 50 |
| 5 | 52 | 75 | 74.0 | 100 |
| | | Loss of home | | |
| I | 0 | 2 | 2.5 | 5 |
| 2 | 6 | 10 | 9.3 | 10 |
| 3 | 11 | 20 | 19.1 | 25 |
| 4 | 27 | 40 | 41.6 | 50 |
| 5 | 51 | 70 | 74.1 | 100 |
| | | Loss of hours at work | | |
| I | 0 | 1 | 1.4 | 3 |
| 2 | 4 | 5 | 5.5 | 8 |
| 3 | 9 | 10 | 11.5 | 15 |
| 4 | 16 | 25 | 23.9 | 30 |
| 5 | 32 | 50 | 50.6 | 100 |
| | | Major medical out-of-pocket expenditure | | |
| I | 0 | 3 | 3.1 | 5 |
| 2 | 6 | 10 | 9.3 | 10 |
| 3 | 11 | 15 | 16.9 | 20 |
| 4 | 21 | 30 | 29.7 | 40 |
| 5 | 41 | 55 | 61.9 | 100 |
| | | Loss of spouse | | |
| I | 0 | 3 | 2.9 | 5 |
| 2 | 6 | 10 | 11.5 | 18 |
| 3 | 19 | 25 | 24.3 | 30 |
| 4 | 31 | 45 | 44.3 | 50 |
| 5 | 52 | 75 | 74.1 | 100 |
| | | Family help | | |
| I | 0 | 3 | 3.1 | 5 |
| 2 | 6 | 10 | 11.4 | 15 |
| 3 | 16 | 22 | 22.4 | 25 |
| 4 | 26 | 40 | 41.2 | 50 |
| 5 | 52 | 75 | 75.3 | 100 |
| | | Victim of a crime | | |
| I | 0 | 1 | 1.1 | 2 |
| 2 | 3 | 5 | 4.3 | 5 |
| 3 | 6 | 10 | 10.8 | 15 |
| 4 | 16 | 25 | 24.1 | 30 |
| 5 | 32 | 50 | 53.3 | 100 |

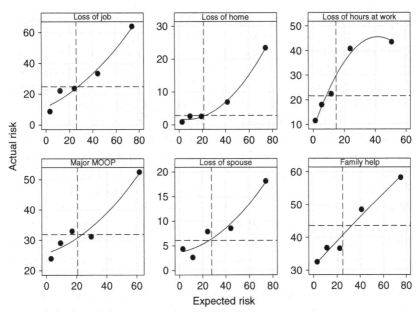

FIGURE 4.1: Expected probabilities and risk experiences.

their overall averages (dashed horizontal and dashed vertical lines). Several noteworthy patterns emerge from the figure. First, the correlation between the ranks of risk expectations and the ranks of realized risk is perfect: on average, respondents in the lowest risk expectation quintile have the lowest probability of losing their jobs; respondents in the second quintile have the second lowest probability of losing their jobs; and so on. Second, risk perceptions are biased (though the fact that I scaled risk experiences from 6 to 12 months makes this statement somewhat speculative): respondents in the group of low expected risk underestimate actual risk (optimism bias), while respondents in the two high-risk expectation groups overestimate actual risk (pessimism bias). Third, the risk expectations of the middle quintile are almost exactly right (again, let me caution that risk experiences were scaled up to 12 months). The average answer to the risk expectation item ("Out of 100 people like you, how many will lose their jobs during the next year?") was 24.2. And the percentage of respondents who were "unemployed not by personal choice" within the next 12 months was 23.7 percent ($11.84 \times 2$) – very close to 24.2 percent. Fourth, all data points are in either the northeast or the southwest quadrant defined by the averages, indicating that groups are always right in terms of whether they will be above or below the average risk.

These findings suggest that respondents' (or, more precisely: groups') risk expectations are remarkably accurate in terms of future job loss, at least in relative terms. Do these patterns hold for risk assessments in other domains as well? As the other panels in Figure 4.1 show, they generally do. The figure plots the average expected risk of a group against the percentage of group members who actually experienced that risk in the future and adds a horizontal and a vertical line that indicates the average expected and average realized risk, respectively. This allows me to assess whether groups are aware whether they are above or below the average risk, among other things. The figure shows that the correlation in terms of ranks is almost perfect in all six domains (there are a few minor exceptions, which tend to occur at the middle of the distribution in cases when the distances between groups are small). To the degree that one can make meaningful statements on the scaled data, the pattern of optimism bias at the bottom of the risk expectation distribution and pessimism bias at the top holds for four out of six examples: loss of job, loss of hours at work, major medical out-of-pocket (MOOP) expenditures, and family help. There is no optimism bias in the examples of loss of home and loss of spouse. In these domains, the majority of groups reveal a pessimism bias: that is, they overestimate risk. To speculate, this could be because these are the two areas with the lowest actual risk – making assessing probabilities particularly difficult. These two bad events (losing one's spouse or home) are also particularly serious – it could be that "risk" is not just a probability of a bad event, but also increases on the basis of the expected loss. Despite the pessimism bias, in most cases groups that expect to be below the mean risk are actually below it, while groups that anticipate being above the mean risk are actually above it.[3] There are a few exceptions, but these are mainly in groups that are very close to the middle of the risk distribution.

## 4.2  WHAT PREDICTS RISK PERCEPTIONS?

Groups defined by risk expectations seem to have fairly accurate perceptions of their own risk exposure, at least in relative terms. Because risks are probabilistic, it is not possible to perform a parallel analysis at the individual level. However, it is possible to explore the correlates of risk perceptions at the individual level, including future risk realization

---

[3] I did not add confidence intervals to the estimates because they are generally very small. Moreover, I performed a similar analysis using deciles (not quintiles). While there is a bit more noise – unsurprisingly – the findings are substantively the same.

recorded at the individual level. The existing literature on non-social policy risks points to various individual level factors that are potentially important predictors of risk perceptions.

First, it has been argued that a host of sociodemographic variables correlate with risk perceptions (Boholm 1998), most prominently race and gender. Perhaps the most consistent finding in this line of research is the so-called white male effect (for a review see Olofsson and Rashid 2011), that is, the regularity with which white male Americans have a relatively low perception of risks. Consequently, the empirical analysis will control for race and gender. Second, one may reason that risk aversion could influence risk perceptions.[4] In the empirical analysis that follows, I will therefore include measures of risk aversion as a control variable. Third, the perhaps most influential account of risk perceptions besides the psychometric approach is cultural theory.[5] The cultural theory of risk perception was presented by Douglas and Wildavsky in their book *Risk and Culture: An Essay on the Selection of Technical and Environmental Dangers* (Douglas and Wildavsky 1982). Building on a grid-group analysis, the theory suggests that people are one of four types[6] – egalitarian,

---

[4] However, it also seems plausible that risk preferences only play a role in one's reaction to risks, not their perception. It is not obvious that the risk assessment itself will be biased by different degrees of risk aversion, although risk preferences and perceptions may share an underlying cause that influences both of them (e.g., a certain degree of anxiousness), which would lead to a correlation between the two.

[5] For an overview of the two approaches, see Weber and Ancker (2011). Psychometric approaches propose that risk perceptions are influenced by characteristics of hazards that exceed the probability of their occurrence or the severity of their consequences. Empirically, a small set of characteristics are found on a regular basis, most importantly the familiarity of a risk (observable, known, old, immediate effects, vs. the opposites) and its dreadness (controllable, voluntary, non-fatal consequences, vs. the opposites) (Sjöberg 2000; Slovic 1987). The findings from psychometric approaches – which are almost entirely inductive – are, however, not particularly relevant to risks that are covered by social insurance. The very fact that social insurance schemes are established – or could plausibly be set up – implies that these risks share similar characteristics. For example, they are all observable (unlike, say, radiation), known (unlike, say, mad cow disease), old (unlike, say, cell phone radiation), immediate (unlike, say, exposure to asbestos), controllable (unlike, say, global warming), and typically not fatal. However, different social policy risks also do have different characteristics. For example, the risk of losing one's job, or losing one's spouse, or becoming old, is qualitatively different in terms of stress, emotional valence, impact on the future, and other factors. I believe that when it comes to social policy risks, systematic psychometric studies are an important and promising field of future research.

[6] The four combinations of high versus low group and grid yield the four types, according to cultural theory: high group, high grid = hierarchists; high group, low grid = egalitarians; low group, high grid = fatalists; low group, low grid = individualists.

individualistic, hierarchic, or fatalistic – and that each type of person "will 'choose' to be concerned with different types of hazards" (Sjöberg 2000, 5). Egalitarians worry about technology and the environment; individualists are concerned about war and other threats to markets; hierarchists prioritize "law and order"; and fatalists are not worried about any of these hazards. Cultural theory has been criticized from a theoretical and empirical perspective (Boholm 1996, 1998; Sjöberg 1996, 1998a, 2000, 2006) – one critic has noted that its success "is largely an example of the persuasive power of speculation" (Sjöberg 2000, 6), while its "results show clearly that general value dimensions are not very promising for understanding risk perception" (Sjöberg 2000, 7). Moreover, it is not obvious how cultural theory helps in explaining social policy risk perceptions in general and their accuracy in particular.[7] But since different "types" of respondents (should they exist) may have different biases in risk perceptions, I will control for a respondent's ideology in various ways.

In summary, I include the factors suggested by existing scholarship – sociodemographics, risk preferences, and values – along with other standard controls in my analyses of the individual-level correlates of risk perceptions. Table 4.3 displays OLS regression results in which the subjective probability of experiencing a bad event (which ranges from 0 to 100) is regressed on the future experience of a bad event (a dummy variable equaling 1 if the respondent will experience the risk in the next 6 months, 0 otherwise), as well as a set of control variables. For each domain, two models are presented. Odd-numbered models only include sociodemographic predictors, along with two measures of risk aversion and a variable that contains information on the capacity of respondents to buffer income losses. Even-numbered models include variables that proxy, more or less, the concepts that cultural theory cares about: party

---

[7] Lennart Sjöberg, who is one of the most vocal critics of cultural theory, suggests that attitudes should be factored in when considering risk perceptions (Sjöberg 2000): "The fact that attitude plays such a prominent role in the models is interesting. It suggests that risk perception is to a large extent a question of ideology in a very specific sense, not in the general sense that is posited by Cultural Theory. People who, for some reason, are strongly in favor of nuclear power tend to see it as risk free, and vice versa. This is a specific case of the general principle that people tend to see mostly good properties of those concepts or objects that they like and mostly bad properties in those that they dislike" (Sjöberg 2000, 9). Yet, at least in terms of social policy risk perceptions, these are more likely causes of attitudes rather than determinants.

TABLE 4.3: *Risk perceptions*

| | (1) | (2) | (3) | (4) | (5) | (6) | (7) | (8) | (9) | (10) | (11) | (12) | (13) | (14) |
|---|---|---|---|---|---|---|---|---|---|---|---|---|---|---|
| | Loss of job | | Loss of home | | Loss of spouse | | Family help | | Loss of hours at work | | Major MOOP | | Victim of crime | |
| Shock in domain in the future | 9.64** (1.47) | 9.61** (1.55) | 10.58** (3.01) | 10.98** (3.13) | 10.80** (2.75) | 5.71# (2.92) | 6.24** (1.28) | 6.49** (1.32) | 4.17** (1.13) | 4.43** (1.17) | 4.96** (1.26) | 4.08** (1.31) | 4.78 (3.25) | -5.56 (3.47) |
| Income (quintiles) | -1.76** (0.42) | -1.77** (0.43) | -1.64** (0.41) | -1.68** (0.42) | -2.74** (0.44) | -2.74** (0.45) | -1.29** (0.43) | -1.40** (0.45) | -1.68** (0.32) | -1.61** (0.32) | -2.49** (0.39) | -2.50** (0.40) | -1.95** (0.33) | -1.85** (0.33) |
| Education (three groups) | -5.17** (0.85) | -3.49** (0.89) | -5.68** (0.82) | -4.34** (0.86) | -2.89** (0.89) | -1.39 (0.93) | -3.30** (0.87) | -2.52** (0.92) | -2.42** (0.64) | -1.83** (0.67) | -3.53** (0.79) | -3.42** (0.84) | -4.27** (0.67) | -4.04** (0.69) |
| Age | -0.21** (0.03) | -0.20** (0.04) | -0.17** (0.03) | -0.15** (0.03) | -0.04 (0.04) | -0.01 (0.04) | -0.16** (0.04) | -0.17** (0.04) | -0.00 (0.03) | -0.00 (0.03) | 0.02 (0.03) | 0.02 (0.03) | -0.15** (0.03) | -0.18** (0.03) |
| Female | 7.37** (1.03) | 6.93** (1.06) | 5.42** (0.99) | 5.08** (1.03) | 6.41** (1.08) | 6.47** (1.12) | 7.87** (1.06) | 8.09** (1.11) | 3.83** (0.78) | 3.31** (0.81) | 4.40** (0.96) | 3.85** (1.01) | 3.24** (0.81) | 2.67** (0.83) |
| Black | 4.71** (1.60) | 2.07 (1.74) | 6.54** (1.54) | 4.44** (1.70) | 9.83** (1.67) | 9.35** (1.84) | 10.19** (1.65) | 7.61** (1.82) | 8.72** (1.22) | 5.68** (1.34) | 4.71** (1.48) | 2.14 (1.65) | 7.55** (1.26) | 4.87** (1.36) |
| Hispanic | 7.37** (2.02) | 7.02** (2.06) | 10.65** (1.94) | 11.73** (2.01) | 5.87** (2.09) | 6.19** (2.16) | -0.88 (2.07) | -0.76 (2.14) | 4.26** (1.51) | 3.84* (1.55) | 2.19 (1.87) | 0.65 (1.95) | 9.77** (1.57) | 10.48** (1.60) |
| No. of kids | 0.26 (0.41) | -0.24 (0.43) | 1.02* (0.40) | 0.67 (0.42) | 0.33 (0.43) | 0.06 (0.46) | -0.27 (0.42) | -0.56 (0.45) | 0.66* (0.31) | 0.52 (0.33) | 0.85* (0.38) | 0.92* (0.41) | 1.32** (0.32) | 0.98** (0.33) |

*(continued)*

69

TABLE 4.3: (continued)

| | (1) | (2) | (3) | (4) | (5) | (6) | (7) | (8) | (9) | (10) | (11) | (12) | (13) | (14) |
|---|---|---|---|---|---|---|---|---|---|---|---|---|---|---|
| | Loss of job | | Loss of home | | Loss of spouse | | Family help | | Loss of hours at work | | Major MOOP | | Victim of crime | |
| Married | 0.14 | 1.11 | -0.92 | 0.12 | 1.76 | 1.38 | 4.61** | 5.77** | 0.77 | 1.16 | 0.35 | 0.22 | 0.00 | -0.21 |
| | (1.21) | (1.25) | (1.16) | (1.22) | (1.29) | (1.36) | (1.25) | (1.31) | (0.91) | (0.95) | (1.12) | (1.19) | (0.95) | (0.98) |
| How long until in financial trouble? [1-6] | -2.16** | -2.35** | -2.48** | -2.46** | -1.04** | -1.07** | -1.47** | -1.09** | -1.64** | -1.54** | -1.70** | -1.55** | -1.44** | -1.32** |
| | (0.36) | (0.36) | (0.34) | (0.35) | (0.37) | (0.38) | (0.36) | (0.38) | (0.27) | (0.27) | (0.33) | (0.35) | (0.28) | (0.28) |
| Risk averse (job) [1-6] | 0.64* | 0.51 | 0.92** | 0.69* | 0.96** | 1.16** | 0.35 | 0.21 | 0.34 | 0.38 | 0.53# | 0.54# | 0.49# | 0.57* |
| | (0.32) | (0.33) | (0.31) | (0.32) | (0.34) | (0.35) | (0.33) | (0.34) | (0.24) | (0.25) | (0.30) | (0.31) | (0.25) | (0.26) |
| Risk averse (general) [1-7] | 0.96 | 1.03 | -0.00 | -0.22 | -0.04 | 0.58 | 1.15# | 1.20# | 0.19 | -0.11 | 0.01 | -0.45 | 1.56** | 1.31* |
| | (0.65) | (0.66) | (0.63) | (0.65) | (0.68) | (0.71) | (0.67) | (0.70) | (0.49) | (0.51) | (0.60) | (0.63) | (0.51) | (0.52) |
| Party ID: Democrat | | Ref cat | | Ref cat | | Ref cat | | Ref cat | | Ref cat | | Ref cat | | Ref cat |
| Party ID: Independent | | -1.12 | | -1.64 | | -2.36 | | -0.86 | | -2.24# | | -1.37 | | -1.10 |
| | | (1.79) | | (1.75) | | (1.88) | | (1.85) | | (1.36) | | (1.69) | | (1.39) |
| Party ID: Republican | | -4.45** | | -2.45# | | -1.28 | | -2.99* | | -2.96** | | -2.11 | | -2.09# |
| | | (1.43) | | (1.39) | | (1.51) | | (1.49) | | (1.09) | | (1.37) | | (1.12) |
| Ideology: Liberal | | Ref cat | | Ref cat | | Ref cat | | Ref cat | | Ref cat | | Ref cat | | Ref cat |
| Ideology: Moderate | | 2.32 | | 1.31 | | 1.70 | | -0.49 | | 2.30# | | 0.12 | | 1.28 |
| | | (1.65) | | (1.60) | | (1.74) | | (1.71) | | (1.26) | | (1.56) | | (1.28) |

| | | | | | | | | | | | | | | |
|---|---|---|---|---|---|---|---|---|---|---|---|---|---|---|
| Ideology: Conservative | | | -2.51 | -2.58# | | 0.47 | | 0.21 | | -0.72 | | -1.09 | | 1.02 |
| | | | (1.54) | (1.49) | | (1.62) | | (1.61) | | (1.18) | | (1.46) | | (1.20) |
| Index for being Authoritarian [0-4] | | | 1.69** | 1.87** | | 0.57 | | 0.52 | | 0.03 | | -0.26 | | -0.70 |
| | | | (0.55) | (0.54) | | (0.58) | | (0.58) | | (0.42) | | (0.53) | | (0.43) |
| Church attendance [1-10] | | | -0.05 | -0.09 | | -0.35* | | -0.14 | | 0.10 | | 0.04 | | 0.25* |
| | | | (0.15) | (0.15) | | (0.16) | | (0.16) | | (0.12) | | (0.14) | | (0.12) |
| Constant | 49.11** | 48.49** | 45.66** | 45.09** | 37.25** | 31.14** | 34.92** | 33.45** | 24.83** | 25.63** | 34.23** | 38.42** | 28.01** | 31.08** |
| | (4.04) | (3.88) | (4.36) | (4.25) | (4.22) | (4.61) | (4.13) | (4.53) | (3.09) | (3.34) | (3.76) | (4.15) | (3.13) | (3.37) |
| No. of cases | 2016 | 2004 | 1868 | 1862 | 2023 | 1876 | 2013 | 1866 | 2007 | 1860 | 2012 | 1865 | 2009 | 1864 |
| Adj $R^2$ | 0.212 | 0.218 | 0.228 | 0.218 | 0.127 | 0.116 | 0.127 | 0.112 | 0.154 | 0.140 | 0.132 | 0.113 | 0.214 | 0.197 |

Notes: #$p < 0.1$, *$p < 0.05$, **$p < 0.01$. OLS coefficients above standard errors in parentheses

identification, ideology, authoritarianism,[8] and church attendance.[9] I do not control for egalitarian preferences – in my theoretical framework, these should be a consequence of risk perceptions, not a cause.

The results in Table 4.3 corroborate the findings from the previous figures: future experience of a bad event is a significant predictor of someone's risk perception of that bad event for all social policy-related bad events. The subjective probability of being a victim of a violent crime, in contrast, cannot be predicted by actually being a victim of a violent crime (see Models 13 and 14). In terms of control variables, richer people have lower risk perceptions, as do respondents with higher education and financial buffers. Being female is a large and consistent predictor of higher risk perceptions, as is being black or Hispanic. This is some suggestive evidence for the so-called white male effect (an explicit test would interact ethnicity and gender). Being married increases risk perceptions with respect to family. Risk aversion does not play a large role when it comes to risk perceptions. None of the ideological right-hand-side variables (partisanship, ideology, being authoritarian, church attendance) are consistently significantly correlated with risk perceptions (though authoritarians have higher risk perceptions of losing one's job or home), with the partial exception of being Republican. Compared to Democrats, Republicans have a tendency to have lower risk expectations, especially with respect to unemployment risk – whether this is justified or not cannot be judged from the results in Table 4.3.

Actual future experience of risk is an excellent predictor of risk perceptions, in terms of statistical significance. The coefficients are between 4 and 11, depending on the domain. In most cases, this implies a reasonably large substantive effect. With respect to job loss, the mean subjective probability is about 26 (the median is 20), and actual future experience of job loss increases the subjective probability by about 10, *ceteris paribus*. The substantive impact of future loss of home is even larger (11 points on

---

[8] The measure of authoritarianism ranges from 0 (not authoritarian) to 4 (most authoritarian) and is based on a series of items from wave 22. This four-item series asks respondents to choose one desirable quality "for a child to have" over another. The pairs of attributes are independence versus respect for elders, obedience versus self-reliance, curiosity versus good manners, and being considerate versus being well behaved. Those who value "respect for elders," "obedience," "good manners," and being "well behaved" score at the maximum of the scale, while those who value "independence," "self-reliance," "curiosity," and "being considerate" score at the minimum (www.thedemocraticstrategist.org/archives/0609/weilera.php).

[9] "On a scale of 1 to 10, where 1 means strongly disagree and 10 means strongly agree, how much do you agree with the following statement: I attend church frequently?"

a variable with a mean of 22 and a median of 15). The substantive effects for the other domains are not far from these.

In summary, the individual-level analysis reveals that actual future experience with risk is a powerful predictor of risk expectations, controlling for a wide range of variables. Respondents seem to have fairly accurate perceptions of their own risk exposure on average, at least in relative terms. In particular, they not only seem to know whether they are above or below the average ($\overline{p}$), but also whether they are at the bottom or at the top of the risk distribution.[10] Furthermore, the group-level optimism and pessimism biases strengthen these perceptions (i.e., make them more extreme). To the degree that one can infer this from the scaled data, risks are, on average, overestimated – potentially one more reason why social insurance is so popular. Respondents, it seems, are capable of figuring out their relative position in the risk distribution – an important mechanism in my framework, in which $(p_i/\overline{p})$ plays a prominent role. This raises the intriguing question of how respondents form their risk expectations. I offer my conjectures on this question in the next section.

## 4.3 HOW ARE RISK PERCEPTIONS FORMED?

Most existing literature deals with risks related to technology (nuclear waste, industrial pollution, traffic accidents, x-rays), biotechnology (genetically modified food, mad cow disease), the environment (lightning, ozone layer, global warming, pollution), lifestyles (AIDS, alcohol, smoking, driving), and crime (crime, terrorism).[11] Objective risk and subjective risk perceptions are not well correlated in these instances – this is the motivation and starting point of the field of risk research. However, in relation to risks related to social policy, objective reality and subjective

[10] I cannot assess whether respondents know the average, but since respondents in the middle of the risk distribution seem to have a good sense of their absolute position in the risk distribution (which roughly is the average), it is not too far-fetched to conclude that average risk levels are known. In some instances, such as in the domain of unemployment, average risk is also widely discussed in the media (since this is simply the economy-wide unemployment rate).

[11] Dake and Sjöberg analyze a richer set of "concerns about society today" (rated by respondents from 1 "not a problem at all" to 7 "a very extreme problem"), which cover technology, environment, war, social deviances, and economic troubles (concerns about inflation, poverty and unemployment, national debt, etc.), as well as some other political topics such as the Middle East conflict. But even in this richer set of concerns, risks covered by social policy play no role, with the exception of the "poverty and unemployment" item (Sjöberg 1998a; Wildavsky and Dake 1990).

perceptions match quite well, as shown previously. Realistic risk perceptions can be expected for hazards "with which people have some experience, direct or indirect" (Sjöberg 2000, 2). Direct personal experiences
and interpersonal experiences of one's network are therefore plausible
sources for the formation of risk perceptions.

But past direct personal and interpersonal experiences can only be
informative if history repeats itself, so to speak, that is, if past and future
shocks are correlated and/or if the experience of one's network is informative for one's own fate. Both scenarios seem plausible. With respect to
the relevance of past experiences, it is the case that many bad events or
"shocks" are clustered both temporally (having experienced a shock in the
past makes it more likely that one experiences it again) and across different
domains (experiencing a shock in one domain, either in the past or present,
makes it more likely that one experiences a different shock as well) (Hacker,
Rehm, and Schlesinger 2010, 2013). With respect to the relevance of the
experiences of one's network, it is important to note that people's networks
tend to be homophilic, that is, "people's personal networks are homogeneous with regard to many socio-demographic, behavioral, and intraperso-
nal characteristics. Homophily limits people's social worlds in a way that
has powerful implications for the information they receive, the attitudes
they form, and the interactions they experience" (McPherson, Smith-Lovin,
and Cook 2001, 415). It is likely that risk exposure differs systematically
across different networks, but remains fairly similar within networks.
Homophily in education and occupations, for example, should lead to fairly
similar risk exposure of losing one's job. Likewise, isomorphic social positions imply similarity in risk profiles across a range of domains.

Drawing conclusions about one's future from one's own experiences
and the experiences of one's network, therefore, can help individuals to
arrive at fairly accurate risk expectations. In the next section, I explore
whether past experiences and the experiences of one's network have an
impact on risk perceptions. I start with correlational evidence, and then
present evidence that arguably allows for causal interpretation.

### 4.3.1 Correlational Evidence

To check the plausibility of the claim that shocks are clustered over time,
I explore how novel shocks (realized bad events) are when they occur. To
this end, I take a broad range of bad events and combine them into four
different domains: employment, health, family, and wealth (Hacker,
Rehm, and Schlesinger 2013). Table 4.4 shows how this is done.

TABLE 4.4: *List of shocks, grouped by domain*

| Domains and shocks |
| --- |

**Employment**
Been unemployed not by personal choice
Had other working adults in your household unemployed, not by personal choice[a]
You or someone in your immediate family lost more than a month from work due to serious illness or injury
**Health**
Had to pay a lot more for your health insurance than expected
Had major out-of-pocket medical expenses as the result of serious illness or injury to you or your immediate family
Lost your health insurance
**Family**
Spent a substantial sum helping out your extended family
Been divorced or separated from your spouse
Had your spouse/partner pass away
**Wealth**
Had the value of your investments or retirement funds decline substantially
Had the value of your house decline substantially
Had your retirement benefits at work cut substantially (including having employer ask you to cover more of these costs)

*Notes:* Shocks experienced in March–September 2009 (wave 21) ("At any time since March 2009, have you: ... ").
Shocks experienced between March 2008 and 2009 (wave 15) ("At any time in the past 12 months, have you: ... ").
Shocks experienced by members of extended family or close friends, between March 2008 and 2009 (wave 15) ("At any time in the past 12 months, have members of your extended family or close friends (not living with you) experienced any of the following?").
Shocks experienced before March 2008 (wave 15) ("Not counting this past 12 months, at any time since you became an adult living out on your own, have you: ... ").
[a]This item was not asked in the series on experiences of members of extended family or close friends.

The SERPI was designed to provide a long window of experiences with these shocks. In particular, four series of questions on shocks were asked:

- Shocks experienced in March–September 2009 (administered in wave 21, i.e., September 2009) ("At any time since March 2009, have you: ... ")
- Shocks experienced between March 2008 and 2009 (administered in wave 15, i.e., March 2009) ("At any time in the past 12 months, have you: ... ")

- Shocks experienced by members of extended family or close friends, between March 2008 and 2009 (wave 15) ("At any time in the past 12 months, have members of your extended family or close friends (not living with you) experienced any of the following: ... ")
- Shocks experienced before March 2008 (wave 15) ("Not counting this past 12 months, at any time since you became an adult living out on your own, have you: ... ")

This information allows me to look at an individual's historical experience with shocks. In particular, I can see whether respondents who reported a shock between March and September 2009 (i.e., in wave 21 of the survey) had experienced a similar shock before, either for themselves (between March 2008 and March 2009; or even before that) or within their personal network (between March 2008 and March 2009). Table 4.5 displays the results, which suggest that experiences with shocks between March and September 2009 were widespread (Hacker, Rehm, and Schlesinger 2010, 2013). More than 21 percent of respondents experienced a shock in the family domain (i.e., spent a substantial sum helping out extended family; had been divorced or separated from their spouse; had their spouse/partner pass away); more than 29 percent experienced an employment shock; more than 33 percent experienced a shock in the health domain; and more than 56 percent of respondents experienced a shock in the wealth domain. To be sure, 2009 was probably a particularly volatile year, and some shocks are more consequential than others. Nevertheless, the breadth of economic insecurity is remarkable.

Table 4.5 also shows past experiences with shocks for those who experienced a shock between March and September 2009. Past experiences with shocks in the same domain are indicated by a sequence of 0s and 1s, where 1s indicate a shock, and 0s the absence thereof. The results indicate that for those who experienced a shock between March and September 2009 this was hardly a new experience. In the employment domain, 88.2 percent (100 − 11.8) who experienced a shock had experienced it before, either between March 2008 and 2009, in their close networks in the same period, or in their adult lives. And 40.4 percent of those experiencing an employment shock between March and September 2009 had experienced at least one employment shock in all three of these ways (between March 2008 and March 2009, in their close networks in the same period, and ever in their adult lives).

The serial correlation of shocks is also apparent in other domains. In the health domain, 90.7 percent (100 − 9.3) of those who experienced

TABLE 4.5: *Shocks, clustered over time*

| Employment domain | |
|---|---|
| No shock | 70.9 |
| At least one shock | 29.1 |
| If at least one shock | |
| 1 0 0 0 | 11.8 |
| 1 0 0 1 | 9.4 |
| 1 0 1 0 | 8.1 |
| 1 0 1 1 | 11.6 |
| 1 1 0 0 | 2.5 |
| 1 1 0 1 | 8.7 |
| 1 1 1 0 | 7.5 |
| 1 1 1 1 | 40.4 |
| **Family domain** | |
| No shock | 78.5 |
| At least one shock | 21.5 |
| If at least one shock | |
| 1 0 0 0 | 12.4 |
| 1 0 0 1 | 11.4 |
| 1 0 1 0 | 6.1 |
| 1 0 1 1 | 12.8 |
| 1 1 0 0 | 2.7 |
| 1 1 0 1 | 11.7 |
| 1 1 1 0 | 4.5 |
| 1 1 1 1 | 38.5 |
| **Health domain** | |
| No shock | 66.9 |
| At least one shock | 33.1 |
| If at least one shock | |
| 1 0 0 0 | 9.3 |
| 1 0 0 1 | 7.3 |
| 1 0 1 0 | 5.2 |
| 1 0 1 1 | 10.4 |
| 1 1 0 0 | 4.2 |
| 1 1 0 1 | 9.6 |
| 1 1 1 0 | 7.0 |
| 1 1 1 1 | 47.0 |
| **Wealth domain** | |
| No shock | 43.4 |
| At least one shock | 56.6 |
| If at least one shock | |
| 1 0 0 0 | 4.1 |
| 1 0 0 1 | 1.1 |

(continued)

TABLE 4.5: *(continued)*

| Employment domain | |
|---|---:|
| 1 0 1 0 | 2.8 |
| 1 0 1 1 | 0.9 |
| 1 1 0 0 | 4.5 |
| 1 1 0 1 | 4.0 |
| 1 1 1 0 | 26.9 |
| 1 1 1 1 | 55.7 |

*Notes:* The patterns for "If at least one shock" are the following:
- Shock experienced in March–September 2009 (always 1, since percentages are conditional on having experienced a shock)
- Shock experienced between March 2008 and March 2009
- Shocks experienced by members of extended family or close friends, between March 2008 and 2009
- Shock experienced before March 2008
A 1 indicates that shock was experienced; a 0 indicates that it was not. For example, a pattern of 1101 indicates that the respondent experienced a shock between March and September 2009, between March 2008 and March 2009, no shock in his or her network, but a shock before March 2008.

a shock between March and September 2009 had experienced one before in one way or another. These numbers are 87.6 percent (100 – 12.4) and 95.9 percent (100 – 4.1) in the family and wealth domain, respectively. To be sure, I am aggregating multiple different bad events that can be considered shocks into domains (three bad events per domain), and the displayed results do not indicate whether it is the exact same bad event that repeats itself over time. But most bad events that are aggregated in each domain are fairly similar (with the partial exception of the family domain). Moreover, even somewhat different bad events within one domain should be informative for the overall risk exposure in that domain.

Overall, then, the table clearly shows that shocks are serially correlated: respondents who experienced a shock in the past are more likely to experience it in the future. This suggests that risk expectations can be meaningfully informed by past experiences and the experiences of one's network. The table also suggests – and additional analysis confirms – that shocks in one's personal network are significantly correlated with one's own shock experiences: the correlations are 0.21 (employment), 0.23 (health), 0.17 (family), and 0.25 (wealth). Typically, one's own history is a better predictor of one's future, but the experience of close friends is nevertheless informative.

TABLE 4.6: *Shocks, clustered across domains*

| Cluster of shocks | Shock experience | | | |
|---|---|---|---|---|
| Empl I Health I Family I Wealth | March 2009 and September 2009 | March 2008 and March 2009 | March 2008 and March 2009 (family or close friends) | Before March 2008 |
| **No shock** | | | | |
| 0 0 0 0 | 22.7 | 14.8 | 14.3 | 19.0 |
| **Shock in one domain** | | | | |
| 1 0 0 0 | 6.2 | 4.3 | 2.4 | 3.8 |
| 0 1 0 0 | 3.1 | 3.7 | 1.5 | 4.0 |
| 0 0 1 0 | 3.3 | 2.7 | 1.7 | 4.4 |
| 0 0 0 1 | 21.3 | 24.4 | 13.6 | 4.0 |
| Sum | 33.9 | 35.1 | 19.2 | 16.2 |
| **Shocks in two domains** | | | | |
| 1 0 0 1 | 3.7 | 4.7 | 3.8 | 3.1 |
| 1 0 1 0 | 1.4 | 1.0 | 1.5 | 3.0 |
| 1 1 0 0 | 3.5 | 3.3 | 2.7 | 5.9 |
| 0 0 1 1 | 4.1 | 5.7 | 5.1 | 3.9 |
| 0 1 0 1 | 9.7 | 12.2 | 7.0 | 4.5 |
| 0 1 1 0 | 0.7 | 0.6 | 1.0 | 2.4 |
| Sum | 23.1 | 27.5 | 21.1 | 22.8 |
| **Shocks in three domains** | | | | |
| 1 0 1 1 | 2.6 | 3.6 | 4.6 | 3.3 |
| 1 1 0 1 | 7.0 | 7.3 | 9.8 | 7.0 |
| 1 1 1 0 | 1.1 | 1.5 | 2.1 | 8.7 |
| 0 1 1 1 | 3.9 | 4.7 | 6.5 | 4.7 |
| Sum | 14.6 | 17.1 | 23.0 | 23.7 |
| **Shocks in four domains** | | | | |
| 1 1 1 1 | 5.7 | 5.4 | 22.5 | 18.3 |

Shocks are also heavily clustered across domains: having a shock in one domain (employment, health, family, wealth) increases the odds of having a shock in one or more of the other domains. This pattern shows up no matter what kind of shock experience one examines, as shown in Table 4.6. For example, the table shows that, between March and September 2009, only 22.7 percent of respondents did not experience a shock in any domain, while 33.9 percent experienced a shock in exactly one domain, 23.1 percent in two domains, 14.6 percent in three domains, and 5.7 percent in all four domains. Put differently, the probability of experiencing a shock in more than one domain, conditional on having at least one shock, is 56.1 percent. These conditional probabilities in the other measures of experience are 58.8 percent (March 2008 and March 2009), 77.6 percent (family or close friends, March 2008 and March 2009), and 80 percent (before March 2008). When it rains, it pours!

Since shocks are clustered over time, across domains, and correlated with the experiences of one's network, individuals have a multitude of direct and interpersonal experiences to draw from in order to form risk expectations. An exploration of the correlation between past shock experiences and future subjective probabilities shows that they do just that. In Table 4.7, the dependent variables are the subjective probabilities of experiencing a bad event within the next 12 months. The control variables are as before (Table 4.3) and include sociodemographic and ideological variables (party identification, ideology, authoritarianism, and church attendance). The explanatory variables of interest are past experiences with shocks in the same domain, and there are three different types of experiences: shocks between March 2008 and March 2009; shocks within the same period, but experienced by one's extended family or close friends; and shocks experienced before March 2008, in adulthood.[12] In most cases, past experiences with shocks are significantly correlated with the risk perception of future shocks in the same area, and more recent shocks tend to be better predictors than more distal shocks.

Of the seven bad events, recent personal shock experiences (March 2008–March 2009) are significantly correlated in all but two cases: the probability of losing one's home and that of being a victim of a crime. We encountered the latter result repeatedly previously: when it comes to crime, risk perceptions are not explainable by past or future risk exposure. The finding that the probability of losing one's home cannot be predicted by one's experience within the last 12 months is, perhaps, not very surprising: a respondent who has just lost his or her home is unlikely to lose it immediately again. Also noteworthy is the result for the subjective probability of losing one's spouse "due to death, divorce or some

[12] Note that I am returning to the specific shocks (Table 4.1) that closely match the subjective probabilities.

TABLE 4.7: *Past shock experiences and future subjective probabilities*

| Shock experience in domain (0: no, 1: yes) | (1) Loss of job | (2) Loss of home | (3) Loss of spouse | (4) Family help | (5) Loss of hours at work | (6) Major MOOP | (7) Victim of crime |
|---|---|---|---|---|---|---|---|
| | Out of 100 people like you, how many (will experience/will need/will be ... within the next 12 months)[a] | | | | | | |
| Within the last 12 months | 7.94** | 3.35 | 9.00** | 4.91** | 5.07** | 9.28** | 0.64 |
| | (1.53) | (3.38) | (2.68) | (1.46) | (1.25) | (1.39) | (3.44) |
| Within the last 12 months (extended family or close friends) | 3.86** | n.a. | -1.00 | 1.88 | 2.57** | 2.19* | -0.17 |
| | (1.04) | | (1.20) | (1.20) | (1.00) | (1.11) | (1.68) |
| Before the last 12 months (ever) | 1.82# | n.a. | 1.00 | 6.99** | 1.23 | 2.78* | 2.57* |
| | (1.10) | | (1.30) | (1.28) | (0.94) | (1.12) | (1.30) |
| Income quintiles | -1.88** | -1.83** | -2.65** | -1.45** | -1.69** | -2.35** | -2.05** |
| | (0.43) | (0.42) | (0.45) | (0.44) | (0.32) | (0.40) | (0.32) |
| Education (1-3) | -3.26** | -4.41** | -1.51 | -2.64** | -1.49* | -3.41** | -3.44** |
| | (0.88) | (0.86) | (0.93) | (0.91) | (0.67) | (0.82) | (0.67) |
| Age | -0.19** | -0.16** | -0.02 | -0.23** | -0.03 | 0.00 | -0.22** |
| | (0.04) | (0.03) | (0.04) | (0.04) | (0.03) | (0.03) | (0.03) |
| Female | 7.21** | 4.96** | 6.44** | 7.35** | 2.93** | 3.84** | 2.42** |
| | (1.06) | (1.03) | (1.12) | (1.09) | (0.81) | (0.99) | (0.80) |
| Black | 0.70 | 4.14* | 9.06** | 7.22** | 5.83** | 2.63 | 5.45** |
| | (1.74) | (1.70) | (1.84) | (1.79) | (1.34) | (1.63) | (1.32) |

(*continued*)

TABLE 4-7: (continued)

| Shock experience in domain (0: no, 1: yes) | (1) Loss of job | (2) Loss of home | (3) Loss of spouse | (4) Family help | (5) Loss of hours at work | (6) Major MOOP | (7) Victim of crime |
|---|---|---|---|---|---|---|---|
| | Out of 100 people like you, how many (will experience/will need/will be ... within the next 12 months)[a] | | | | | | |
| Hispanic | 7.07** | 11.86** | 6.22** | -0.08 | 3.87* | 0.47 | 6.99** |
| | (2.03) | (2.02) | (2.16) | (2.13) | (1.54) | (1.92) | (1.59) |
| No. of kids | -0.18 | 0.78# | 0.06 | -0.54 | 0.47 | 0.79# | 0.84* |
| | (0.43) | (0.42) | (0.46) | (0.45) | (0.33) | (0.40) | (0.33) |
| Married | 0.60 | -0.28 | 1.84 | 5.80** | 1.30 | 0.07 | 0.99 |
| | (1.25) | (1.22) | (1.38) | (1.30) | (0.95) | (1.17) | (0.96) |
| How long until in financial trouble? (1–6) | -2.40** | -2.49** | -1.16** | -1.01** | -1.42** | -1.36** | -1.24** |
| | (0.36) | (0.36) | (0.38) | (0.37) | (0.28) | (0.34) | (0.27) |
| Risk averse (job) (1–6) | 0.65* | 0.64* | 1.20** | 0.21 | 0.45# | 0.60# | 0.44# |
| | (0.33) | (0.32) | (0.35) | (0.34) | (0.25) | (0.31) | (0.25) |
| Risk averse (general) (1–7) | 0.89 | -0.31 | 0.97 | 1.77* | -0.19 | -0.02 | 1.28* |
| | (0.66) | (0.65) | (0.71) | (0.71) | (0.51) | (0.62) | (0.51) |
| Party ID: Democrat | Ref cat | Ref cat | Ref cat | Ref cat | Ref cat | Ref cat | Ref cat |
| Party ID: Independent | -1.68 | -1.27 | -2.35 | 0.23 | -1.98 | -2.57 | -1.19 |
| | (1.81) | (1.74) | (1.89) | (1.83) | (1.36) | (1.67) | (1.35) |
| Party ID: Republican | -4.86** | -2.77* | -1.36 | -2.54# | -2.98** | -2.16 | -2.13# |
| | (1.43) | (1.39) | (1.51) | (1.47) | (1.09) | (1.34) | (1.09) |
| Ideology: Liberal | Ref cat | Ref cat | Ref cat | Ref cat | Ref cat | Ref cat | Ref cat |

82

| | | | | | | | |
|---|---|---|---|---|---|---|---|
| Ideology: Moderate | 3.38* | 1.27 | 1.88 | -1.14 | 2.43# | 0.44 | 2.13# |
| | (1.65) | (1.60) | (1.75) | (1.69) | (1.25) | (1.54) | (1.25) |
| Ideology: Conservative | -1.51 | -2.63# | 0.89 | -0.09 | -0.67 | -0.97 | 1.96# |
| | (1.53) | (1.50) | (1.62) | (1.58) | (1.17) | (1.44) | (1.17) |
| Index for being authoritarian (0–4) | 1.56** | 1.88** | 0.52 | 0.31 | 0.16 | -0.28 | -0.54 |
| | (0.55) | (0.54) | (0.58) | (0.57) | (0.42) | (0.51) | (0.42) |
| Church attendance (1–10) | 0.02 | -0.07 | -0.34* | -0.16 | 0.12 | 0.00 | 0.14 |
| | (0.15) | (0.15) | (0.16) | (0.16) | (0.12) | (0.14) | (0.12) |
| Constant | 42.81** | 46.91** | 29.62** | 31.76** | 24.78** | 34.07** | 31.66** |
| | (4.40) | (4.27) | (4.63) | (4.53) | (3.32) | (4.08) | (3.32) |
| No. of cases | 1863 | 1865 | 1876 | 1863 | 1853 | 1862 | 1858 |
| Adj $R^2$ | 0.237 | 0.214 | 0.121 | 0.136 | 0.157 | 0.148 | 0.202 |

*Note:* #$p < 0.1$, *$p < 0.05$, **$p < 0.01$. OLS coefficients above standard errors (in parentheses)

[a]"People face certain risks that can affect their economic situation or other important aspects of their lives. We'd like you to indicate how likely each of the following risks might be, in terms of the chance that they'll affect the lives of people like you over the next year. Out of 100 people like you, how many …"

other circumstance" within the next 12 months: the experience within the last 12 months is a very strong predictor here. This hardly makes sense – someone who just lost his or her spouse is very unlikely to lose him/her again; the recent past should not be a strong predictor. Yet it is, and this helps to explain the finding reported earlier that the risk of losing one's spouse is greatly overestimated (in levels, but not in ranks).

This raises the question of what happens when we test the predictive power of recent (within the last 12 months) and future (within the next 6 months) shock experiences simultaneously. This is done in Table 4.8, which parallels the even-numbered models in Table 4.3, except that past experiences are now an additional explanatory variable. In about half the cases, future experiences within the next 6 months are a significant predictor of risk perceptions for the next 12 months, even if we control for past experiences (note that this difference in reference periods makes this test extremely conservative). The exceptions are losing one's spouse and major medical out-of-pocket expenditures (for which past experiences are very powerful predictors of risk expectations) and being a victim of a crime. When it comes to the estimated probability of losing one's job or one's home, future experience is a better predictor than one's experience within the last 12 months (Table 4.8). The reverse is true for losing one's spouse, having to help out one's family, losing hours at work as a result of illness, and major medical out-of-pocket spending. Once again, being a victim of a crime is not predictable in a consistent way with past or future experiences.

Overall, these investigations then suggest at least two points. First, respondents extrapolate from their own past experiences, and the past experience of their close networks, to form risk expectations. When not controlling for past experiences, future experiences are significant and meaningful predictors of subjective probabilities – people get it roughly right. Given the data, this test is very conservative (the survey item about the future refers to the next 12 months, while we observe the realization of risk only over the next 6 months; surely, more of the expected risk was realized in the 6 months after that, increasing the predictive power of future risk experiences for subjective probabilities). When controlling for past and future experiences at the same time, past experiences are better predictors in various areas. But since risks are serially correlated (as shown earlier), this means that relying on past experiences to predict the future leads to fairly accurate risk assessments.

The evidence presented up to this point is correlational: I have shown that past and future experiences with bad events are positively correlated

TABLE 4.8: *Past and future shock experiences and future subjective probabilities*

| Shock experience in domain (0: no, 1: yes) | (1) Loss of job | (2) Loss of home | (3) Loss of spouse | (4) Family help | (5) Loss of hours at work | (6) Major MOOP | (7) Victim of crime |
|---|---|---|---|---|---|---|---|
| | Out of 100 people like you, how many (will experience/will need/ will be ... within the next 12 months)[a] | | | | | | |
| Within the next 6 months | 6.78** | 13.52** | 2.73 | 3.13* | 2.84* | 0.21 | -5.76# |
| | (1.69) | (3.78) | (3.07) | (1.43) | (1.21) | (1.38) | (3.48) |
| Within the last 12 months | 6.74** | -4.79 | 8.32** | 8.05** | 5.75** | 11.23** | 2.45 |
| | (1.63) | (4.07) | (2.72) | (1.41) | (1.19) | (1.39) | (3.29) |
| Income quintiles | -1.65** | -1.70** | -2.68** | -1.74** | -1.67** | -2.39** | -1.84** |
| | (0.43) | (0.42) | (0.45) | (0.44) | (0.32) | (0.40) | (0.33) |
| Education (1-3) | -3.25** | -4.42** | -1.40 | -2.24* | -1.68* | -3.46** | -4.06** |
| | (0.89) | (0.87) | (0.93) | (0.91) | (0.67) | (0.83) | (0.69) |
| Age | -0.20** | -0.15** | -0.02 | -0.20** | -0.01 | 0.01 | -0.18** |
| | (0.04) | (0.03) | (0.04) | (0.04) | (0.03) | (0.03) | (0.03) |
| Female | 7.20** | 5.06** | 6.55** | 7.99** | 3.02** | 3.97** | 2.64** |
| | (1.06) | (1.04) | (1.12) | (1.09) | (0.80) | (0.99) | (0.83) |
| Black | 1.17 | 4.39** | 9.22** | 8.04** | 5.85** | 2.14 | 5.02** |
| | (1.75) | (1.70) | (1.84) | (1.80) | (1.34) | (1.62) | (1.37) |
| Hispanic | 6.83** | 11.27** | 6.27** | -0.29 | 3.97** | 0.46 | 10.43** |
| | (2.06) | (2.03) | (2.16) | (2.11) | (1.54) | (1.93) | (1.60) |
| No. of kids | -0.20 | 0.63 | -0.01 | -0.63 | 0.47 | 0.69# | 0.93** |
| | (0.43) | (0.42) | (0.46) | (0.44) | (0.33) | (0.40) | (0.34) |

*(continued)*

TABLE 4.8: (continued)

|  | (1) | (2) | (3) | (4) | (5) | (6) | (7) |
|---|---|---|---|---|---|---|---|
| | Out of 100 people like you, how many (will experience/will need/ will be ... within the next 12 months)[a] | | | | | | |
| Shock experience in domain (0: no, 1: yes) | Loss of job | Loss of home | Loss of spouse | Family help | Loss of hours at work | Major MOOP | Victim of crime |
| Married | 0.89 | 0.21 | 2.05 | 6.13** | 1.35 | 0.42 | -0.07 |
| | (1.25) | (1.23) | (1.37) | (1.30) | (0.95) | (1.17) | (0.98) |
| How long until in financial trouble? (1–6) | -2.38** | -2.48** | -1.07** | -0.95* | -1.42** | -1.37** | -1.31** |
| | (0.36) | (0.36) | (0.38) | (0.37) | (0.28) | (0.34) | (0.28) |
| Risk averse (job) (1–6) | 0.59# | 0.68* | 1.19** | 0.16 | 0.43# | 0.60# | 0.60* |
| | (0.33) | (0.32) | (0.35) | (0.34) | (0.25) | (0.31) | (0.26) |
| Risk averse (general) (1–7) | 1.06 | -0.29 | 0.78 | 1.19# | -0.04 | -0.29 | 1.41** |
| | (0.66) | (0.65) | (0.71) | (0.69) | (0.51) | (0.62) | (0.52) |
| Party ID: Democrat | Ref cat | Ref cat | Ref cat | Ref cat | Ref cat | Ref cat | Ref cat |
| Party ID: Independent | -1.20 | -1.65 | -2.19 | 0.03 | -2.29# | -1.90 | -1.10 |
| | (1.80) | (1.75) | (1.88) | (1.83) | (1.35) | (1.67) | (1.39) |
| Party ID: Republican | -4.47** | -2.53# | -1.16 | -2.62# | -2.94** | -2.25# | -2.22* |
| | (1.43) | (1.39) | (1.50) | (1.47) | (1.09) | (1.35) | (1.12) |
| Ideology: Liberal | Ref cat | Ref cat | Ref cat | Ref cat | Ref cat | Ref cat | Ref cat |
| Ideology: Moderate | 2.27 | 1.27 | 1.74 | -0.64 | 2.60* | 0.82 | 1.33 |
| | (1.65) | (1.60) | (1.74) | (1.69) | (1.25) | (1.54) | (1.29) |

| | | | | | | |
|---|---|---|---|---|---|---|
| Ideology: Conservative | -2.12 | -2.78# | 0.57 | 0.53 | -0.95 | 1.14 |
| | (1.54) | (1.50) | (1.62) | (1.59) | (1.44) | (1.21) |
| Index for being authoritarian (0–4) | 1.67** | 1.86** | 0.55 | 0.40 | -0.32 | -0.71 |
| | (0.55) | (0.54) | (0.58) | (0.57) | (0.52) | (0.43) |
| Church attendance (1–10) | -0.02 | -0.08 | -0.35* | -0.20 | 0.04 | 0.26* |
| | (0.15) | (0.15) | (0.16) | (0.16) | (0.14) | (0.12) |
| Constant | 43.68** | 46.08** | 29.75** | 33.99** | 36.29** | 30.53** |
| | (4.39) | (4.29) | (4.62) | (4.48) | (4.10) | (3.40) |
| No. of cases | 1858 | 1851 | 1875 | 1862 | 1862 | 1860 |
| Adj $R^2$ | 0.235 | 0.218 | 0.120 | 0.129 | 0.143 | 0.198 |

*Notes:* #$p < 0.1$, *$p < 0.05$, **$p < 0.01$. OLS coefficients above standard errors (in parentheses)

[a] "People face certain risks that can affect their economic situation or other important aspects of their lives. We'd like you to indicate how likely each of the following risks might be, in terms of the chance that they'll affect the lives of people like you over the next year. Out of 100 people like you, how many…"

with risk perceptions. To be sure, using future experiences to predict (past) risk expectations goes a long way in testing whether risk perceptions are rational in the sense that they are based on reality, and there are few endogeneity concerns here. But the correlation between past shocks and risk expectations is just that – a correlation. Whether there is a causal connection between past experience and risk perceptions is explored in the next section.

### 4.3.2 Causal Evidence

Since the SERPI is a panel survey, one obvious way to gauge causality is to explore whether risk experiences *change* risk perceptions.[13] Unfortunately, the series of questions on risk expectations was asked only in one wave (wave 15) – a difference-in-difference analysis is therefore not possible. However, the SERPI includes a series of questions on "worries" that were asked twice. Arguably, worries tap into risk expectations as well, although they clearly are less purely cognitive and more emotional in nature than subjective probabilities (Sjöberg 1998b). The survey includes a rich set of questions on worries about different areas, 20 of which have been asked repeatedly.[14] Most of these worries, which were asked in March 2009 and September 2009, can be matched closely with shocks experienced between March 2009 and September 2009.[15] This allows me to explore whether the experience of a shock changes one's worries.

To explore this, I estimate a series of logit regressions in which the dependent variable is 1 for respondents who are "fairly" or "very" worried, and 0 for respondents who are "slightly" or "not at all" worried about a specific risk. These worries are measured in September 2009.

---

[13] There are a couple of studies that look at changes in job security perceptions with panel data (Cebulla 2004; Dickerson and Green 2012).

[14] One item asks about worries about economic insecurity in general: "To begin, I'd like you to think about your and your family's economic security. By economic security I mean your security in being able to keep your job, maintain your income, have health insurance coverage, and retire comfortably. Overall, how worried are you about your economic security?" Answer categories: very worried, fairly worried, slightly worried, and not worried at all. The other worry items are specific about the target of worry ("Are you very worried, fairly worried, slightly worried, or not worried at all about: ...?" Answer categories: very worried, fairly worried, lightly worried, and not worried at all).

[15] For the following analysis, I drop respondents who were interviewed in April, since the item in September asks about shocks experienced "since March." Therefore, it could be that the respondent already experienced the shock when responding to the worry question for the first time.

On the right-hand side, I include the level of worry measured 6 months earlier (in March), measured in the same way. Including the lagged measure of the dependent variable effectively means that changes in worries are explained; that goes a long way toward establishing a causal interpretation of the results (Finkel 1995). The explanatory variable of interest is a dummy variable indicating whether a respondent experienced a shock in the same domain as the worry during the time between the two interviews (i.e., between March and September). I also include a rich set of control variables (the same as before). The estimated models are, for more than a dozen worries and matched risks:

worry (September) = worry (March) + shock (between March and September) + controls (income, education, age, female, black, Hispanic, married, ability to buffer, risk aversion [job], risk aversion [general], party identification, ideology, authoritarianism, church attendance)

In almost all of the 20 worry-shock combinations, experiencing a shock in a domain significantly increases worries about that domain. A few particularly powerful examples are given in Table 4.9. Instead of regression results, simulated effects are displayed. They show that experiencing a shock in a domain substantively increases worries in that domain. For example, respondents who spent a substantial sum helping out their extended family (the shock) were roughly 50 percent more likely to be fairly or very worried about needing to help out a member of their extended family (the predicted probability increased from 29.2 percent to 45.8 percent). In several examples, the predicted probability of being fairly or very worried was more than twice as high for respondents who experienced a shock. For example, respondents who lost their home because they could not pay their mortgage have a predicted probability of being fairly or very worried about paying their mortgage of 79.6 percent, compared to 33 percent for those respondents who did not lose their home.

It is, of course, not very surprising that a respondent who experienced a bad event is more worried about that particular risk. But the (arguably) causal evidence presented in this section corroborates the correlational evidence from the previous sections in which it was shown that risk expectations are predictably and usually strongly correlated with one's own shock experiences and those of one's close network.

\* \* \*

The focus of this and the previous chapter has been on the micro-level: I have shown that risk exposure importantly shapes social policy attitudes

TABLE 4.9: *Shocks and worries (causal)*

| Shock (between March 2009 and September 2009) | Worry (September 2009) | Worries as a function of having experienced a shock (percentage) | | |
|---|---|---|---|---|
| | | Shock: No | Shock: Yes | Yes minus No |
| Spent a substantial sum helping out your extended family | Needing to help out a member of your extended family if he/she gets in financial trouble | 29.2 | 45.8 | 16.5 |
| Been unemployed not by personal choice | Worry about losing/ finding job | 32.8 | 53.8 | 21.1 |
| | General economic security | 41.3 | 61.2 | 19.9 |
| Gotten so far into debt that you felt you could never get out | Getting out of debt | 31.1 | 57.7 | 26.6 |
| Had to pay a lot more for your health insurance than expected | Having health care coverage substantially cut or its costs substantially increased by your employer | 43.5 | 69.7 | 26.2 |
| Had your retirement benefits at work cut substantially (including having employer ask you to cover more of these costs) | Having your retirement benefits cut substantially at your main job | 27.9 | 61.3 | 33.4 |
| Lost your home because you couldn't pay the mortgage | Paying your mortgage | 33.0 | 79.6 | 46.5 |

*Notes:* Shown are the predicted probabilities of being "fairly" or "very" worried about something (as opposed to slightly or not worried), as a function of having experienced a certain shock (column "Shock: Yes") or not ("Shock: No"), as well as the difference between the two ("Yes minus No").

The results are based on logit regressions of the following form: worry_w21 = worry_w15 + shock + controls (income, education, age, female, black, Hispanic, married, ability to buffer, risk aversion [job], risk version [general], party-ideology, ideology, authoritarianism, church attendance).

(Chapter 3), and that risk expectations are fairly accurate (Chapter 4). Since an individual's position in the risk distribution is both theoretically and empirically a crucial determinant of her or his support for social policy, I turn in the following chapters to some key macro-level implications of my framework. The basic intuition of these implications was explained in Chapter 1 and elaborated in Chapter 2. The following chapters will flesh out several of these implications. They are, of course, all concerned with the distribution of risk in a society.

The first implication that I will explore empirically is the prediction that risk inequality and social policy support and supply are negatively correlated (Chapter 5): that is, the more heterogeneous a risk pool is, the lower the aggregate support for social policy and the generosity of benefits. A second and related implication is that we should expect changes in social policy generosity if risk pools change noticeably. In particular, if risk inequality increases sharply, we should observe welfare state retrenchment, or at least an increasing demand for retrenchment. In Chapter 6, I will exploit German unification as an exogenous change of the risk pool. I will show that unification resulted in a sharp increase in unemployment risk inequality and will argue that this helps to explain the far-reaching labor market reforms of the early 2000s (the so-called Hartz reforms). The third implication relates to the likelihood of social policy adoption. Reiterating a common theme of this book, we would expect social policy adoption to occur in times of more homogeneous risk pools. In Chapter 7, I will show that in all cases of unemployment insurance (UI) adoption in the last few decades, risk inequality markedly decreased in the years before eventual adoption. In a similar vein, I show in Chapter 7 that American states were quicker to adopt UI when their risk distributions were more characterized by lower inequality (or "more flipped" risk distributions).

Chapter 8 argues that social policy development in the last 150 years was (partially) driven by dynamics of risk distributions. In particular, I highlight the role of economic or societal crises for social policy development. I will argue that my risk pool perspective offers a way to theorize about the role of crises and social policy, and will empirically explore the relationship between social policy milestones and crises between 1870 and 1950 (and even 2000).

# 5

# Risk Pools and Social Policy Generosity

Citizens' demand for social insurance is as emphatic as is its supply. Surveys reveal that citizens overwhelmingly agree that it should be the government's responsibility to provide health care for the sick (98 percent); to provide a decent standard of living for the old (96.1 percent); and to provide a decent standard of living for the unemployed (67.8 percent).[1] And, indeed, every rich democracy has social policy programs addressing these (and other) risks. But support for social insurance varies across countries, as does its supply. In fact, there is a fairly close correlation between how supportive citizens are of social policy and how generous social policy programs are. This correlation is well documented (see also Figure 2.2 and Figure 2.3), especially in the work by Clem Brooks and Jeff

---

[1] See Table 1.1. One may wonder whether I conflate support for social policy in principle with support for a particular (or support for more or less generous) social policy. This is a legitimate point. Simply put, existing survey items that are used to compare cross-national patterns of social policy are of two types: (i) the "it should be the government's responsibility to do X" variety and the (ii) "would you like to see more or less government spending in area X" variety. The problem with (i) is that these items may conflate support in principle with support for particular levels; the problem with (ii) is that these survey items are not really comparable across countries, because a respondent's answer to a "more or less" question should critically depend on the status quo, which varies across countries. Fortunately, these two kinds of survey items are quite highly correlated (respondents who think it should be the government's responsibility to provide social policy also tend to prefer increased spending). Perhaps more importantly, I could replicate Table 1.1 with the "spending more or less" data, and it would show that the median respondent tends to prefer more spending (even relative to the often very generous status quo). I think it is fair to conclude that there is strong evidence that citizens in rich democracies are strongly supportive of generous social policy.

Manza (Arts and Gelissen 2001; Brooks and Manza 2006a, 2006b, 2007; Burstein 1998, 2003; Coughlin 1980; Flavin 2012; Gelissen 2002; Gilens 2005, 2009). But the relationship between public opinion and social policy making is not well understood: "mass opinion is ... the great black box of contemporary welfare state politics" (Brooks and Manza 2007, 16).

The long neglect of citizen preferences as a core ingredient of social policy making is surprising, for a variety of reasons. First, the welfare state literature typically restricts its sample to (rich) democracies. Therefore, the idea that public policy reflects citizen preferences should not be controversial, at least with respect to important, visible, and durable policies such as those underpinning welfare states. In fact, congruence between citizen preferences and policy output is a core part of many definitions of democracy.[2] Second, and as previously mentioned, Clem Brooks and Jeff Manza have convincingly argued that existing accounts are "reaching for, but not grasping, public opinion" (Brooks and Manza 2007, 25).[3] Although citizen preferences are greatly understudied in the welfare state literature (or were until very recently), all main welfare state theories are, in principle, compatible with the conjecture that social policy making reflects citizen preferences; some theories even heavily rely on a link between mass preferences and outcomes (the Power Resources Theory, for example, assumes that parties aggregate and implement distinct citizen preferences). Third, the relatively close correlation between support for social policy and its generosity is widely documented, although typically from perspectives that claim that social policy programs generate their own support; for skeptical views, see (Kenworthy 2009; Kenworthy and McCall 2008; Kenworthy and Owens 2011).

The difficult question any account that relies on a link between citizen preferences and social policy making will eventually face is *why* social policy support varies across countries (and across social policy domains, and over time). Existing accounts have little to offer to this question. For example, the workhorse model in the political economy of the welfare state

---

[2] According to John May, for example, democracy can be defined as "necessary correspondence between acts of governance and the wishes with respect to those acts of the persons who are affected" (May 1978, 1).

[3] As cited before: "Analysts within multiple theoretical traditions have anticipated the possibility that mass opinion is a factor relevant to shaping social policymaking, and perhaps in accounting for differences between countries. But none of these scholars has taken the next steps of explicitly theorizing and attempting to measure its policy impact" (Brooks and Manza 2007, 25–26).

literature – the model due to Meltzer and Richards (1981) – makes no direct prediction in that regard. To be sure, the key insight of the model is that a larger gap between mean and median income leads to more redistribution – but the mechanism here is the position of the median voter in the income distribution, not aggregate demand for social policy. In fact, the model predicts that citizens with above-average income are opposed to redistributive taxation – a proposition that has no empirical support. On the contrary, social policy is widely popular. The Nobel laureate economist James Buchanan has called the widespread popularity of social policy the "paradox of support" (Buchanan 1983, 340, 341, 342 [footnote 4]).[4] Another difficult issue one has to face is the potential of reverse causality: that social policy programs influence social policy support, not the other way around (Pierson 1994, 1996). I will address this problem in the following.

In my framework, differences in support for social insurance stem from differences in risk distributions (across countries, time, or domains). There are two ways in which risk distributions can be linked to social benefit generosity: via the preferences of the decisive (median) voter and via public opinion. Both approaches yield the same prediction: benefits are more generous the more equal the distribution of risk is. I discuss the details of both links in turn.

The *median voter* approach posits a link between the preferences of an electorally decisive individual or group and policy outcomes. The formal model sketched previously suggests that demand for social insurance is proportional to one's relative position in the risk distribution $(p_i/\bar{p})$. From a median voter perspective, the predicted social benefit generosity is then simply proportional to $(p_m/\bar{p})$, where $p_m$ is the risk exposure of the median voter. Since risk distributions are right-skewed in normal times, we know that median risk exposure is below the mean $(p_m < \bar{p})$. In this situation, if risk inequality increases ($\bar{p}$ increases; $p_m$ stays the same), the median voter's preferred benefit generosity decreases, *ceteris paribus*: hence the prediction that lower risk inequality (more risk homogeneity) is associated with higher social benefit generosity. But few political observers think that the median voter model is an accurate description of reality.

Fortunately, my framework also generates predictions linking risk distributions with social insurance generosity via *public opinion*. Unlike

---

[4] Referring to Social Security in the United States, James Buchanan asks, "Why is the support for the system [Social Security in the United States] so universal?" "Are there rationally derived reasons for the near universal support for the [Social Security] system"?

in the median voter scenario, where outcomes narrowly follow the preferences of a particular individual or group, social policy outcomes perhaps more likely follow aggregate support for social policy, or popular
demand. In my framework, popular support of social policy is driven by
risk distributions: more homogeneous risk distributions should be associated with higher support for – and supply of – generous benefits. There
are two closely related reasons for this expectation. First, theoretically we
can expect that social insurance is generally popular because people are
risk averse and because it is difficult or impossible to self-insure risks such
as unemployment, health, accidents, and even old age. Citizens who have
high (above average) risk emphatically support generous benefits – and
their support should not change (much) when risk inequality changes (in
normal times, when risk distributions are bottom-heavy). In contrast,
while citizens with below-mean risk levels are supportive of social insurance, their support wanes as risk inequality increases: the more heterogeneous the risk pool, the worse the deal low-risk citizens get out of social
insurance.

Second, and closely related, social insurance is empirically so popular
that aggregate support can only decrease if opposition against it increases.
In other words, given the popularity of the policy, contestation about it
can only be generated by more opposition. The overwhelming support for
government responsibility for social policy has been cited at the beginning
of this chapter. But it can be documented with support for redistribution
as well: even on survey items inquiring about respondents' position on
plain zero-sum income redistribution, widespread support is found. For
example, one ISSP 2006 Role of Government item asks: "On the whole,
do you think it should or should not be the government's responsibility to
reduce income differences between the rich and the poor [Q.7g]?" In
every single one of the 33 countries for which the item is available, more
than 50 percent of respondents indicate that it "definitely should be" or
"probably should be" the government's responsibility to reduce income
differences between the rich and the poor. Support is highest in Portugal
with 93.5 percent respondents in favor, and lowest in New Zealand, with
50.2 percent in favor (see Table 1.1). Widespread support implies little
opposition, and lowering support requires more opposition (Rehm,
Hacker, and Schlesinger 2012). The two panels of Figure 5.1 show a
fairly close correlation between average support for redistribution and
polarization on the issue (measured by the kurtosis).

In sum, both approaches to thinking about preference aggregation –
the median voter model as well as the public opinion model – yield the

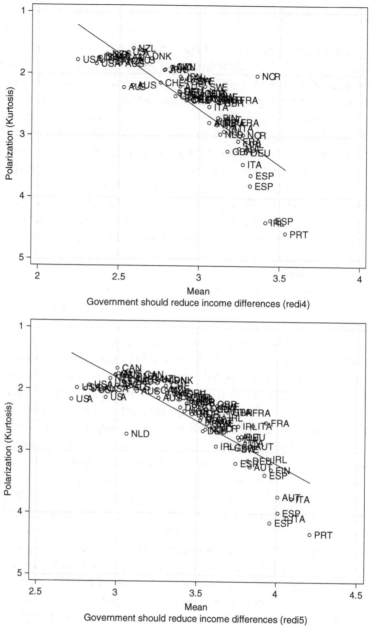

FIGURE 5.1: Mean and polarization on redistribution items.

*Note*: redi5 "What is your opinion of the following statement: It is the responsibility of the government to reduce the differences in income between people with high incomes and those with low incomes?" 1 Disagree strongly, 2 Disagree, 3 Neither agree nor disagree, 4 Agree, 5 Agree strongly

redi4 "On the whole, do you think it should be or should not be the government's responsibility to reduce income differences between the rich and poor?" 1 Definitely should not be, 2 Probably should not be, 3 Probably should be, 4 Definitely should be

*Source*: ISSP, Role of Government I–IV.

same prediction: *The lower risk inequality is, the more generous is social insurance.*

I believe my framework offers a new explanation both for why public support for social policy differs and for why benefit generosity differs, building on my previous work (Rehm 2011b; Rehm, Hacker, and Schlesinger 2012). However, this does not mean that the distribution of risk has not been a topic in existing scholarship. In political science, the incidence of risk across groups plays a prominent role in Baldwin (1990) and Mares (2003). It also receives attention in Iversen (2001, 56),who highlights the distinction between level of risk and its distribution, but then concentrates on the determinants and effects of the former; in Hacker (2004, 2008), who shows that Americans bear an increasing burden of risks; as well as in Korpi and Palme (1998, 2003).[5] Iversen and Soskice (2001) suggest that skill specificity increases the demand for social protection and find empirical support for that conjecture at the micro-level. They further suggest that cross-national differences in skill composition might explain differences in redistribution, but their argument is about levels, not the distribution, of risk. Moene and Wallerstein (2001, 2003) offer a model in which citizens have both redistributive and insurance motives for supporting welfare spending.[6] The insider-outsider

---

[5] Korpi and Palme's (1998) observation that there exists a trade-off between the degree of low-income targeting and the generosity of benefits implicitly relies on the logic outlined in this chapter: targeting tax-financed benefits makes it rather unattractive to support risk pooling since the benefits and costs are rather unfavorable for most taxpayers ex ante. As a result, benefit generosity should be low. However, their typology is based on the structure of old age pension and sickness insurance "since they cover risks that are relatively equally shared by all socio-economic categories" (Korpi and Palme 2003, 432), unlike, for example, unemployment (p. 431). Empirically, there is large within-type variance with respect to benefit generosity – see their table 1 (Korpi and Palme 2003, 435). In robustness checks later, I will control for their types.

[6] It is the mixture of these two motives that determines the correlation between income inequality and support for welfare expenditures. A critical assumption in their model is that the coefficient of relative risk aversion (RRA) is larger than 1, an assumption "which implies that the demand for insurance rises as income increases" (Moene and Wallerstein 2003, 490). However, empirical investigations of preferences for insurance always find the opposite: controlling for risk, demand for insurance and income are negatively correlated, a result that I have presented previously and that has been shown elsewhere (Cusack, Iversen, and Rehm 2006; Iversen and Soskice 2001; Rehm 2009). Moene and Wallerstein's predictions, therefore, are problematic (Iversen and Soskice 2001, 879). More importantly, they assume that the distribution of risk is identical across countries (Moene and Wallerstein 2003, 495), as is clearly not the case, as shown later. But it goes without saying that their work importantly shaped my thinking about risk and social policy.

argument advanced in the literature (Lindbeck and Snower 1989; Rueda 2005, 2007; Saint-Paul 2000) is, in a sense, a special case of the conjecture that the homogeneity of the risk pool matters with respect to social policy outcomes in which one part of the population has very low risk (the insiders), while others have a high degree of risk exposure (the outsiders). To that extent, my theoretical framework is compatible with David Rueda's important work on the topic, albeit his work is primarily concerned with employment protection and active labor market policies. Most work on the topic by economists is either purely formal or based on simulations (Pallage and Zimmermann 2001, 2005, 2006; Pollak 2007).[7] One of the earliest formal models of unemployment benefit determination stresses the importance of unequal unemployment risks (Wright 1986).[8]

The reminder of this chapter will test two central claims: that risk inequality is correlated with popular social policy support and that risk inequality is associated with social policy generosity. I will begin with an exploration of the link between risk pools and public opinion, offering three different tests: a purely cross-national test, a time-series test, and a cross-domain test. I will then investigate the hypothesis that lower risk inequality is correlated with more generous social insurance. These tests are performed on cross-national and cross-national time-series data.

---

[7] Di Tella and MacCulloch (2002) explore the topic formally and econometrically. They find, theoretically and empirically, a negative correlation between unemployment rates and benefit generosity, and weak partisan effects. They call for further research on the role of "risk" (p. 419, 422), which is what this chapter does. Neugart (2005a) suggests a model in which the probability of unemployment varies across regions within countries, which he shows to lead to different URRs, depending on the electoral system. Saint-Paul (1996, 277) provides a simple numerical example that shows that different hypothetical distributions of unemployment risk can change the median voter. In their cross-national simulation study of 11 OECD countries, Pallage and Zimmermann (2005) focus on differences in moral hazard but also incorporate differences in socioeconomic characteristics in their calibration study. Most relevant here is their distinction of different unemployment risk groups, based on four educational groups. They encounter the unexpected finding that unemployment inequality and benefit generosity are negatively correlated (as predicted by my framework), for which they have no explanation.

[8] While the literature on the *causes* of unemployment benefits is small, there is a large and controversial literature on the *effects* of unemployment benefits. A recent study and review by Howell and M. Rehm (2009) finds no correlation between unemployment rates and unemployment generosity.

## 5.1 RISK POOLS AND SOCIAL POLICY POPULARITY

### 5.1.1 Cross-National Evidence

As a first test, I explore the correlation between unemployment risk pool homogeneity and popular support for unemployment benefit generosity. I concentrate on the risk of unemployment because this is the quantity of interest in the model as well as the focus of the micro-level empirical investigations presented in Chapter 3. And, as mentioned previously, the unemployment domain is a particularly promising area for studying the politics of social solidarity for the twin reasons that the incidence of risk is more unequally distributed than other "old risks" (old age and sickness, in particular) and that unemployment was historically regarded as an uninsurable risk. In these situations, the emergence of mandatory unemployment insurance (UI) systems in virtually all rich democracies is all the more puzzling.

To measure the *inequality of risk* (the heterogeneity/homogeneity of the risk pool), I use the occupational unemployment rates described and employed earlier to calculate Gini coefficients of unemployment rates in a given country-year (using the size of occupations as weights). Higher Gini coefficients indicate higher risk inequality. The distribution of unemployment rates – and therefore the incidence of risk – varies widely across countries, as is shown in Figure 5.2.

To measure aggregate support for unemployment benefit generosity I rely on one of the "government responsibility" items mentioned at the beginning of this chapter. Specifically, the ISSP 2006 contains a question that reads, "On the whole, do you think it should or should not be the government's responsibility to provide decent standard of living for the unemployed?" Aggregate support for generous unemployment benefits is measured by the percentage of respondents who reply that it "definitely" or "probably should be" the government's responsibility to "provide a decent standard of living for the unemployed."[9]

---

[9] Note that the displayed levels of support are slightly different from the ones reported in FN 5 (and Table 1.1), because the sample here is restricted to employed respondents aged 25–60. The ISSP also contains an item reporting whether respondents want more or less spending for unemployment benefits (as is employed in the micro-level analysis earlier; see Chapter 3). However, that item references the status quo, and as such it would be problematic to compare mean values across countries.

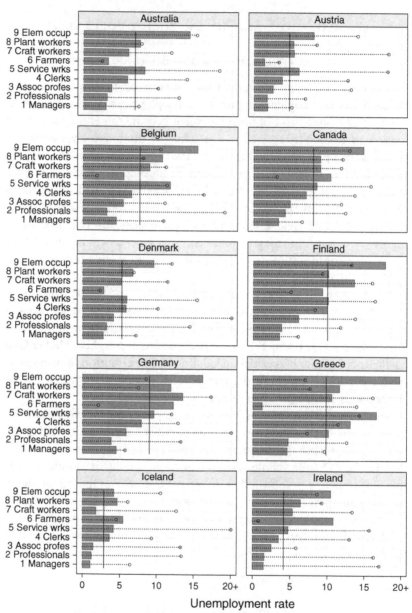

FIGURE 5.2: Occupational unemployment rates and size of occupations (2001–04 averages).

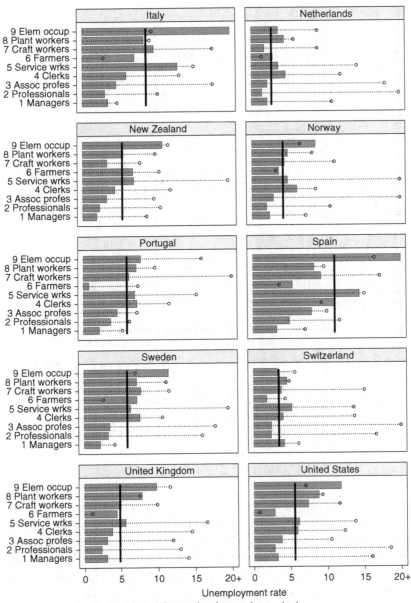

Vertical solid black line: national unemployment rate
Horizontal bars: occupational unemployment rates (capped at 20)
Horizontal dotted lines: size of occupation (capped at 20)

FIGURE 5.2: (*continued*)

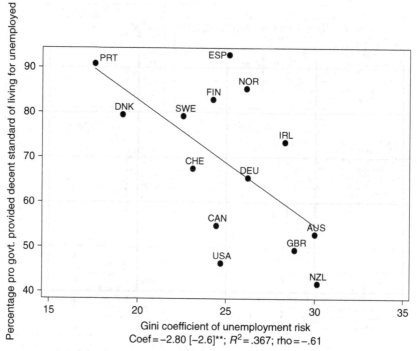

FIGURE 5.3: Risk inequality and support for unemployment benefit generosity (cross-national).

*Notes*: The y-axis displays the percentage of respondents (employed, ages 25–60) who reply it "definitely should be" or "probably should be" the government's responsibility to "provide a decent standard of living for unemployed," on ISSP 2006 (question wording is "On the whole, do you think it should or should not be the government's responsibility to ...?").

Figure 5.3 displays the bivariate correlation between support for generous unemployment benefits on the vertical axis and risk inequality on the horizontal axis. As hypothesized, there is a clear, statistically significant, negative correlation between risk inequality and public support for unemployment benefit generosity: where risk inequality is higher, aggregate support for generous benefits is lower.[10] While the fit is surely not perfect, the patterns clearly suggest that support for unemployment benefits is lower in countries with higher unemployment risk inequality.

[10] The results do not change much if we control for the level of unemployment.

### 5.1.2 Time-Series Evidence

As a second test, I explore the correlation of public support for unemployment policies and unemployment risk inequality over time within the United States. The Policy Agendas Project[11] provides estimates of "policy moods" on different topics. Mood number 103 relates most closely to unemployment-related attitudes and is derived from seven different survey items that were administered a total of 99 times to the American public between 1966 and 2007. These survey items are the following:

- INFLJOBS: If the government had to choose between keeping down inflation or keeping down unemployment to which do you think it should give highest priority?
- JOBS-TR: I would like to get your opinion on several areas of important government activities. As I read each one, please tell me if you would like to see the government do more, less or do about the same amount as they have been on ... expanding employment.
- RPUNEMP: There are many problems facing our nation today. But at certain times some things are more important than others, and need more attention from our federal government than others. I'd like to know for each of the things on this list whether you think it is something the government should be making a major effort on now, or something the government should be making some effort on now, or something not needing any particular government effort now. Trying to reduce unemployment.
- CUTHOURS: Here are some things the government might do for the economy. Circle one number for each action to show whether you are in favor of it or against it. Reducing the workweek to create more jobs
- JOBSALL: On the whole, do you think it should or should not be the government's responsibility to ... Provide a job for everyone who wants one?
- SAVEJOBS: Here are some things the government might do for the economy. Circle one number for each action to show whether you are in favor of it or against it. Support declining industries to protect jobs.

[11] www.policyagendas.org. "The data used here were originally collected by Frank R. Baumgartner and Bryan D. Jones, with the support of National Science Foundation grant numbers SBR 9320922 and 0111611, and were distributed through the Department of Government at the University of Texas at Austin. Neither NSF nor the original collectors of the data bear any responsibility for the analysis reported here."

- NYTENV2: Do you agree or disagree with the following statement: We must protect the environment even if it means jobs in your community are lost because of it.

The mood variable is coded in such a way that higher values indicate more liberal (progressive) attitudes, that is: average response = [liberal response/(conservative response + liberal response)]. As before, the unemployment risk variable is calculated as the Gini coefficient from the distribution of occupational unemployment rates (based on the March Current Population Surveys). Estimates of both variables are available from the 1970s until the 2000s, and Figure 5.4 shows their bivariate correlation. Once again, the correlation between these two variables is not perfect (rho = -0.47), but it is quite strong and statistically significant: when risk inequality is high, support for policies in favor of the unemployed is low; in contrast, when risk inequality is lower, support

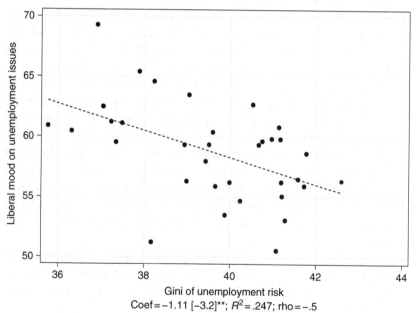

FIGURE 5.4: Risk inequality and policy mood on unemployment benefit generosity (time-series).
*Note*: The dependent variable is policy mood number 103 from the Policy Agendas Project, which relates quite closely to unemployment-related attitudes. It is derived from seven different survey items that were administered a total of 99 times to the American public between 1966 and 2007. The mood variable is coded in such a way that higher values indicate more liberal (progressive) attitudes. See text for more details

TABLE 5.1: *Risk inequality and policy mood on unemployment benefit generosity (time-series)*

|  | (1) | (2) | (3) |
|---|---|---|---|
|  | Support for unemployment benefit generosity (policy mood) | | |
| Gini of unemployment risk | −1.12** | −1.10** | −1.23** |
|  | (0.34) | (0.34) | (0.41) |
| Unemployment rate |  | −0.68 | −1.21* |
|  |  | (0.43) | (0.54) |
| Years 1968–70 |  |  | Ref |
|  |  |  | cat |
| Years 1971–82 |  |  | 3.67 |
|  |  |  | (2.66) |
| Years 1983–91 |  |  | 3.41 |
|  |  |  | (2.75) |
| Years 1992–02 |  |  | 0.21 |
|  |  |  | (2.64) |
| Years 2003–07 |  |  | 0.44 |
|  |  |  | (2.78) |
| Constant | 102.93** | 106.31** | 112.48** |
|  | (13.65) | (13.52) | (16.89) |
| N. of cases | 34 | 34 | 34 |
| Adj. $R^2$ | 0.223 | 0.257 | 0.313 |

Notes: $\#p < 0.10$, $^*p < 0.05$, $^{**}p < 0.01$.
Dummies for periods are inserted in Model 3 because of breaks in occupational classifications.
The dependent variable is policy mood number 103 from the Policy Agendas Project, which relates closely to unemployment-related attitudes. It is derived from seven different survey items that were administered a total of 99 times to the American public between 1966 and 2007. The mood variable is coded in such a way that higher values indicate more liberal (progressive) attitudes. See text for more details.

for these policies is higher. The fit considerably increases once we control for the level of unemployment and for breaks in the occupational classifications (Table 5.1).

### 5.1.3 Causal Evidence

The previous two tests cannot address an obvious problem, namely, reverse causality: social policy programs may generate their own support (Pierson 1994, 1996), rather than the other way around. As a third test, therefore, I explore the relationship between risk inequality in different social policy domains and support for *hypothetical* social policy programs in these domains. This addresses the reverse causality concern because hypothetical programs cannot possibly have an impact on risk inequality/ risk perceptions. I rely, once again, on the *Survey of Economic Risk Perceptions and Insecurity* (SERPI). The SERPI contains a set of questions asking respondents about their attitudes toward programs that do not exist. Respondents were asked the following:

With each new Administration in Washington, our political leaders consider a variety of new policies. How much would you support or oppose each of the following new ways of having government address social issues?

Seven hypothetical new programs were then listed and respondents were asked how much they support these hypothetical programs that cover different domains, such as unemployment, health, and family (strongly oppose, moderately opposed, neither support nor oppose, moderately support, strongly support):

- Offering tax breaks to people who financially support or personally care for family members not living with them, such as an elder parent (this would increase your taxes by $50 per year)
- Providing short-term financial support for people whose incomes drop substantially because of unexpected events and who don't have other help (this would increase your taxes by $50 per year)
- Providing short-term financial support for people whose incomes drop substantially following a divorce or other family dissolution (this would increase your taxes by $50 per year)
- Allowing all Americans to buy coverage from Medicare at a premium that is set based on their age (this would increase your taxes by $50 per year)
- Protecting homeowners against financial practices or circumstances that might threaten their credit or cause them to lose their home (this would increase your taxes by $50 per year)
- Providing free access to a trained patient advocate who can help you navigate the health care system and assist you in disputes with health insurers (this would increase your taxes by $50 per year)
- Providing up to two years of job retraining or support for higher education for people who have been laid-off from work (this would increase your taxes by $50 per year)

It is possible to match risk-related items (subjective probabilities and worries) in the SERPI with the hypothetical programs, as shown in Table 5.2. In that way, risk pools (measured by subjective probabilities and worries)

TABLE 5.2: *Mapping of risk items and hypothetical programs*

| Worries: "Are you very worried, fairly worried, slightly worried, or not worried at all about:" | Hypothetical program: "With each new Administration in Washington, our political leaders consider a variety of new policies. How much would you support or oppose each of the following new ways of having government address social issues?" | Subjective probabilities: "People face certain risks that can affect their economic situation or other important aspects of their lives. We'd like you to indicate how likely each of the following risks might be, in terms of the chance that they'll affect the lives of people like you over the next year." |
| --- | --- | --- |
| Needing to help out a member of your extended family if he/she gets in financial trouble | Offering tax breaks to people who financially support or personally care for family members not living with them, such as an elder parent (this would increase your taxes by $50 per year) | Out of 100 people like you, how many will need to help out someone in their extended family with a substantial amount of money during the next year? |
| Getting out of debt | Providing short-term financial support for people whose incomes drop substantially because of unexpected events and who don't have other help (this would increase your taxes by $50 per year) | |
| Getting by without spouses'/ partners' income if they were no longer around due to death, divorce, or other circumstances | Providing short-term financial support for people whose incomes drop substantially following a divorce or other family dissolution (this would increase your taxes by $50 per year) | Out of 100 people like you, how many will need to start getting by with less money because their spouse/partner is no longer there during the next year, due to death, divorce, or some other circumstance? |
| Having a serious illness in your immediate family that creates | Allowing all Americans to buy coverage from Medicare at a premium that is set based on | Out of 100 people like you, how many will have a serious illness in their immediate |

(continued)

TABLE 5.2: (*continued*)

| Worries: "Are you very worried, fairly worried, slightly worried, or not worried at all about:" | Hypothetical program: "With each new Administration in Washington, our political leaders consider a variety of new policies. How much would you support or oppose each of the following new ways of having government address social issues?" | Subjective probabilities: "People face certain risks that can affect their economic situation or other important aspects of their lives. We'd like you to indicate how likely each of the following risks might be, in terms of the chance that they'll affect the lives of people like you over the next year." |
|---|---|---|
| major out-of-pocket medical expenses | their age (this would increase your taxes by $50 per year) | family that creates major out-of-pocket medical expenses during the next year? |
| Paying your mortgage | Protecting homeowners against financial practices or circumstances that might threaten their credit or cause them to lose their home (this would increase your taxes by $50 per year) | Out of 100 people like you, how many will lose their homes during the next year because they won't be able to pay their mortgages? |
| Getting seriously ill and not being able to figure out what your insurance will cover | Providing free access to a trained patient advocate who can help you navigate the health care system and assist you in disputes with health insurers (this would increase your taxes by $50 per year) | |
| Losing your job | Providing up to two years of job retraining or support for higher education for people who have been laid-off from work (this would increase your taxes by $50 per year) | Out of 100 people like you, how many will lose their jobs during the next year? |

*Source:* SERPI.

can be mapped onto aggregate support for non-existing social policies. On the basis of my theoretical framework, we would expect that differences in risk pools are correlated with differences in support for social policy programs. In particular, my theoretical framework does have three direct and testable implications here: the more homogeneous risk pools are, that is, the lower risk inequality is, (i) the lower is opposition to new social policy programs; (ii) the less contested are new social policy programs; and (iii) the higher is support for new programs.

To test these propositions, I regress in separate models three measures of support for hypothetical programs (share opposed, coefficient of variation, mean) on the Gini coefficient of risk (where risk is measured by either subjective probabilities or worries), the mean level of risk, and a couple of dummy variables (for the type of risk item, i.e., subjective probabilities vs. worries and for the wave of the panel survey, i.e., wave 21 vs. wave 15). The results yield the expected positive correlations between opposition to new programs and their contestedness (Table 5.3, Models 1 and 2): if risk is more heterogeneous, new programs face stronger opposition and more heterogeneous support. The results also

TABLE 5.3: *Support for hypothetical programs as a function of risk pools*

|  | (1) | (2) | (3) |
| --- | --- | --- | --- |
|  | Support for hypothetical programs | | |
|  | Share opposed | Coefficient of variation | Mean |
| Gini of risk (worry or subjective probability) | 2.78# | 2.21# | −14.38* |
|  | (1.48) | (1.04) | (6.47) |
| Mean risk (worry or subjective probability) | 0.02 | 0.02 | −0.11# |
|  | (0.01) | (0.01) | (0.05) |
| Dummy for risk = worry | 1.32# | 0.99* | −6.82* |
| (vs. risk = subjective probability) | (0.63) | (0.45) | (2.77) |
| Dummy for wave 21 | 0.03 | 0.02 | −0.13 |
| (vs. wave 15) | (0.04) | (0.03) | (0.17) |
| Constant | −1.72# | −1.03 | 12.80** |
|  | (0.90) | (0.64) | (3.96) |
| N. of cases | 17 | 17 | 17 |
| Adj. $R^2$ | 0.046 | 0.066 | 0.134 |

*Note*: #$p < 0.1$, *$p < 0.05$, **$p < 0.01$
*Source*: SERPI.

yield the expected negative correlation between overall support for new hypothetical programs and risk pools (Table 5.3, Model 3): the lower risk inequality is, the more popular are the new programs. Figure 5.5 maps these findings – shown are partial correlations between risk pools on the horizontal axes and support for hypothetical programs on the vertical axes. The findings suggest that the correlation between risk inequality and patterns of social policy support may well be causal: it is difficult to see how a hypothetical program can shape risk inequality.

In summary, all three ways to explore the correlation between risk inequality and support for social policy yield the expected relationship: the higher risk inequality is, the lower is support for social policy programs. The next section cuts out the attitudinal middleman, so to speak, and relates risk inequality directly with social policy generosity, comparing countries (and countries over time).

## 5.2 RISK POOLS AND SOCIAL POLICY GENEROSITY

To investigate the relationship between risk inequality and social policy generosity,[12] I return to the unemployment domain, and risk pool homogeneity will, once again, be captured by the Gini coefficient of occupational unemployment risk. Measuring the generosity of unemployment benefits across time and space in a comparable way is complicated, but there has been much progress in recent years. Howell and M. Rehm (2009) provide a detailed discussion of the strength and weaknesses of existing benefit generosity measures. I will employ the net unemployment replacement rates (URRs) published by the OECD.[13]

Figure 5.6 displays the correlation between risk inequality – measured by the Gini coefficient of unemployment risk – and unemployment benefit

---

[12] I focus on benefit generosity, but historically there were two issues that were more contested (Mares 2003). First, the coverage rate (the boundary of the risk pool, as Mares [2003, 107] calls it); second, the question of control (or design). Contemporaneously, these issues are largely settled: coverage rates are high in most rich democracies, and the institutional arrangements are largely fixed.

[13] The OECD "initial net replacement rates" are simulated for six family types at three different earnings levels, yielding 18 different net URRs. Fortunately, the OECD also publishes a summary measure, which averages various scenarios (dx.doi.org/10.1787/182506528237). This is the measure I employ later (averaged for 2001–04).

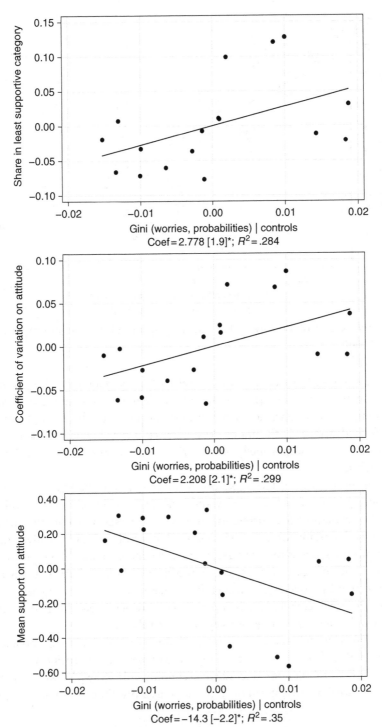

FIGURE 5.5: Real risk pools, support for hypothetical programs.

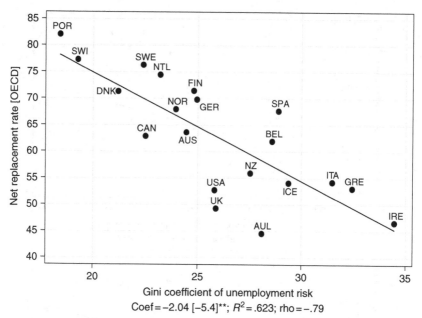

Coef = −2.04 [−5.4]**; $R^2$ = .623; rho = −.79

FIGURE 5.6: Risk pool inequality and unemployment benefit generosity (cross-national).

generosity – measured by OECD's net URRs (the data are averaged over the years 2001 to 2004). As conjectured, there is a clear negative correlation ($\rho$ = −0.79, statistically significant): the more equally unemployment risk is distributed, the more generous are unemployment benefits. As expected, the homogeneity of the risk pool shapes the generosity of benefits.

In the following, I will explore whether – and argue that – this relationship between risk inequality and benefit generosity is robust. I explore the robustness of this correlation in two ways. First, to explore the impact of time-invariant (or only once observed) control variables I will average all variables across the period 2001 to 2004 and estimate OLS regressions with a set of control variables. A second robustness check extends the country-year coverage considerably. These various tests suggest that the negative correlation between unemployment risk inequality and unemployment benefit generosity is rather robust.

With respect to control variables, I want to make sure that potential alternative determinants of unemployment benefit generosity are taken into account. I therefore include the economywide *unemployment rate* ($\bar{p}$) as a control because it can be understood as a price for insurance. Despite its importance in the literature, we lack a high quality measure of *income inequality* with broad country coverage. Conceptually, earnings inequality is the appropriate measure, which is usually proxied with the $p90/p10$ earnings ratios published by the OECD. However, the country-year coverage is spotty. I therefore employ OECD's "Gini coefficient based on equivalized household market income, before taxes and transfers (18–65 years only)." Finally, for maximum country-year coverage and despite theoretical reservations, I also employ "Gini coefficient based on equivalized household disposable income, after taxes and transfers (18–65 years only)" (OECD 2008a). Since it is conceivable that the self-employed have no interest in generous unemployment benefit systems (or no access to them), I include a measure of the prevalence of *self-employment* as control variable. Several contributions apply partisan arguments to unemployment benefits (Allan and Scruggs 2004; Boadway and Oswald 1983; Boix 1998; Di Tella and MacCulloch 2002; Korpi and Palme 2003; Martin and Swank 2004; Scruggs and Allan 2006; Swank and Martin 2001). My theoretical framework puts citizen preferences first, but it is not incompatible with the possibility that parties play an important role. To take into account potential partisan effects, I control for *partisanship of the government*. Since my test is cross-national and hardly captures time dynamics, I employ a cumulative measure of right-wing party strength (the percentage of total cabinet posts held by the right-wing party, weighted by days, cumulative since 1990). To take into account the possibility that *corporatist bargaining arrangements* matter, I include a measure of union density. This is, of course, a very rough proxy, but replacing it with superior approximations[14] (at the cost of much smaller sample sizes) does not change the results. Regarding other control variables, I follow Allan and Scruggs (2004) and control for *GDP growth* (one may expect that higher growth rates relax the budget constraint), *trade openness* ([imports + exports]/GDP), and *budget deficits* (as percentage of GDP).[15]

Finally, the political economy literature often groups countries into "types." As discussed previously, skill specificity plays an important role in the Varieties of Capitalism literature (Iversen 2005), and I therefore

---

[14] Such as the "Index of Government Involvement in Wage-Setting" or the "Index of Confederal Involvement in Wage-Setting."

[15] Allan and Scruggs (2004) also control for institutional veto points and financial openness. These variables have only limited country-year coverage and are never significant in the Allan-Scruggs model.

include an indicator variable for *liberal market economies* (LMEs). We should expect lower unemployment benefit generosity in these countries. Vroman (2007) classifies unemployment *benefit systems* into those that primarily provide unemployment assistance, those that primarily provide UI, and those that are a mix of the two, and I control for that. UI systems should be more generous than unemployment assistance systems. Finally, Korpi and Palme (2003, 435) classify countries by their *type of dominant social insurance institution* (targeted, basic security, state corporatist, encompassing). Table 5.4 contains the definition and sources of all macro-level variables employed in this chapter.

The first set of robustness checks are contained in Table 5.5, which shows the results from OLS regressions. Model 1 in Table 5.5 contains the estimate of the regression line displayed in Figure 5.6. Models 2 and 3 control for income inequality, measured in different ways. In both cases, income inequality is negatively correlated with unemployment benefit generosity, but the coefficient is not significant. Model 4 shows that unemployment systems that mix assistance and insurance elements are more generous than their pure counterparts, especially relative to pure assistance levels. Model 5 includes an indicator variable for LMEs, which is negative and significant. As expected, LMEs have less generous net URRs. Finally, Model 6 includes controls for the "types of dominant social insurance institutions" due to Korpi and Palme (1998, 2003). Although it is unclear whether these types should have much explanatory power in terms of URRs, the results show some moderate differences across regimes. Most important for the purposes of this chapter, however, is the finding that the Gini coefficient of unemployment risk is stable across these models and always statistically and substantively significant. The higher unemployment inequality is, the lower are unemployment benefits.

The second set of robustness checks extends the country and time coverage considerably. The previous analysis was based on data for the years 2001 to 2004 only, because I could assemble a data set with highly comparable information on unemployment risk distributions only for this period. But if one is willing to trade data quality for year and country coverage, it is possible to extend the data set significantly. I calculate Gini coefficients of unemployment risk, based on ILO's LABORSTA data, where unemployment risk is provided either in the ISCO-88 or in the ISCO-68 classification, at the one-digit level. Since the OECD net URR data are not available before 2001, I make use of an update of the Scruggs data (Vliet and Caminada 2012). This data set contains six

TABLE 5.4: *Variable definitions and sources*

| Measure | Source |
|---|---|
| **Unemployment benefit generosity:** | |
| (1) OECD's net URR | (1) OECD: Benefits and Wages (gross/net replacement rates, country specific files and tax/benefit models; update: March 2006) |
| (2) net URRs [OECD] * coverage [Scruggs] | (2) Coverage (insured population) from Scruggs (2004) (Version 1.2 [http//sp.uconn.edu/~scruggs/cwed/generosity12.xls]) |
| Homogeneity of risk pool: Gini coefficient of occupational unemployment rates (ISCO88-1d level), weighted by size of occupation | Based on CPS (http://cps.ipums.org/cps), EU-LFS (http://epp.eurostat.ec.europa.eu/portal/page/portal/microdata/lfs), ILO (http://laborsta.ilo.org) |
| National unemployment rate | Occupation-size weighted mean of occupational unemployment rates OECD (http://stats.oecd.org/wbos/Index.aspx?DataSetCode= INEQUALITY), mildly interpolated (in-between missing years). |
| **Income inequality** | |
| (1) OECD's "Gini coefficient based on equivalised household market income, before taxes and transfers" (18–65 years only) | |
| (2) Gini coefficient based on equivalised household disposable income, after taxes and transfers (18–65 years only) | |
| Self-employment as percentage of civilian employment | OECD's "Annual Labour Force Statistics summary tables," available at http://stats.oecd.org/Index.aspx?DataSetCode=ALFS_SUMTAB |
| Partisanship of the government: the percentage of total cabinet posts held by right-wing party, weighted by days, cumulative since 1990 | "Comparative Political Data Set III" (Armingeon et al. 2009); calculated from variable gov_right1 |

(continued)

| Measure | Source |
|---|---|
| Corporatist bargaining arrangements: Trade union density (= wage and salary earners that are trade union members/total number of wage and salary earners) | OECD (http://stats.oecd.org/Index.aspx?DataSetCode=UN_DEN), mildly interpolated (in-between missing years) |
| Growth of GDP (expenditure approach) | Calculated from OECD's National Accounts of OECD Countries (http://stats.oecd.org/Index.aspx?DatasetCode=SNA_TABLE1) |
| Trade openness ([imports + exports]/GDP) | Calculated from OECD's National Accounts of OECD Countries (http://stats.oecd.org/Index.aspx?DatasetCode=SNA_TABLE1) |
| Budget deficit: Government net lending, as percentage of GDP | OECD: Economic Outlook No. 86: Annual and Quarterly data (http://oecd-stats.ingenta.com/OECD) |
| Skill specificity: indicator variable for liberal market economies | Dummy for Australia, Canada, Ireland, New Zealand, UK, and the US |
| Unemployment system | Unemployment assistance only: AUL, NZ<br>Unempl. insurance only: BEL, CAN, DNK, GRE, ITA, NOR, SWI, USA<br>Mixed systems: AUS, FIN, GER, IRE, NTL, POR, SPA, SWE, UK (Vroman [2007]) |
| Type of dominant social insurance institutions | Targeted: Australia<br>Basic security: CAN, DEN, IRE, NTL, NZ, SWI, UK, US<br>State corporatist: AUS, BEL, FRA, GER, ITA<br>Encompassing: FIN, NOR, SWE<br>(Korpi and Palme 2003, 435) |

TABLE 5.5: *Determinants of unemployment benefit generosity I (OLS on 2001–04 averages)*

| | (1) | (2) | (3) | (4) | (5) | (6) |
|---|---|---|---|---|---|---|
| | Dependent variable Net unemployment replacement rates (OECD), 2001–04 average | | | | | |
| Gini coefficient of unemployment risk | -2.04** (0.38) | -2.19** (0.48) | -1.84** (0.38) | -1.88** (0.37) | -1.74** (0.24) | -2.05** (0.41) |
| Income inequality: | | | | | | |
| Household market inc. inequality (18–65 years old) | | -0.22 (0.52) | | | | |
| Household disposable inc. inequality (18–65 years old) | | | -0.74# (0.40) | | | |
| Unemployment system: | | | | | | |
| Assistance | | | | ref. category | | |
| Assistance/insurance | | | | 11.79* (5.21) | | |
| Insurance | | | | 8.40 (5.24) | | |
| Asset specificity regime: | | | | | | |
| Dummy for LME | | | | | -11.81** (2.18) | |
| Dominant social insurance: | | | | | | |
| Basic security | | | | | | ref. category |

(continued)

TABLE 5.5: (continued)

| | (1) | (2) | (3) | (4) | (5) | (6) |
|---|---|---|---|---|---|---|
| | Dependent variable Net unemployment replacement rates (OECD), 2001–04 average | | | | | |
| State corporatist | | | | | | 6.00 |
| | | | | | | (3.59) |
| Encompassing | | | | | | 8.00# |
| | | | | | | (3.86) |
| Targeted (= Australia) | | | | | | –10.38 |
| | | | | | | (6.12) |
| Constant | 115.77** | 127.79** | 132.72** | 102.52** | 111.35** | 112.58** |
| | (9.83) | (19.90) | (13.46) | (11.17) | (6.19) | (10.42) |
| N. of countries | 20 | 16 | 19 | 19 | 20 | 16 |
| Adj. $R^2$ | 0.602 | 0.616 | 0.638 | 0.654 | 0.845 | 0.727 |

*Note:* OLS estimates on 2001–04 averaged values.
Displayed are coefficients above standard errors (in parentheses).
#$p < 0.1$, *$p < 0.05$, **$p < 0.01$

measures of unemployment benefit generosity, for wide country-year coverage:

- RRAPW: Net Unemployment Replacement Rate for an Average Production Worker, Single Person
- RRAPW: Net Unemployment Replacement Rate for an Average Production Worker, One Earner Couple with Two Children
- RRAW: Net Unemployment Replacement Rate for an Average Worker, One Earner Couple with Two Children
- RRAW: Net Unemployment Replacement Rate for an Average Worker, Single Person
- GRRAPW: Gross Unemployment Replacement Rate for an Average Production Worker, One Earner Couple with Two Children
- GRRAPW: Gross Unemployment Replacement Rate for an Average Production Worker, Single Person
- GRRAW: Gross Unemployment Replacement Rate for an Average Worker, One Earner Couple with Two Children
- GRRAW: Gross Unemployment Replacement Rate for an Average Worker, Single Person

I use these as dependent variables, and the ILO-based measures of unemployment risk inequality as key explanatory variable, with unemployment rates (levels) and a dummy variable for different occupational classifications (ISCO88 vs. ISCO68) as controls. This gives me a data set with information on 22 countries, with an average of about 22 years of observation.[16] With so many data points, a wider and arguably stronger set of robustness checks can be performed. In particular, I estimate five models for each of the eight dependent variables, for a total of 40 estimations:

- Pooled OLS
- Panel-corrected standard errors
- Random effects
- Fixed effects
- Between effects

---

[16] AUS (1972–2008), AUT (1984–2008), BEL (1983–2008), CAN (1973–2008), CHE (2002–2008), CZE (1993–2008), DEU (1996–2008), DNK (1984–2008), ESP (1979–2008), FIN (1977–2008), GRC (1981–2008), HUN (1995–2008), IRL (1983–1997), ITA (1993–2008), JPN (1978–2008), NOR (1972–2008), NZL (1987–2008), POL (1995–2008), PRT (1979–2008), SVK (1994–2008), SWE (1971–2008), USA (1971–2002).

In all 40 estimations, unemployment risk inequality is a statistically significant and negative predictor of unemployment benefit generosity: higher risk inequality is associated with less generous benefits. The results for the first dependent variable (Net Unemployment Replacement Rate for an Average Production Worker, Single Person) are shown as an example in Table 5.6. These robustness checks confirm the strong and robust negative cross-country correlation between the unemployment risk pool and unemployment benefit generosity: the more heterogeneous the risk pool is, the lower are benefits.

\* \* \*

TABLE 5.6: *Determinants of unemployment benefit generosity II (OLS, RE, FE, BE)*

| | (1) | (2) | (3) | (4) | (5) |
|---|---|---|---|---|---|
| | Dependent variable: Net Unemployment Replacement Rate for an Average Production Worker, Single Person | | | | |
| | OLS | PCSE | RE | FE | BE |
| Gini coefficient of | −1.843** | −0.498** | −0.469** | −0.412** | −2.592** |
| unemployment risk | (0.134) | (0.109) | (0.091) | (0.091) | (0.662) |
| Unemployment rate | −0.001 | 0.000 | 0.003* | 0.003** | 0.004 |
| (level) | (0.001) | (0.002) | (0.001) | (0.001) | (0.008) |
| Dummy for ISCO88 | 0.027# | −0.019# | −0.021** | −0.023** | 0.076 |
| (vs. ISCO-68) | (0.015) | (0.011) | (0.008) | (0.008) | (0.091) |
| Constant | 0.981** | 0.674** | 0.646** | 0.636** | 1.088** |
| | (0.029) | (0.027) | (0.033) | (0.023) | (0.124) |
| No. of cases | 485 | 485 | 485 | 485 | 485 |
| No. of countries | 22 | 22 | 22 | 22 | 22 |
| Obs. per group: min | | 7 | 7 | 7 | 7 |
| Obs. per group: mean | | 22 | 22 | 22 | 22 |
| Obs. per group: max | | 37 | 37 | 37 | 37 |
| $R^2$ | 0.335 | 0.646 | | 0.140 | 0.527 |
| Adj. $R^2$ | 0.331 | | | 0.095 | 0.448 |
| Overall $R^2$ | | | 0.239 | 0.208 | 0.317 |
| Within $R^2$ | | | 0.139 | 0.140 | 0.082 |
| Between $R^2$ | | | 0.409 | 0.358 | 0.527 |

Notes: #$p < 0.1$, *$p < 0.05$, **$p < 0.01$
Model 1: pooled OLS; Model 2: panel-corrected standard errors; Model 3: random effects; Model 4: fixed effects; Model 5: between effects.
The dependent variable ranger from 0.23 to 0.93, with a standard deviation of 0.16 and a mean of 0.55. The Gini coefficient of unemployment risk ranges from 0.108 to 0.357, with a standard deviation of 0.0547 and a mean of 0.238

In this chapter, I have focused on a key macro-level implication that follows from my theoretical framework – namely, that lower risk inequality is associated with more generous social insurance, via popular support – and subjected it to various empirical tests. I found strong empirical support for the claim. An obvious limitation of most of these tests is the problem of reverse causality. There are two related problems here. A first problem is the possibility that social policy programs generate their own support, rather than that social policy support influences social policy programs. This chapter has addressed this problem directly by exploring the link between real risk pools and support for hypothetical programs (which cannot possibly influence risk distributions, for the simple reason that they do not exist).

A second problem is the possibility that social policy programs shape risk pools, leading to a circular relationship among risk pools, public opinion, and social insurance. The following two chapters will cope with this issue. In Chapters 6 and 7, I will address this endogeneity problem by looking at the impact of shocks to risk pools and the role of risk pools before social insurance is adopted. I will analyze a case of a clearly exogenous shock to risk pools – German reunification – and its impact on benefit generosity (Chapter 6). I will also analyze the distribution of risk pools *before* social insurance adoption, making them again clearly exogenous (Chapter 7). In particular, I will explore whether social insurance adoption is more likely if risk pools become more homogeneous, as predicted by my theoretical framework.

# 6

# Risk Pools and Retrenchment – German Reunification

On February 25, 2002, the German chancellor, Gerhard Schröder, heading a coalition of the Social Democratic Party (SPD) with the Green Party (Greens), instituted what became known as the "Hartz Commission."[*] Charged with the organizational restructuring of the Federal Labor Office (*Bundesanstalt für Arbeit*), the commission presented its suggestions in August of the same year. These suggestions included several far-reaching labor market reforms, most importantly the merging of the unemployment and social assistance systems. Immediately before the federal election on September 22, 2002, Schröder announced his intention to implement the proposed reforms "one-by-one." After a narrow win, the reelected red-green coalition initiated and eventually passed legislation to that effect. Of these so-called Hartz reforms, the merging of unemployment and social assistance was particularly consequential. For those unemployed for longer than 12 months – in Germany typically more than half of the unemployed (Duell and Vetter 2012, 2) – the reforms meant deep cuts in benefits. Arguably, the German labor market reforms are among the most significant examples of welfare state retrenchment in Western Europe.

How can we understand far-reaching structural reforms of a statist welfare state in a gridlocked political system known for its *Reformstau* (reform backlog)? How can we make sense of the fact that a left government initiated some of the deepest cuts in welfare state benefits in the post–World War II era? In other words, what explains the Hartz reforms?

* I am grateful for discussions about the Hartz Reforms with Achim Kemmerling, Philip Manow, Kai Muehleck, Alexander Petring, Georg Picot, and Hanna Schwander. I also thank Lauren Stabler for her competent research assistance.

In this chapter, I apply my theoretical framework to make sense of the German experience.

From the perspective of my theoretical framework, German reunification can be understood as an exogenous shock, combining two risk pools (West and East Germany) into one, while maintaining the social policy arrangement of West Germany. This led to a sharp increase in risk inequality – the result of adding the high-unemployment Länders from the former East Germany to the existing West German social insurance system – and made risk pooling for a majority of West Germans much more expensive and a lot less attractive, and it eroded support for generous unemployment benefits. Risk pool and benefit generosity were out of equilibrium. Contrary to conventional wisdom, I argue that Schröder had a clear mandate for labor market reforms and retrenchment – a mandate to synchronize risk pool and generosity benefits, so to speak. From my theoretical perspective, the puzzle is not why he followed through with the agenda, but why he did it so late – and why the SPD suffered major electoral losses afterward.

The following case study complements the (largely) correlational analysis in the previous chapter: because German reunification can be interpreted as an exogenous shock to a risk pool, the following analysis can directly test the consequences of a change in risk inequality on social policy generosity, avoiding the problem of reverse causality (that social policy shapes risk pools, not the other way around). I develop the case study as follows. I first outline the German unemployment insurance UI system and the Hartz reforms. After a review of existing explanations of the Hartz reforms, I present my account. I first empirically confirm that German reunification sharply increased risk inequality; I then show that reunification and the way it was financed also sharply weakened the actuarial elements of the UI system. Finally, I present evidence based on opinion surveys that suggests that a broad majority in Germany was well aware of these developments; that support for generous benefits eroded; that demand for far-reaching reforms was high; and that the Hartz reforms were welcome by large parts of the population.

## 6.1 GERMAN UNEMPLOYMENT INSURANCE

The German UI program is administered by the federally organized *Bundesagentur für Arbeit* (BA).[1] It is funded by employees and employers

---

[1] The German employment office (labor office) was founded in 1952 as the "*Bundesanstalt für Arbeitsvermittlung und Arbeitslosenversicherung*." It was renamed the *Bundesanstalt*

(via a contribution rate paid to 50 percent by each), as well as the federal government (more on that later). Until the Hartz IV reform, which took effect in 2005, Germany's unemployed could rely on one of three benefits: income-related unemployment benefits (*Arbeitslosengeld*), income-related unemployment assistance (*Arbeitslosenhilfe*), and flat-rate social assistance (*Sozialhilfe*). Unemployment benefits were financed by contributions and were paid to qualifying individuals for typically 12 months (but up to 32 months for certain older age groups). Benefits were proportional to previous income and depended on the family situation (number of dependents and the like). *Arbeitslosenhilfe* was administered by the BA but financed by the federal budget and available to qualifying individuals who ran out of *Arbeitslosengeld*; it was proportional to previous income levels, was means-tested, and was offered for an unlimited period. *Sozialhilfe* was administered and largely financed by the municipalities (*Kommunen*) and was a means-tested social assistance system for those eligible for neither *Arbeitslosengeld* nor *Arbeitslosenhilfe*. Unemployment assistance and social assistance were two parallel systems covering the same need – but they followed very different logics: *Arbeitslosenhilfe* was income-related, while *Sozialhilfe* was not. The Hartz IV reforms combined the two systems into one that provides flat-rate, not income-related, means-tested benefits (*Arbeitslosengeld II*). As such, these reforms were structural in nature.

Many elements of the German welfare state more or less follow the "equivalence principle" (*Äquivalenzprinzip*) – "the principle that benefits have to be basically proportionate to contributions, which in turn are proportionate to earned income" (Streeck and Trampusch 2005, 191). This is true for Germany's UI system as well (more so for the *Arbeitslosengeld*, and much less so for the *Arbeitslosenhilfe*), but it deviates from actuarial principles in three main ways. First, UI redistributes across risk groups. As in all social insurance systems, premiums are not scaled to risk. This has redistributive consequences, depending on the relationship between income and risk. If income and risk are negatively correlated – as they typically are – the system redistributes from low-risk (and rich) to high-risk (and poor) citizens. Second, the German UI system redistributes across regions. The reason, again, is that premiums are not scaled to risk; they neither differ across individuals nor across regions. As a consequence, resources are transferred from low to high unemployment

---

*für Arbeit* (1969) and is called *Bundesagentur für Arbeit* since 2004. I will refer to the institution as the employment office, the labor office, or the BA.

regions (Beramendi 2012; Ziblatt 2002). Third, the UI system is often subsidized by the federal government, using general tax revenues. The federal government is legally obligated to keep the UI system solvent and it has done so frequently and with large sums. Politicians have "with increasing skill hidden rising contribution rates and avoided spending cuts" by infusing federal tax revenues into the social insurance system (Streeck and Trampusch 2005, 177). Since reunification, all three violations of actuarial principles have become particularly significant, as will be documented in the following.

## 6.2 THE HARTZ REFORMS

In August 2002, the Hartz committee – a 15-member committee called *Moderne Dienstleistungen am Arbeitsmarkt* (Committee for Modern Services in the Labor Market), instituted by the federal government – proposed far-reaching social policy reforms, including the merging of the separate unemployment and social assistance systems. With the federal elections being only five weeks away (September 22, 2002), Chancellor Schröder could not pursue legislative changes, but promised to implement the proposed reforms in full, and in consensus with the Christian Democrats (who dominated the Bundesrat).[2] Schröder's red-green coalition narrowly won reelection. In their coalition negotiations, the SPD and the Green Party decided to implement the Hartz proposals "one-by-one."[3] Wolfgang Clement, the designated minister for the newly created "super ministry," a combination of the Economic and Labor Ministries, became a particularly vocal supporter of the reforms and remained so during his tenure as federal minister of economics and labor (*Bundesminister für Wirtschaft und für Arbeit*) between 2002 and 2005 (Stiller 2007, 162).

The coalition got busy turning the Hartz proposals into law, and they were ultimately implemented in four bundles (Hartz I to Hartz IV), taking effect in January 2003 (Hartz I and II), January 2004 (Hartz III), and January 2005 (Hartz IV). Hartz I and II tightened the rules according to which an unemployed worker could reject a job offer as well as the conditions for claiming unemployment assistance (Streeck and Trampusch 2005, 184). Other changes included the expansion of low-paid

---

[2] Handelsblatt August 16, 2002.    [3] FAZ October 8, 2002.

jobs exempted from social insurance contributions, as well as measures to promote the employment of older people and the transition from unemployment into self-employment (Streeck and Trampusch 2005, 185). In March 2003, Chancellor Schröder presented Agenda 2010, a series of planned reforms. The Hartz III and IV reforms were cornerstones of that agenda. The most consequential part of these reforms was the merging of *Arbeitslosenhilfe* (unemployment assistance) and *Sozialhilfe* (social assistance) into one system (*Arbeitslosengeld*). But UI benefits were changed as well: their maximum duration was decreased for older groups and sanctions were harshened.

As mentioned, a critical difference between *Arbeitslosenhilfe* and *Arbeitslosengeld* is that the former paid proportional benefits for an unlimited amount of time, while the latter provides flat-rate benefits. This is hugely consequential for those out of work for more than 12 months. This can be seen in Table 6.1, which compares the status quo before and after the Hartz reforms in terms of benefits, their duration, and sanctions.[4]

To give a sense of the differences between unemployment related benefits before and after the Hartz Reforms let us consider the income consequences of becoming unemployed in Germany under the two different systems (before and after Hartz IV), for two different hypothetical workers: (i) an average worker (unmarried, no children), full-time employed, whose wage earnings are equal to the average wage earnings of a full-time worker (100 percent AW), and (ii) the same worker, but with earnings equal to 1.5 the average wage earnings (150 percent AW).[5] In 2012, the 100 percent AW's yearly gross income was about €44,000, and net income was €26,000. For the 150 percent AW, these values are €66,000 (yearly gross) and €37,000 (yearly net), respectively.[6] For workers younger than 45 years of age, UI payments are fairly similar before and after the Hartz Reforms:

---

[4] Shown is the state of affairs in 2004 and 2012, respectively. Several changes due to the Hartz Reforms were somewhat weakened in later years. These changes are generally documented in later footnotes.

[5] Note that this example is for a West German worker. The unemployment benefit system in the East differed in one respect: it had a somewhat (~15 percent) lower benefit ceiling (*Bemessungsgrundlage*; in 2012, €67,200 in the West vs. €57,600 in the East), which would lead to a slightly lower benefit in the example for an unemployed worker in East Germany.

[6] Source: OECD's Benefits and Wages: Tax-Benefit calculator (www.oecd.org/social/soc/benefitsandwagestax-benefitcalculator.htm). See www.pub.arbeitsagentur.de/alt.html for a benefit calculator.

TABLE 6.1: *Unemployment benefits before and after the Hartz Reforms*

| | Before Hartz Reforms | | After Hartz Reforms | |
|---|---|---|---|---|
| | Arbeitslosengeld | Arbeistlosenhilfe | Arbeitslosengeld I | Arbeitslosengeld II |
| Benefits | Proportional to net earnings 67% (60% w/o children) | Proportional to net earnings 57% (53% w/o children) | Proportional to net earnings 67% (60% w/o children) | 1. Flat cash benefit, per month (Regelbedarfe) €374 (single person) €337 (partners above the age of 18) €219–€299 per child, depending on age<br>2. Reasonable costs for accommodation and heating<br>3. One-time benefits for the initial equipment of a flat including household appliances and clothing<br>4. Some school related expenses<br>5. Some other expenses<br><br>The financial benefits mentioned are reduced by the income and assets to be credited |
| Duration | Duration of benefits (DB) depends on duration of insurance coverage (DI) and age, but is 12 months for someone | Unlimited, renewable at least every 12 months | Duration of benefits (DB) depends on duration of insurance coverage (DI) and age, but is 12 months for someone | Unlimited, renewable at least every 6 months |

(continued)

TABLE 6.1: (continued)

| | Before Hartz Reforms | | After Hartz Reforms | |
| --- | --- | --- | --- | --- |
| | Arbeitslosengeld | Arbeitslosenhilfe | Arbeitslosengeld I | Arbeitslosengeld II |
| | with 24 months of DI Maximum DB: 32 months (above 57 years, 64 months of DI) | | with 24 months of DI Maximum DB: 24 months (above 58 years, 48 months of DI)* | |
| Sanctions | Under certain circumstances, entitlement to unemployment benefit (Arbeitslosengeld) is suspended during 12 weeks (i.e., unemployment caused by the person) and for up to 12 weeks in the event of an unjustified refusal of a reasonable job | | Under certain circumstances, entitlement to unemployment benefit (Arbeitslosengeld) is suspended during 12 weeks (i.e., unemployment caused by the person) and for up to 12 weeks in the event of an unjustified refusal of a reasonable job (which includes a much larger set of jobs than before) | Sanctions possible for capable beneficiaries who do not make an effort to participate in the labor market or do not accept reasonable employment. Reduction of Arbeitslosengeld II by 30% of the relevant normal requirements (Regelbedarf) for three months if the beneficiary fails to comply with his or her duties for the first time and by further 30% of the relevant normal requirements if the beneficiary fails to comply with his or her duties for a second time; in the case of repeated failure of the beneficiary within a 12-month period unemployment benefit II will cease |

*Source:* Based on MISSOC (Mutual Information System on Social Protection / Social Security), www.missoc.org. Entries refer to January 2004 (Arbeitslosengeld and Arbeitslosenhilfe) and January 2012 (Arbeitslosengeld I and II).

* According to the initial Hartz Reforms (in force since January 1, 2004, for new entitlements after February 1, 2006), the maximum DB was 18 months (for those 55 years or older, with 36 months of DI). This was changed starting in 2008 to 24 months (for those 58 years or older, with 24 months of DI).

60 percent of net income for 12 months, that is, €1,300/month for the 100 percent AW, and €1,850/month for the 150 percent AW. In the most generous scenario, these monthly payments would continue for 32 months before the reform (for an unemployed worker 57 years or older who contributed at least 64 months to the UI system), and for 24 months after the reforms[7] (for an unemployed worker 58 years or older who contributed at least 48 months to the UI system).

After the expiration of benefits (typically after 12 months), the situation of the still unemployed AW dramatically differs, comparing the pre- and post-Hartz regimes. Before Hartz, the AW would receive *Arbeitslosenhilfe*, that is, 50 percent of previous net earnings (~€1080 for the 100 percent AW, ~€1540 for the 150 percent AW), for an unlimited amount of time. The unlimited duration of unemployment benefit payments before the reforms "was an extraordinary feature of the German unemployment benefit system" (Jacobi and Kluve 2006, 6).[8] Since the Hartz Reforms, the still unemployed worker receives *Arbeitslosengeld II*, that is, €374 per month, plus "reasonable costs" for accommodation (rent for an apartment with up to 50 m² [538 ft²] and heating, but not electricity and phone). This benefit is means-tested; that is, (certain types of) assets and savings have to be used up before eligibility.[9] It is easy to see, then, that the Hartz Reforms meant a dramatic reduction in benefits for those unemployed for 12 months or longer. But not only the long-term unemployed fared worse after the Hartz Reforms – many social assistance recipients did so as well. While the

---

[7] According to the initial Hartz Reforms (in force since January 1, 2004, for new entitlements after February 1, 2006), the maximum duration of benefits (DB) was 18 months (for those 55 years or older, with 36 months of duration of insurance contributions [DI]). This was changed starting in 2008 to 24 months (for those 58 years or older, with 24 months of DI).

[8] This system created incentives to stay on benefits: "Engels (2001) calculates that a typical family with three children receiving social assistance in West Germany in the year 2000 received an income that was only 15.3% below the income of a comparable family with a single earner receiving an average unskilled worker's wage. In East Germany the respective difference was only 11.5%" (Jacobi and Kluve 2006, 7).

[9] The allowance for savings is €150 per year of age (minimum €3,100, maximum €9,750). Certain pension-related savings (€250 per year of age, increased to €750 in 2010), housing assets (self-used house of up to 130 m² living space), and a car up to €7,500 are not counted against the allowance. Recipients of *Arbeitslosengeld II* can earn income from a job: 100 percent of €100 per month without a reduction in benefit, 20 percent of €100–1,000 per month without a reduction in benefit, 10 percent of €1,000–1,200 without a reduction in benefit. Therefore, one can interpret *Arbeitslosengeld II* as a sort of minimum wage paid by the government.

benefits paid by *Arbeitslosengeld II* look more generous than *Sozialhilfe*, in practice the latter had a variety of extra payments that totaled more than *Arbeitslosengeld II*.

## 6.3 LITERATURE REVIEW

How does the existing scholarship explain the Hartz Reforms?[10] For the longest time, political scientists have been occupied analyzing the causes of welfare state persistence, not change. The immobility of the German welfare state drew special attention, as it perfectly demonstrated the institutional constraints for which the Bismarckian model is well known. However, significant measures of retrenchment began to sweep across Europe in the 1990s, challenging analysts to reconsider old explanations. During this time, Germany adopted only minor legislation in order to "trim back" social spending; it was not until the Hartz labor reforms, adopted under Chancellor Schröder, that explaining reform rather than *Reformstau* (reform backlog) became a priority.

When it comes to structural reforms, Germany is seen as an unlikely case.[11] Not only does much existing scholarship predict that welfare states will remain resilient to widespread retrenchment (Pierson 1994) – together

---

[10] See also Clasen and Clegg (2011) and Dingeldey (2011).

[11] Not all scholars agree that the German welfare state has undergone significant restructuring. While Kemmerling and Bruttel concede that there exists "evidence for both policy diffusion and retrenchment," they believed it was too early (in 2006) to suggest a change in profile. In fact, they argue that the Hartz Reforms and blocked proposals often ignored in the literature "follow a traditional German logic of strong institutional resistance" (Kemmerling and Bruttel 2006, 90). First, organizational implementation revealed strong institutional obstacles; the one-stop shop idea, as one example, was diluted by conflicts about autonomy among municipalities and the local Public Employment Service (PES) branches (Kemmerling and Bruttel 2006, 107). Second, "the new instruments for the contracting-out of employment services are still used by the PES in a legalistic 'commissioning tradition' rather than in a modern management approach in the spirit of 'quasi-markets'" as a result of strong collective bargaining in German politics. To support their claim further, the authors provide evidence from Elmeskov's summary index released in 1998, which measured the degree to which countries implemented policy recommendations endorsed by the Organisation for Economic Co-operation and Development (OECD), of Germany's exceptionally slow and loose implementation – which they then attribute to its corporatist-federal profile. Others agree: "Reforms in German labour market and social policy have tended to be slow or, in some cases, blocked altogether by political opposition" (Kemmerling and Bruttel 2006, 12). Most importantly, Kemmerling and Bruttle suspect that "Hartz may prove to have a reinforcing rather than a path switching effect in the mid to long term" (2006, 19) as the oddity of the tax-funded unemployment assistance system is now gone.

with institutional "stickiness," the unpopularity of retrenchment among voters should stall cutbacks in social policy. Moreover, Germany's political system is characterized by a large number of "veto players" that are predicted to slow change (Tsebelis 2003). These include the *Bundesrat* (Germany's upper chamber representing the Länders), the Central Bank, the Constitutional Court, and powerful concertation (Clasen 2007). The party system with a relatively weak liberal party (FDP) and two strong centrist and Social Democratic parties (SPD and CDU) does not encourage reform either (Kitschelt 2001; Stiller 2007). The "weak" liberal party, which is expected to encourage retrenchment, was overpowered by the SPD and CDU, which are expected to encourage welfare state expansion and/or persistence. Moreover, Germany's strong federal profile leads to budgetary complexities that are difficult to overcome (Clasen 2007). For example, activation policies for claimants of means-tested support, often suggested by reformers, would create budgetary conflicts among the federal government, the UI fund, and local authorities. In Germany, labor market programs are financed out of the same fund as the insurance benefits, which are regionally managed (by the Bundesländer), meaning, expenditure on the latter "tends to crowd out the [former] whenever unemployment goes up" (Clasen 2000, 104). This budgeting nightmare results in strong resistance from regional governments, which often materializes in blocked legislation in the *Bundesrat* – the "joint decision trap" snaps (Scharpf 1988).

A widespread perception of the German welfare state is its immobility, yet eventually there were reforms. Which factors help in explaining the Hartz Reforms? What ultimately "triggered" the creation of the Hartz Commission was the so-called *Vermittlungsskandal* (placement scandal). In January 2002, the German Federal Court of Auditors went public with information that the statistics of the Employment Office (*Bundesanstalt für Arbeit*) were manipulated: only one-third of reported placements were plausible. The information that 85,000 of the employment office's 100,000 employees were working in administrative jobs unrelated to job placement drew further criticism in the German public. The *Vermittlungsskandal* was uncovered relatively close to the September 2002 federal elections, making it a particularly salient topic (Davidsson and Marx 2012, 15).[12] It became a hot issue in the German press (Dyson 2005) and

---

[12] Given the political environment in Germany prior to the election, Davidsson and Marx argue that the SPD-Grünen coalition under Schröder had strong motivation to adopt serious welfare reform in order to be seen as competent in "dealing with the labour

gave Chancellor Schröder in Feburary 2002 – "when the government faced certain defeat in the upcoming federal election" – an opportunity to "show the public that he was taking action 'to clean up the mess'" (Streeck and Trampusch 2005, 184). The composition of the commission represented a break with the tripartite tradition because only 2 of its 21 members represented trade unions (Streeck and Trampusch 2005, 184). "Governing" by commission – and a commission of that composition – was a deliberate strategy of "hand binding" at the end of Schröder's first executive term. According to Dyson, Schröder used the "tight electoral timetable" and placement scandal as means to restrict the influence of the SPD and trade unions. In this narrative, timing is everything. The labor market was in clear need of reform (see later discussion); after the Federal Audit Court's discovery of false statistics on job placements, Schröder was forced to act, and he ultimately seized the opportunity to "take the issue out of the hands of the traditionalists in the Federal Labor and Social Affairs Ministry" (Dyson 2005, 234) The commission operated as a powerful agenda setting tool and, despite strong opposition, largely determined the direction of reform. The assumption is that SPD

market crisis." "It was the combination of the high salience of unemployment and significant shifts in competence ratings that triggered competition over issue ownership, which, in turn, manifested itself in credit-claiming strategies of radical reform" (Davidsson and Marx 2012, 15). Although the SPD and CDU have both promoted welfare expansion in the past and continue to compete for welfare state supporters in present-day elections, high unemployment at the turn of the century had a greater impact on public opinion than general welfare attitudes. "The literature on economic voting typically holds that a rise in unemployment tends to punish the incumbent government, given clarity of responsibility." This makes sense in the case of Germany, where its citizens hold the government partly responsible for labor market crises: "In 2005, 71 per cent of West and 84 per cent of East Germans believed that the government is at least partly responsible for providing a job for anybody who wants to work" (Davidsson and Marx 2012, 8). In 1997, almost the entire West German population considered unemployment the most pressing issue; as a result campaigns for the 1998 federal election were characterized by attempts by both sides to obtain greater legitimacy in dealing with the labor market crisis (Jung and Roth 2002). Ultimately, the retrenchment policies of the presiding CDU government were unsuccessful and led to their defeat in the 1998 election. Six years later, unemployment threatened the SPD reelection as unemployment staggered on. In the polls, the CDU was viewed as more competent in dealing with the labor market crisis, forcing the SPD to adopt "radical retrenchment as a way to claim credit for overcoming Germany's structural problems" (Davidsson and Marx 2012, 9). Because of a severe decline in political support, the SPD agreed to adopt a policy of liberal reform in order to gain centrist voters (Kitschelt and Streeck 2003, 29). The government tried to present itself as the political force finding the courage to accept this "inconvenient truth" and to fulfill its responsibility. This line of reasoning clearly belonged to a credit-claiming strategy (Hegelich 2011, 114–18).

traditionalists would have acted upon their vocal opposition; however, they were held back by the upcoming elections.[13] Fleckenstein also recognizes the advantages provided by the placement scandal and party politics, stating that "the up-coming general election had a disciplinary effect on the opposition to Schröder within the SPD" because, although the left wing of the SPD was reluctant to accept proposals of the Hartz Commission, it could not afford interparty conflict while leading up to the 2002 race against a conservative-liberal coalition (Fleckenstein 2008, 181).

The placement scandal and the proximity to federal elections are important situational factors that explain the timing of the Hartz Commission. But there was already fertile ground for labor market reforms: since the 1980s, the perceived threat to international competitiveness and job growth posed by globalization dominated the political debate. This long-standing discourse in Germany about "*Standort D*" fueled the perception – right or wrong – that Germany was about to lose its competitiveness; some other countries in Western Europe reformed their social insurance systems, and these experiences led to policy learning, which was heavily promoted by OECD's best practices recommendations; and the Hartz Committee had an unofficial precursor hosted by the Bertelsmann Foundation. The discourse was powerful: "As the new diagnosis of the problem came to the fore they condensed into irrefutable facts justifying more serious social policy changes" (Hinrichs 2010, 55). Seeleib-Kaiser and Fleckenstein also believe the "perceived threat" of globalization pushed labor market reforms – not globalism itself, because "German companies on the aggregate were not priced out of the market by new, fierce international competition" (Seeleib-Kaiser and Fleckenstein 2007, 436). Yet still, "the Red–Green Alliance had accepted the need to reduce the level of social insurance contributions due to the perceived negative effects of high rates on the international competitiveness of German firms" (Seeleib-Kaiser and Fleckenstein 2007, 438). From this perspective, public discourses may create the need for reform regardless of contextual factors. Although the SPD–Green Party coalition did not agree that labor market reforms were necessary prior to their 1998–2002 term, their acceptance of a new "interpretative pattern, whereby globalization … necessitates social as well as labour market policy reforms, was the result of power struggles as well as effective persuasion of the party majority by

---

[13] In Dyson's words, "The labour market crisis and the uphill task facing the SPD in the federal elections in September were used by Schröder to tie the hands of traditionalists" (Dyson 2005, 235).

the so-called 'modernizers' within the Social Democratic Party" (Seeleib-Kaiser and Fleckenstein 2007, 443).

The discourse about Germany's lack of competitiveness was nurtured by "lesson drawing" and policy learning. Two features of the German labor market were identified as particularly disadvantageous, from a comparative perspective: (1) the institutional separation of the benefit schemes (unemployment and social assistance) and (2) "reintegration of the long-term unemployed into the labor market through activation measures" (Fleckenstein 2008, 182). Other European countries that reformed their social insurance systems became part of the debate. "Policy experiences of other European countries were a constitutive part of the argumentative repertoire of the Christian Democratic–Liberal coalition government to justify its various retrenchment and activation proposals during the 1990s. They specifically emphasized reforms in countries governed by Social Democrats, with a specific reference to the Netherlands' one-stop shops from Centres for Work and Income" (Seeleib-Kaiser and Fleckenstein 2007, 440). In addition, the authors argue that the strong workfare component in the United Kingdom, its emphasis on the "making work pay" philosophy, its reduction in unemployment benefit duration, and lowered generosity level all "inspired" German policy-makers and helped shape discourse (Seeleib-Kaiser and Fleckenstein 2007, 441). Fleckenstein also gives significant credit to universal systems in Anglo-Saxon and Scandinavian welfare states: "UK Job Centre Plus, where jobseekers are assigned a so-called 'personal adviser,' was considered particularly instructive" (Fleckenstein 2008, 185). Germany also adopted mini- and midi-jobs from the United Kingdom and France, and targeting of assistance and the activation of job seekers from Denmark and the United Kingdom (Kemmerling and Bruttel 2006). Besides learning from best practices, Kemmerling and Bruttle find indications for policy learning from policy proposals by the European Union (EU) and the OECD. The EU's European Employment Strategy and the OECD's Jobs Study are perhaps the most relevant policy endorsers and share "extensive similarities in the diagnoses and in the recommendations" (Casey 2004, 348). More specifically, in 1994 the OECD recommended that countries limit unemployment assistance to the period when reemployment is more likely (first year to two years of unemployment) and eliminate indefinite-duration unemployment benefit entitlements. In 2003, the European Employment Strategy gave similar advice to its member states (Kemmerling and Bruttel 2006, 103). They add that the introduction of the "agreement of objectives" contracts between the Federal Ministry of Economics and Labor and the Public

Employment Service (PES) is another instance of policy learning, as well as the "contracting of private providers for the delivery of placement services" – an international trend now evident in the placement vouchers (*Vermittlungsgutschein*) and the PSA (*Personal-Service-Agentur*) (Kemmerling and Bruttel 2006, 104). Overall, threats such as increased unemployment, unbalanced budgets, "globalization," and "generational equity" were common among all European countries in the late twentieth century and were responded to by using similar policies (Hinrichs 2010).

Long before the Hartz Commission, an expert forum on the future of unemployment and social assistance moderated by the Bertelsmann Foundation was initiated in 1999 at the request of the Ministry of Labor. Fleckenstein argues that, here, a common knowledge base was formed. The forum was a "key arena" for policy experts to consider reform options without political influence, as no MPs were able to participate in this expert body in order to prevent politicization (Fleckenstein 2008, 183–84). Studies commissioned by the Bertelsmann Foundation included a "very first study on cooperation projects; a large-scale legal study on different reform options including the integration of both systems and a fiscal study on the integration of both systems. Moreover, the expert group inspected several Mozart co-operation projects, initiated in the meantime, as well as the reformed one-stop job center in the Netherlands" (Fleckenstein 2008, 184). These Mozart pilot projects were initiated to delay legislation and provide policy experts with the opportunity to gather information on limits of cooperation between the PES and the municipalities (Fleckenstein 2008, 183). The Hartz IV commission eventually corresponded in principle with recommendations made by Bertelsmann Foundation's expert forum. Of course, it helped that these reforms were essentially drafted outside government and then legitimately adopted (Hinrichs 2010). It was in this forum that policies that deviated from social insurance schemes and included means-tested basic security for the long-term unemployed began.

German competitiveness may or may not have been under threat, but in the 1990s Germany's labor market was undeniably in crisis. High and persistent unemployment combined with the financial burdens of German reunification led to a "public funding crisis" that forced "political decision makers to act" (Hassel 2010, 111). Because of the fiscal constraints imposed by the Maastricht criteria, delaying reform by increasing deficits was not an option (Neugart 2005b).[14]

---

[14] In essence, the government did not have the freedom to choose from traditional policy options in order to reform Germany's labor market; controversial institutional reform

## 6.4 THE IMPACT OF REUNIFICATION ON
## UNEMPLOYMENT INSURANCE

German reunification "brought West German welfare standards to East Germans nearly overnight" (Streeck and Trampusch 2005, 176) by incorporating the East into the existing social policy arrangements of the West. This hugely expensive undertaking was financed, in large part, via the social insurance system and undermined its actuarial spirit. As mentioned, the German UI system deviates from actuarial principles because premiums are not scaled to risk (leading to redistribution across risk groups and, in the German case, across Länders) and because the federal government subsidizes it. The exogenous shock of reunification sharply increased the redistributive results of the existing social insurance system, in three ways.

First, reunification sharply increased the heterogeneity of the risk pool and hence sharply increased redistribution across risk groups. Figure 6.1 shows the development of the risk pools in West, East, and unified Germany. The combination of the West and East German risk pool led to a sharp increase in unemployment risk inequality (measured, as in previous chapters, by the Gini coefficient of occupational unemployment rates).

Unemployment risk inequality did not increase because good risks were added, but because bad risks were added. In terms of my theoretical framework, risk inequality increased because average risk ($\bar{p}$) increased, while median risk ($p_m$) was fairly constant. The worsening of the risk pool was astonishing. The hemorrhaging of jobs in Eastern Germany – a staggering 36 percent decrease in Eastern employment three years after reunification, a loss of 3.5 million jobs (Hassel 2010) – increased unemployment in the East sharply from 10.2 percent in 1991 to 15.7 percent in 1994 to more than 20 percent in 2003. West German unemployment rates were much lower – 3.2 percent in 1991, 9 percent in 1994, and 9.3 percent in 2003 (see Table 6.2).

To keep the distribution of expected net benefits similar for a majority of citizens, an increase in risk inequality would need to be balanced by a

---

was therefore the only policy option available (Neugart 2005b, 14). Martin Seeleib-Kaiser and Timo Fleckenstein, on the other hand, reject Neugart's claim. In their opinion, the EMU's criteria had no causal effect on German labor reforms; rather, they simply reinforced fiscal conservatism of some Germany policy makers. In other words, the desire to reform the unemployment insurance scheme was already strong and present in Germany for reasons other than EMU pressure.

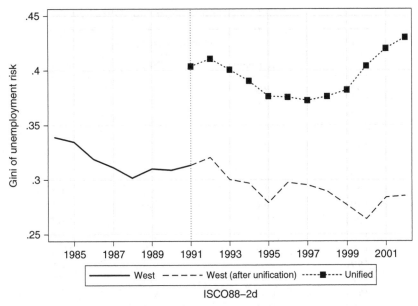

FIGURE 6.1: Risk pool in Germany.

*Note*: Risk pool (inequality of unemployment risk at ISCO88-2d) in West Germany and unified Germany up to the Hartz Reforms.
*Source*: GSOEP.

decrease in the price of insurance, by lowering contributions, benefits, or both. But – initially – the opposite happened (Table 6.3): UI contributions increased from 4.3 percent in 1990 to 6.8 percent in 1991 (and 6.5 percent starting in 1993). This pushed the combined social insurance contribution rate (unemployment, pensions, health care) from 35.5 percent in 1990 to 41.1 percent in 1996, thereby crossing the "magic figure of 40 per cent of gross wages" (Streeck and Trampusch 2005, 176).[15]

Second, reunification sharply increased regional heterogeneity and hence increased redistribution across regions (because risk pools are not regionalized). The UI system has "always entailed an implicit regional redistribution of unemployment insurance money in Germany. ... This system – which has always contained an implicit element of regional redistribution of unemployment resources – has gone totally

---

[15] Interestingly, the pension and health insurance contribution rates initially decreased after reunification.

TABLE 6.2: *Unemployment rate in East and West Germany*

| Year | Unemployment rate | | |
|------|---------|------|------|
|      | Germany | West | East |
| 1985 | 9.3  |      |      |
| 1986 | 9.0  |      |      |
| 1987 | 8.9  |      |      |
| 1988 | 8.7  |      |      |
| 1989 | 7.9  |      |      |
| 1990 | 7.2  |      |      |
| 1991 | 7.3  | 6.2  | 10.2 |
| 1992 | 8.5  | 6.4  | 14.4 |
| 1993 | 9.8  | 8.0  | 15.4 |
| 1994 | 10.6 | 9.0  | 15.7 |
| 1995 | 10.4 | 9.1  | 14.8 |
| 1996 | 11.5 | 9.9  | 16.6 |
| 1997 | 12.7 | 10.8 | 19.1 |
| 1998 | 12.3 | 10.3 | 19.2 |
| 1999 | 11.7 | 9.6  | 18.7 |
| 2000 | 10.7 | 8.4  | 18.5 |
| 2001 | 10.3 | 8.0  | 18.8 |
| 2002 | 10.8 | 8.5  | 19.2 |
| 2003 | 11.6 | 9.3  | 20.1 |
| 2004 | 11.7 | 9.4  | 20.1 |
| 2005 | 13.0 | 11.0 | 20.6 |
| 2006 | 12.0 | 10.2 | 19.2 |
| 2007 | 10.1 | 8.3  | 16.7 |
| 2008 | 8.7  | 7.2  | 14.6 |
| 2009 | 9.1  | 7.7  | 14.5 |
| 2010 | 8.6  | 7.4  | 13.4 |
| 2011 | 7.9  | 6.7  | 12.6 |
| 2012 | 7.6  | 6.6  | 11.9 |

*Note*: Arbeitslosenquote bez. auf abhängige zivile Erwerbspersonen.
*Source*: Statistik der Bundesagentur für Arbeit, Arbeitslosigkeit im Zeitverlauf. Datenstand: März 2013 (DZ/AM).

unquestioned in Germany since its founding in 1952. Only after German reunification, as the amount of transfers from west to east skyrocketed, has it become a political issue" (Ziblatt 2002, 637). In fact, officials at the *Bundesanstalt für Arbeit* became so worried about the disparities that in 1997 they stopped reporting detailed data about regional net contributions to the UI system (the amount of contributions and the amount of expenditures by state), information that is published for 1952–96

TABLE 6.3: *Social insurance contribution rates in Germany*

| Year | Unemployment | Pension | Health care | Total |
|------|------|------|------|------|
| 1950 | 4 | 10 | 6 | 20.0 |
| 1960 | 2 | 14 | 8.4 | 24.4 |
| 1970 | 1.3 | 17 | 8.2 | 26.5 |
| 1980 | 3 | 18 | 11.4 | 32.4 |
| 1990 | 4.3 | 18.7 | 12.5 | 35.5 |
| 1991 | 6.8 | 17.7 | 12.3 | 36.8 |
| 1992 | 6.3 | 17.7 | 12.5 | 36.5 |
| 1993 | 6.5 | 17.5 | 13.2 | 37.2 |
| 1994 | 6.5 | 19.2 | 13.3 | 39.0 |
| 1995 | 6.5 | 18.6 | 13.1 | 39.9 |
| 1996 | 6.5 | 19.2 | 13.7 | 41.1 |
| 1997 | 6.5 | 20.3 | 13.4 | 41.9 |
| 1998 | 6.5 | 20.3 | 13.6 | 42.1 |
| 1999 | 6.5 | 19.5 | 13.6 | 41.3 |
| 2000 | 6.5 | 19.3 | 13.6 | 41.1 |
| 2001 | 6.5 | 19.1 | 13.6 | 40.9 |
| 2002 | 6.5 | 19.1 | 14 | 41.3 |
| 2003 | 6.5 | 19.5 | 14.3 | 42.0 |
| 2004 | 6.5 | 19.5 | 14.2 | 41.9 |
| 2005 | 6.5 | 19.5 | 14.2 | 41.9 |
| 2006 | 6.5 | 19.5 | 14.2 | 41.9 |
| 2007 | 4.2 | 19.9 | 14.8 | 40.6 |
| 2008 | 3.3 | 19.9 | 15.2 | 40.3 |
| 2009 | 2.8 | 19.9 | 15.2 | 39.8 |
| 2010 | 2.8 | 19.9 | 14.9 | 39.5 |
| 2011 | 3 | 19.9 | 15.5 | 40.3 |
| 2012 | 3 | 19.6 | 15.5 | 40.0 |

*Note*: Contribution rates in percentage of gross income: 1949–89: West Germany, since 1990 unified Germany; www.vbgr.de/aktuelle_themen/anlagen/Anlage6_Stellenzulage.pdf; www.sozialpolitik-aktuell.de/tl_files/sozialpolitik-aktuell/_Politikfelder/Finanzierung/Datensammlung/PDF-Dateien/abbII8.pdf.
*Source*: Total: from 1995 including long-term care (1995–96: 1 percent; 1997–2007: 1.7 percent; 2008–12: 1.9 percent); 1949–2003: from (Streeck and Trampusch 2005, 177). 2004–13:
Unemployment: www.sozialpolitik-aktuell.de.
Pension: www.deutsche-rentenversicherung.de/Allgemein/de/Inhalt/4_Presse/infos_der_pressestelle/02_medieninformationen/homepage/entwicklung_beitragssatz.html/.
Health: www.bmg.bund.de/fileadmin/dateien/Publikationen/Gesundheit/Broschueren/Daten_des_Gesundheitswesens_2012.pdf, table 9.10 (p. 14).

(Ziblatt 2002, 637). One reason for this worry was the campaign of the Bavarian government to regionalize the social insurance system. The motivation was neatly expressed by "one official in the Bavarian Social Ministry: 'Why should a hard-working construction worker in Bavaria

TABLE 6.4: *Regional redistribution of the unemployment insurance system (1996)*

| Net receivers | | Net donors | |
|---|---|---|---|
| Thuringia | −4,610,860 | Hesse | 21,234 |
| Berlin/Brandenburg | −2,775,713 | Bavaria | 1,380,997 |
| Saxony-Anhalt | −2,691,129 | Saarland | 1,598,680 |
| Rhineland-Palatinate | −2,215,226 | Lower Saxony | 2,864,572 |
| Hamburg | −1,595,389 | Baden-Wuerttemberg | 4,748,095 |
| Saxony-Anhalt | −1,295,189 | North Rhine-Westphalia | 12,227,990 |
| Mecklenburg-Western Pomerania | −1,056,401 | Schleswig-Holstein | 21,939,568 |
| Bremen | −599,667 | | |

*Note*: Data refer to 1996 (latest available) and are in 1,000 DM.
*Source*: Taken from Ziblatt (2002, 637), based on Bundesanstalt für Arbeit (1996).

have to pay for the problems of unemployment in Mecklenburg-Western Pomerania?'" (Ziblatt 2002, 638).

The regional transfers are rather substantive, and the transfers go from Western Länders to East Germany (and to the city states Hamburg and Bremen), as can be seen in Table 6.4. Länder-level data are not available beyond 1996, but East-West data are (Table 6.5). The numbers suggest that in 1991, every Euro spent in the East was only matched by 15 cents raised in the East. Conversely, for every Euro spent in the West, 1.56 Euros were raised in the West. The ratio of revenue to spending between East and West converged over the years slightly, but not by much. In 2004 (just before the Hartz IV reforms), it was 0.37 in the East and 1.17 in the West, and in 2007 – the last year available – it was 0.5 in the East and 1.4 in the West.[16]

Third, reunification greatly increased federal subsidies to the UI system, which the federal government is legally obligated to keep solvent, using general tax revenues.[17] This further undermined actuarial principles.

---

[16] Since in all likelihood North-South regional redistribution among the Western Länders was occurring at the same time, these revenue/spending ratios underestimate the degree of West-East transfer via the unemployment insurance system.

[17] § 364 SGB III (Liquiditätshilfen): (1) Der Bund leistet die zur Aufrechterhaltung einer ordnungsgemäßen Kassenwirtschaft notwendigen Liquiditätshilfen als zinslose Darlehen, wenn die Mittel der Bundesagentur zur Erfüllung der Zahlungsverpflichtungen nicht ausreichen.

TABLE 6.5: *Expenditures and revenues of the unemployment office and federal subsidies*

| Year | Contribution rate | Expenditures | | | Revenues | | | Revenues/ expenditures | | | Federal subsidy | Federal subsidy percentage of expenditures |
|---|---|---|---|---|---|---|---|---|---|---|---|---|
| | | All | West | East | All | West | East | All | West | East | | |
| 1955 | 4.0 | 3,191 | | | 4,277 | | | 1.34 | | | 0 | |
| 1960 | 2.0 | 1,314 | | | 3,422 | | | 2.60 | | | 0 | |
| 1970 | 1.3 | 6,542 | | | 5,983 | | | 0.91 | | | 0 | |
| 1980 | 3.0 | 22,115 | | | 19,438 | | | 0.88 | | | 1,877 | 8.5 |
| 1990 | 4.3 | 35,171 | | | 34,601 | | | 0.98 | | | 557 | 1.6 |
| 1991 | 6.8 | 54,541 | 31,886 | 22,655 | 53,227 | 49,770 | 3,457 | 0.98 | 1.56 | 0.15 | 777 | 1.4 |
| 1992 | 6.3 | 67,506 | 34,292 | 33,214 | 57,515 | 52,067 | 5,448 | 0.85 | 1.52 | 0.16 | 6,453 | 9.6 |
| 1993 | 6.5 | 75,678 | 40,742 | 34,936 | 58,802 | 51,166 | 7,636 | 0.78 | 1.26 | 0.22 | 16,871 | 22.3 |
| 1994 | 6.5 | 67,187 | 39,186 | 28,001 | 60,320 | 52,196 | 8,124 | 0.90 | 1.33 | 0.29 | 6,823 | 10.2 |
| 1995 | 6.5 | 64,233 | 40,564 | 23,669 | 59,674 | 51,259 | 8,415 | 0.93 | 1.26 | 0.36 | 4,556 | 7.1 |
| 1996 | 6.5 | 68,848 | 43,923 | 24,925 | 59,874 | 51,669 | 8,205 | 0.87 | 1.18 | 0.33 | 8,970 | 13.0 |
| 1997 | 6.5 | 65,706 | 41,002 | 24,704 | 59,582 | 51,635 | 7,946 | 0.91 | 1.26 | 0.32 | 6,124 | 9.3 |
| 1998 | 6.5 | 62,659 | 38,151 | 24,508 | 57,737 | 50,141 | 7,596 | 0.92 | 1.31 | 0.31 | 4,921 | 7.9 |
| 1999 | 6.5 | 63,713 | 39,000 | 24,713 | 59,104 | 51,394 | 7,710 | 0.93 | 1.32 | 0.31 | 4,608 | 7.2 |
| 2000 | 6.5 | 61,325 | 37,582 | 23,743 | 60,272 | 52,551 | 7,721 | 0.98 | 1.40 | 0.33 | 1,053 | 1.7 |
| 2001 | 6.5 | 62,682 | 39,586 | 23,096 | 60,381 | 52,924 | 7,457 | 0.96 | 1.34 | 0.32 | 2,301 | 3.7 |

(*continued*)

TABLE 6.5: *(continued)*

| Year | Contribution rate | Expenditures | | | Revenues | | | Revenues/ expenditures | | | Federal subsidy | Federal subsidy percentage of expenditures |
|---|---|---|---|---|---|---|---|---|---|---|---|---|
| | | All | West | East | All | West | East | All | West | East | | |
| 2002 | 6.5 | 66,379 | 44,283 | 22,097 | 59,774 | 52,510 | 7,264 | 0.90 | 1.19 | 0.33 | 6,605 | 10.0 |
| 2003 | 6.5 | 66,097 | 44,595 | 21,503 | 58,871 | 51,662 | 7,210 | 0.89 | 1.16 | 0.34 | 7,226 | 10.9 |
| 2004 | 6.5 | 62,315 | 43,328 | 18,988 | 57,541 | 50,591 | 6,950 | 0.92 | 1.17 | 0.37 | 4,775 | 7.7 |
| 2005 | 6.5 | 59,788 | 44,682 | 15,106 | 59,341 | 52,571 | 6,771 | 0.99 | 1.18 | 0.45 | 447 | 0.7 |
| 2006 | 6.5 | 48,970 | 37,158 | 11,812 | 61,404 | 54,116 | 7,288 | 1.25 | 1.46 | 0.62 | 0 | |
| 2007 | 4.2 | 39,229 | 29,933 | 9,296 | 46,428 | 41,773 | 4,655 | 1.18 | 1.40 | 0.50 | na | |
| 2008 | 3.3 | 41,615 | | | 40,435 | | | 0.97 | | | na | |
| 2009 | 2.8 | 50,592 | | | 36,061 | | | 0.71 | | | na | |
| 2010 | 2.8 | 47,078 | | | 38,599 | | | 0.82 | | | 5,422 | 11.5 |
| 2011 | 3.0 | 38,278 | | | 38,319 | | | 1.00 | | | na | |
| 2012 | 3.0 | 34,842 | | | 37,429 | | | 1.07 | | | na | |

*Note:* Numbers are in million Euro (2012 = 1).
*Source:* Based on data provided by Bundesagentur für Arbeit.

According to the law, the federal government has to provide interest free loans, which are forgiven if the employment office does not magically manage to pay them back. In practice, the loans are straight subsidies and have become the norm.[18] Between 1975 (the first year in which the federal government provided a subsidy) and 1990, federal subsidies were provided in eight years (1975, 1980–83, 1988–90). Since 1991, federal subsidies were paid every single year but 2006 (Table 6.5). Since 2007, transfers of federal money to the Employment Office have been abandoned and replaced by interest free loans (though there was a one-time 16 billion Euro transfer of the federal government to the Employment Office during the Great Recession).[19] The federal grants to the UI funds were significant, in absolute and relative terms, as Table 6.5 shows. The highest yearly transfer, in 1993, amounted to a staggering 16.8 billion Euros (in 2012 Euros). Since reunification, the yearly transfer amount has been around 5.5 billion Euros (in 2012 Euros) – averaging about 7–8 percent of the Employment Office's budget.[20]

It is difficult to put even a rough estimate on the costs of reunification, and even harder to pin down how exactly it was financed. But it is clear that the social insurance system in general and the unemployment insurance system in particular were used for the purpose of shouldering the

(2) Die Darlehen sind zurückzuzahlen, sobald und soweit am Ende eines Tages die Einnahmen die Ausgaben übersteigen.

[18] German lawyers would say that the "Eventualzuschuss" turned into a "Regelzuschuss."

[19] Until January 1, 2007, § 365 Bundeszuschuß read: "Können Darlehen des Bundes zum Schluß des Haushaltsjahres aus den Einnahmen und der Rücklage der Bundesagentur nicht zurückgezahlt werden, wird aus den die Rücklage übersteigenden Darlehen ein Zuschuß." The paragraph was dropped starting on January 1, 2007 (www.buzer.de/gesetz/6003/al4405-0.htm), via the Haushaltsbegleitgesetz 2006, HBeglG 2006). It was reintroduced in altered form on February 1, 2009 (Artikel 10 G. v. 02.03.2009 BGBl. I S. 416), but now transfers are interest free loans, to be repaid at some point in the future (§ 365 Stundung von Darlehen: "Kann die Bundesagentur als Liquiditätshilfen geleistete Darlehen des Bundes bis zum Schluss des Haushaltsjahres nicht zurückzahlen, gilt die Rückzahlung als bis zum Schluss des folgenden Haushaltsjahres gestundet"; www.buzer.de/gesetz/6003/al17438-0.htm). The legislation in the face of the Great Recession changed the laws once again, authorizing a one-time 16 billion Euro transfer of the federal government to the Employment Office (§ 434 t SGB III, 2010 einmaliger Zuschuss).

[20] These are solely expenditures to keep the Employment Office solvent. The federal government spends vastly more on unemployment related matters. First, it is responsible for the basic needs of those seeking work ("Grundsicherung für Arbeitssuchende") – about 20 billion a year between 1991 and 2004, and about 40 billion a year since the Hartz Reforms in 2005 (in 2012 Euros). Second, an even larger amount of federal money was (and is) spent on active labor market policies, especially immediately after reunification – topping 44.4 billion Euros in 1993 (Bundesministerium für Arbeit und Soziales 2011, sec. 8.11A).

costs of reunification (Beramendi 2012). One official estimate suggests that the employment office (*Bundesanstalt für Arbeit*) contributed 158 billion Euros (in 2012 Euros) between 1991 and 1998 for the financing of reunification (Table 6.6).

## 6.5 A MANDATE FOR REFORM

Much existing scholarship considers welfare state retrenchment as politically risky.[21] Yet, while reform always carries political risks, non-action can be as risky as action. At least in theory, voters have preferred policies, and the status quo of social spending may be too low (in which case a voter should prefer social policy expansion) or too high (in which case a voter should prefer social policy retrenchment). I will next show that, contrary to popular belief, support for labor market reforms in Germany was widespread.

The hefty price tag of German reunification was not unnoticed, although East and West Germans interpreted it very differently. Survey items asking whether reunification had more advantages than disadvantages for the West and East German Länders, respectively, reveal a very large geographical gap. East Germans overwhelmingly believed that reunification benefited West German Länders and much less so East German Länders. West Germans overwhelmingly believed the opposite, namely, that East German Länders benefited from reunification, while West German Länders did so to a much lesser degree. The gap in perceptions of East and West Germans about the advantages and disadvantages of reunification for the old and the new Länders is impressive and narrowed only recently.

The top panel in Figure 6.2 shows that, in 1991, almost 80 percent of East Germans believed that reunification had more advantages than disadvantages for West German Länders, while less than 40 percent of West Germans believed so. Almost 20 years later, in 2010, this perceptional gap narrowed somewhat, but the opinions of East and West

---

[21] The literature on "credit claiming" sometimes treats retrenching reforms as a political asset, not a liability. Clasen, for example, suggests that labor market conditions can provide opportunities for claiming policy success, but that opportunity is not equally granted to all parties. He explains that policies are deemed credible by voters if they are pursued by parties that usually do not support such policies. "It might be politically less problematic for a Social Democratic than a Conservative Party to introduce potentially unpopular welfare reforms" (Clasen 2000, 106).

TABLE 6.6: *The financing of German reunification*

| | 1991 | 1992 | 1993 | 1994 | 1995 | 1996 | 1997 | 1998 | Sum |
|---|---|---|---|---|---|---|---|---|---|
| Bundeshaushalt | 56.9 | 63.5 | 78.8 | 76.7 | 89.3 | 90.0 | 83.8 | 88.1 | 627 |
| Fonds "Deutsche Einheit" | 23.5 | 17.3 | 10.4 | 3.4 | | | | | 55 |
| EU | 3.0 | 3.6 | 3.5 | 4.0 | 4.6 | 4.6 | 4.5 | 4.4 | 32 |
| Rentenversicherung | | 3.6 | 6.2 | 8.1 | 11.2 | 12.4 | 11.5 | 11.4 | 64 |
| Bundesanstalt für Arbeit | 19.0 | 27.4 | 26.3 | 18.8 | 15.2 | 17.0 | 16.6 | 17.7 | 158 |
| Länder/Gemeinden West | 3.8 | 3.6 | 6.9 | 9.4 | 6.6 | 7.2 | 7.0 | 7.0 | 52 |
| Gesamt | 105.4 | 109.0 | 115.4 | 113.7 | 122.4 | 121.9 | 117.1 | 119.8 | 925 |

*Note*: In billion 2012 Euros.

*Source*: Antwort der Parlamentarischen Staatssekretärin Dr. Barbara Hendricks vom 28. März 2006. Deutscher Bundestag – 16. Wahlperiode Drucksache16/1111, p. 7.

(Deutsche Bundestag 2006, 7). See also Beramendi (2012, 152).

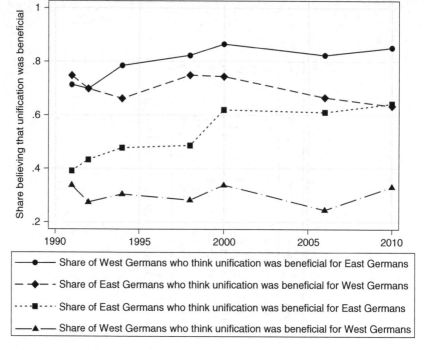

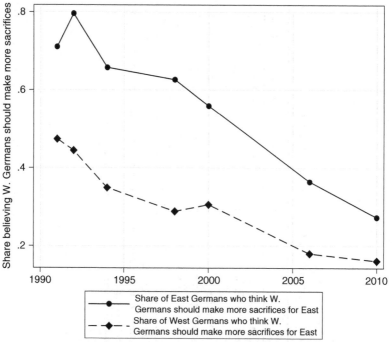

FIGURE 6.2: Divergent views on German reunification.

*Note*: Survey items in top panel: "Die Wiedervereinigung hat für die Bürger in den alten Bundesländern mehr Vorteile als Nachteile gebracht" [vi42] and "Die Wiedervereinigung hat für die Bürger in den neuen Bundesländern mehr Vorteile als Nachteile gebracht" [vi43]. Survey item in bottom panel: "Die Bürger in den alten Bundesländern sollten zu mehr Opfern bereit sein, um die Lage der Bürger in den neuen Bundesländern zu verbessern" [vi40]. Sample: Employed, ages 18–60.

*Source*: (GESIS - Leibniz-Institut für Sozialwissenschaften 2012).

Germans were still very far apart. The pattern is the reverse when asked whether the advantages of reunification outweighed its disadvantages for East German Länders: in 1991, more than 70 percent of West Germans believed that reunification was beneficial for East German Länders – and that percentage has trended upward ever since (about 85 percent in 2010). In 1991, less than 40 percent of East Germans believed that reunification was, on average, beneficial for East Germans – though that percentage had increased to around 65 percent in 2010.

West Germans, then, believe that reunification benefited the East but not the West, while East Germans believe the opposite – with relatively little convergence over time. What did converge, however, are opinions on whether or not West Germans should make more sacrifices in order to improve the situation in the new Länders. The bottom panel in Figure 6.2 shows that in the early 1990s between 70 and 80 percent of East Germans believed so, while only 30–50 percent of West Germans did. But the percentage of respondents who indicated that West Germans should make more sacrifices declined quite rapidly, especially in the East. In 2010, only about 30 percent of East Germans and less than 20 percent of West Germans held that opinion. That West Germans should make more sacrifices to help the East never was a majority position in West Germany, and stopped being one at some point in the early 2000s in East Germany.[22]

Furthermore, there was a sense of urgent need for reforms. In August 1997, a mere 11 percent of citizens believed that the "necessary societal reforms" in Germany were proceeding fast enough, while 84 percent believed they were not. In 2000, 2002, and 2004, these numbers were very similar (Bundesverband deutscher Banken 2002, 4, 2004a, 3).[23] There was also consensus that the German social insurance system was in trouble. In a poll from September 2004,[24] only 4 percent believed that

---

[22] At least if the interpolated trend in Figure 6.2 is not too far off.

[23] "Ergebnisse repräsentativer Meinungsumfragen im Auftrag des Bundesverbandes deutscher Banken. Die telefonischen Befragungen wurden vom 25.9. bis 1.10. und vom 22.10. bis 24.10.2002 unter 1.546 beziehungsweise 1.015 wahlberechtigten Bundesbürgern durch das Mannheimer Institut für praxisorientierte Sozialforschung, ipos, durchgeführt" (Bundesverband deutscher Banken 2002, 1). "Ergebnisse einer repräsentativen Meinungsumfrage des Bundesverbandes deutscher Banken. Die telefonische Befragung wurde Ende April 2004 unter 1.546 wahlberechtigten Bundesbürgern durch das Mannheimer Institut für praxisorientierte Sozialforschung (ipos) durchgeführt" (Bundesverband deutscher Banken 2004a, 1).

[24] "Ergebnisse einer repräsentativen Meinungsumfrage im Auftrag des Bundesverbandes deutscher Banken. Die telefonische Befragung wurde Anfang September 2004 unter

the state of the social insurance systems was "by and large in order," while 50 percent diagnosed "bigger problems" and 44 percent believed they were "about to collapse" (Bundesverband deutscher Banken 2004b, 6).[25] A year later, similar views prevailed.[26] After reunification, unemployment was widely perceived to be "the most important problem in Germany" (Figure 6.3). In 1990, less than 20 percent of the population considered unemployment to be Germany's top problem, down from about 40 percent in 1986. That percentage peaked at above 80 percent in 1998, and was at about 60 percent in 2002, when the Hartz Commission was initiated (Forschungsgruppe Wahlen 2012).

In the aftermath of reunification, support for generous social benefits was sharply declining, especially among West Germans.[27] The percentage of West Germans (employed, aged 18–60) who "fully agreed" that the government ought to be concerned with a decent standard of living in case of sickness, need, unemployment and old age plummeted from 54 percent in 1984 to a low of 34 percent in 2000 (Table 6.7) – it had slightly recovered to 40 percent in 2010.

Given the situation, widespread support for labor market reforms is perhaps not very surprising. And, indeed, a majority welcomed the Hartz Reforms. In September 2004, immediately before the election, support for Schröder's Agenda 2010 reforms was high: 53 percent of respondents thought that the reforms since 2003 were "rather right" (vs. 40 percent who thought they were "rather wrong"). More than 90 percent of respondents also thought that the reforms were not sufficient to solve

1.516 wahlberechtigten Bundesbürgern durch das Mannheimer Institut für praxisorientierte Sozialforschung, ipos, durchgeführt" (Bundesverband deutscher Banken 2004b, 1).

[25] "Wenn Sie einmal an den Zustand unserer sozialen Sicherungssysteme denken, also an Renten-, Kranken- und Arbeitslosenversicherung, meinen Sie, dass da im Grossen und Ganzen alles in Ordnung ist, dass es da groessere Probleme gibt, oder stehen die sozialen Sicherungssysteme kurz vor dem Zusammenbruch?" (Bundesverband deutscher Banken 2004b, 6)

[26] "Ergebnisse repräsentativer Meinungsumfragen im Auftrag des Bundesverbandes deutscher Banken. Die telefonischen Befragungen wurden in der Zeit vom 26. September bis 1. Oktober 2005 (Hauptbefragung) und dem 8. bis 10. November 2005 (Nachbefragung) unter 1.528 bzw. 1.230 Bundesbürgern ab 18 Jahren durch das Mannheimer Institut für praxisorientierte Sozialforschung, ipos, durch-geführt" (Bundesverband deutscher Banken 2005, 1). In 2005, the percentages were 5 percent (social insurance system is "by and large in order"), 56 percent ("bigger problems"), and 37 percent ("about to collapse") (Bundesverband deutscher Banken 2005, 6).

[27] For a broader analysis of social policy attitudes in Germany, see Georg Picot's insightful book (Picot 2012).

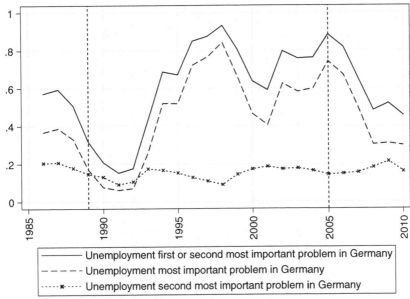

FIGURE 6.3: Most important problem in Germany.

*Notes*: Question wording varies somewhat, but generally is "Was ist Ihrer Meinung nach gegenwärtig das wichtigste Problem in Deutschland?" (1989–2010). Shown are the shares of respondents who identified "Arbeitslosigkeit/Arbeitsplätze (1989–2005), Arbeitsplatz, Arbeitslosigkeit (1986–1988), Arbeitslosigkeit/Arbeitsplätze/Ausbildungsplätze (2006–2010)" as the most important or second most important problem, as well as the sum of these shares. Sample: Employed, ages 18–60.
*Source*: Politbarometer cumulative file (Forschungsgruppe Wahlen 2012).

the existing problems.[28] In October/November 2005,[29] immediately after Schröder had lost the election to Angela Merkel, only 23 percent indicated that the reforms should be reversed, 11 percent thought that the reforms so far were sufficient, and 55 percent said that there should be

---

[28] "Seit 2003 sind eine Reihe von Reformen in den Bereichen Gesundheit, Rente, Arbeitsmarkt und Steuern beschlossen worden. Ganz allgemein gefragt, waren diese Massnahmen eher richtig oder eher nicht richtig?" (Forschungsgruppe Wahlen 2006, sec. Q52a). "Und glauben Sie, dass die beschlossenen Reformen ausreichen, um die Probleme in diesen Bereichen zu loesen?" (Forschungsgruppe Wahlen 2006, sec. Q52b).

[29] "Ergebnisse repräsentativer Meinungsumfragen im Auftrag des Bundesverbandes deutscher Banken. Die telefonischen Befragungen wurden in der Zeit vom 26. September bis 1. Oktober 2005 (Hauptbefragung) und dem 8. bis 10. November 2005 (Nachbefragung) unter 1.528 bzw. 1.230 Bundesbürgern ab 18 Jahren durch das Mannheimer Institut für praxisorientierte Sozialforschung, ipos, durchgeführt" (Bundesverband deutscher Banken 2005, 1).

TABLE 6.7: *Support for social policy*

| Year | "Average" support | | | Share who "strongly agree" | | | Share who "agree" or "strongly agree" | | |
|---|---|---|---|---|---|---|---|---|---|
| | Germany | West | East | Germany | West | East | Germany | West | East |
| 1984 | 3.41 | 3.41 | | 0.54 | 0.54 | | 0.90 | 0.90 | |
| 1991 | 3.45 | 3.38 | 3.74 | 0.54 | 0.49 | 0.76 | 0.92 | 0.90 | 0.99 |
| 1994 | 3.34 | 3.28 | 3.63 | 0.49 | 0.44 | 0.69 | 0.87 | 0.86 | 0.95 |
| 2000 | 3.19 | 3.14 | 3.37 | 0.37 | 0.34 | 0.49 | 0.84 | 0.83 | 0.90 |
| 2004 | 3.18 | 3.14 | 3.36 | 0.37 | 0.35 | 0.48 | 0.82 | 0.81 | 0.89 |
| 2010 | 3.20 | 3.19 | 3.24 | 0.40 | 0.40 | 0.42 | 0.83 | 0.83 | 0.84 |

*Note:* "Ich habe hier einige Meinungen über Staat und Wirtschaft in Deutschland (1984: in der Bundesrepublik). Sagen Sie mir bitte zu jeder Meinung, ob Sie ihr voll zustimmen, eher zustimmen, eher nicht zustimmen oder überhaupt nicht zustimmen." "Der Staat muß dafür sorgen, daß man auch bei Krankheit, Not, Arbeitslosigkeit und im Alter ein gutes Auskommen hat" (4 Stimme voll zu; 3 Stimme eher nicht zu; 2 Stimme eher nicht zu; 1 Stimme überhaupt nicht zu [this is reversed from original]) (GESIS - Leibniz-Institut für Sozialwissenschaften 2012). Sample restricted to those employed and aged 18–60.

more reforms.[30] Of respondents 55 percent anticipated that there would be more reforms, and 50 percent deemed it necessary to cut benefits (vs. 44 percent).[31]

Labor market issues also dominated the campaigns in the run-up of both elections that resulted in the red-green governments led by Chancellor Schröder (Jung and Roth 1998, 2002). Schröder's campaign in 1998 promised to reduce unemployment significantly, and he repeatedly went on record stating that his government's performance should be judged vis-à-vis this goal (September, November, and December 1998)[32] – these statements were widely repeated, including often during the 2005 campaign (Schröder's third, last, and unsuccessful bid). For example, the largest German weekly – *Der Spiegel* – decided to put the following famous quote by Schröder on its front page, white letters on black background:

"If we don't manage to significantly reduce the unemployment rate, we don't deserve to be re-elected." Gerhard Schröder, Chancellor, December 1998.[33]

In early 2002, when Schröder decided to form the Hartz Commission, the upcoming federal elections (September 2002) already cast a long shadow (Dyson 2005, 235; Fleckenstein 2008, 181). Schröder's first term was coming to an end. The SPD had suffered a series of election losses at the

---

[30] "Was meinen Sie zu den von Bundeskanzler Schröder im Rahmen der Agenda 2010 begonnenen Reformen? Sollte es bei den bislang schon umgesetzten Reformen bleiben, sollten die Reformen in absehbarer Zeit weiter fortgeführt werden, oder sollten die bisherigen Reformen wieder zurückgenommen werden?" (Bundesverband deutscher Banken 2005, 5).

[31] "Im Wahlkampf wurde ueber Kuerzungen im Sozialsystem gesprochen. Wie ist das bei Ihnen: Halten sie Kuerzungen im Sozialsystem für notwendig, oder halten Sie die nicht für notwendig?" (Bundesverband deutscher Banken 2005, 5).

[32] The German weekly *Der Spiegel* (DER SPIEGEL 10/2005, p. 3) summarizes some of these public statements: "Wenn wir es nicht schaffen, die Arbeitslosigkeit signifikant zu senken, dann haben wir es weder verdient, wiedergewählt zu werden, noch werden wir wiedergewählt" [September 21, 1998], hatte er kurz vor der Wahl im SPIEGEL-Gespräch mit Olaf Ihlau, Stefan Aust und Gabor Steingart gesagt. Im September 1998 hatten 3,97 Millionen Menschen keinen Job. Schröder war es wirklich ernst: "Wir wollen uns jederzeit - nicht erst in vier Jahren - daran messen lassen, in welchem Maße wir zur Bekämpfung der Arbeitslosigkeit beitragen," versicherte er in seiner Regierungserklärung im November 1998. Und kurz darauf wiederholte er in kleiner Runde: "Wenn wir die Arbeitslosenquote nicht spürbar senken, dann haben wir es nicht verdient, wiedergewählt zu werden." [December 1998] Die Quote sank weder spürbar noch signifikant, sondern gar nicht."

[33] The quote reads: "Wenn wir die Arbeitslosenquote nicht spürbar senken, dann haben wir es nicht verdient, wiedergewählt zu werden." Gerhard Schröder, chancellor, December 1998 [my translation].

Länder level since the government's inception, and the government's popularity poll numbers were low (Jung and Roth 2002). In fact, the German public expressed more positive judgments of the opposition starting in January 2002, despite the epic financial scandals of the CDU. The CDU/CSU had just decided to nominate Edmund Stoiber (CSU) as its candidate for chancellor and was planning an election campaign centering on economic and labor market issues. Much of the discontent with Schröder's first government was related to his self-proclaimed "Politik der ruhigen Hand" (the politics of the steady hand) in 2001/2002, that is, his decision not to do much, despite promising the opposite. As a result of a severe decline in political support, the SPD agreed to adopt a policy of liberal reform in order to gain centrist voters (Kitschelt and Streeck 2003, 29; Picot 2012).

In sum, the evidence suggests that East and West Germans perceived the pros and cons of reunification very differently – believing that the "other Germany" got the better deal. But there was widespread consensus that the social insurance system was in trouble, not least because of Germany's perceived number one problem, namely, unemployment. Willingness for fast and furious social insurance and labor market reforms was high and widespread, and support for generous benefits was eroding. The labor market crisis was the defining campaign topic in 1998 and 2002, and Schröder's government won with a clear mandate to reform. Immediately before the 2002 election that resulted in reelection, the coalition announced it would implement the Hartz Reforms "one-by-one" and the majority of Germans viewed the Hartz and Agenda 2010 reforms favorably.

While there was a lot of visible protest against the Hartz Reforms (on the streets and in op eds), the evidence suggests that the idea of labor market reforms enjoyed widespread support – and that a majority of Germans had favorable views of the Hartz IV reforms. This is consistent with the prediction of my theoretical framework, which suggests that German reunification – which sharply increased risk inequality overnight – should lead to demand for less generous benefits. The exogenous shock of reunification triggered social policy generosity adjustments. My interpretation of the Hartz Reforms, then, is this: German reunification without social policy changes transformed passive labor market policies from an insurance program to a pretty obvious West-East transfer program. The sharp increase in risk inequality led to more diverse interests and preferences and resulted in plummeting support for generous benefits. The Hartz Reforms can be seen as a reaction to these developments.

From this perspective, the Hartz Reforms are not puzzling because they happened, but because they happened so late, and because the SPD suffered massive electoral losses afterward. There are many plausible reasons for the tardiness of the reforms – Germany's political system is well known for its *Reformstau* (reform backlog). Moreover, the massive transfers from West to East via the social insurance system were also meant to prevent migration in the other direction (Beramendi 2012) and therefore had some positive externalities for West German workers (such as less competition and lower downward pressure on wages). The electoral misfortunes of the SPD are somewhat more difficult to understand. I see three main reasons for the SPD's electoral losses. First, most traditionally large parties in Europe saw their vote shares dwindle in the last few decades. From this perspective the electoral successes of the SPD in 1998 and 2002 are outliers and the decline is due to regression to the mean. Second, the SPD lost votes because of the surprising and unlikely emergence of a competitor on the left (PDS/"Die Linke").[34] In fact, the combined vote share of the three left parties in the German parliament (PDS-Die Linke/Greens/SPD) between 1994 and 2013 is fairly constant (around 48 percent). The electoral success of the PDS/"Die Linke" was highly unlikely and could not be anticipated by the actors at the time (Picot 2012). Third, the red-green government also significantly retrenched pension systems. These reforms were less popular than the Hartz Reforms and more likely led to electoral losses. Recent research has shown that the electoral consequences of the Hartz Reforms were, indeed, relatively minor (Schwander and Manow 2014).

---

[34] Though Kemmerling argues that the strong electoral performance of the PDS in East Germany changed the electoral game for the SPD from the early 2000s onward (Kemmerling 2009).

# 7

## Risk Pools and Social Policy Adoption

Within a few decades, every rich democracy adopted social policy programs to cover all main risks (old age, health, accident, and unemployment), a remarkable transition "from poor house[s] to welfare states" (Alber 1982). The specifics of these roughly 100 or so programs (23 rich democracies times 4 risks) vary widely, as do their conception, birth, and maturation (Alber 1981; Carroll 1999; Flora and Alber 1981). The complex history of social policies cannot be reduced to simple models of their development, and it is easy to point out specific examples that contradict existing generalizations of welfare state politics: industrialization nurtured social policy development, but a late-industrializing nation was the first to adopt social insurance programs (Germany); left parties and unions were often supportive of social policy development, but sometimes vigorously opposed it; it was often liberal, not social democratic, parties that initiated social policy legislation; employers often opposed the welfare state, but were sometimes instrumental in advancing it; and so on.

The diversity of unemployment insurance (UI) systems, and the diversity of opinions toward these systems, are well documented in a report prepared by Hugh S. Hanna of the U.S. Bureau of Labor Statistics. The report provides a description of all "unemployment-insurance systems in effect in the 18 countries which . . . had adopted such systems up to May, 1931. The descriptive reports for these countries were prepared by the consular representatives of the United States Department of State in the several countries concerned, in accordance with an outline and a memorandum of instructions prepared by the Bureau of Labor Statistics" (Hanna 1931, 1). One particularly useful aspect of these reports is that they include, for many countries, "a statement of the attitude of representative individuals and organizations toward the system" (Hanna 1931, 178).

The reports prepared by the Bureau of Labor Statistics reveal that (in 1931) in some countries, the (voluntary or mandatory) UI system enjoyed general support from employers, employees, and the public (Ireland, Italy, Belgium, Netherlands) while in other countries, no group was enthusiastic about the system (Czechoslovakia). In various cases, employers were initially opposed to (specifics of) the unemployment system (Austria, Bulgaria, Germany, others), while employees supported it. But the reverse – support from employers, opposition from employees – can also be found (Denmark). And in some countries, we find the familiar split of the left: some actors representing the interest of workers – typically Social Democratic parties – supported UI, while other actors – typically Communist parties – opposed it. The Bureau of Labor Statistics' publication reports the attitudes of employers, employees, and the public toward the existing UI system – and the various positions are clearly influenced by specifics of the system. Likewise, careful historical research that elicits the preferences of different actors before the introduction of UI also shows a very wide range of different patterns of support for UI (Black 1991; Mares 2003; Quirk 2010; Swenson 2002).

Despite the particularities of each individual case, a common theme in the discussions and controversies about UI was the distribution of risk, either across occupations/industries (almost everywhere), and/or across regions (Australia, Canada, the United States, France, and many other cases),[1] and/or across class (Germany), and/or across race (the United States) (Andersson 1938, 171; Baldwin 1990, 119, 121; Beramendi 2012; Garside 2002, 35, 37; Hellwig 2005; King 1995; Mares 2003; Swenson 2002). This theme is particularly prominent in Isabela Mares's important work that predicts – and empirically confirms – employer preferences regarding social policy design based on risk exposure: low-risk producers favor occupational or other actuarial systems while high-risk producers have an interest in redistributing risk, for example, via universalistic social policies (Mares 2003, 31–32 and passim).

---

[1] Advising against separate schemes for each Australian state, Godfrey Ince acknowledges that "some lack of uniformity is inevitable as between one State and another owing to the varying incidence of unemployment in the different States" (Ince 1937, 9).

While simple generalizations of diverse and complex historical processes seem futile, my theoretical framework does make predictions about
the conditions under which social insurance adoption is more likely: in
cases in which risk distributions are (or become) more homogeneous and
in cases in which they "flip" from being bottom-heavy to being top-heavy.
This chapter's ambition is not to offer a general theory of social policy
(adoption), but to highlight an arguably important and common mechanism suggested by my theoretical framework: that social policy adoption is
more likely in conditions of low(ering) risk inequality or in the presence of
risk flips.

In the following sections, I will explore the plausibility of this proposition in two different ways. First, I analyze the American experience in
the 1930s, when the New Deal legislation emerged. In particular, I will
explain the order in which the American states adopted UI systems (an
established dependent variable in the literature on American political
development) by the homogeneity of their unemployment risk pools.
I will show that, *ceteris paribus*, states with a more equal distribution of
risk adopted UI faster. Second, I trace the historical development of
unemployment risk pools in all countries that adopted UI in the last
couple of decades or so, namely, South Korea (1995), Taiwan (1999 or
2003, depending on point of view), Turkey (2002), and Thailand (2004).[2]
In all of these cases, risk inequality markedly fell in the years before UI
was adopted. In contrast, this pattern is not found in "comparable
countries" that did not adopt UI (Singapore, Hong Kong, and the
Philippines).

### 7.1 NEW DEAL LEGISLATION

The New Deal – the series of economic and social policy programs
enacted in the 1930s in the United States – has attracted much scholarly
attention. In large part, the debates parallel those in comparative politics,
although the discussions in American political development are often (but
not always) richer in historical detail. In fact, the American case has
played an important role in the development of the comparative literature.
For example, Theda Skocpol's forceful call to "bring the state back in" has

---

[2] Vietnam also adopted social insurance relatively recently (2009), but I could not collect the
data necessary for an empirical investigation of this case.

resonated widely in the comparative welfare state literature. The American experience is not only an inspiration for comparativists – it often is also an ideal testing ground for comparative arguments, thanks to the relative autonomy of the American states. The 48 to 50 states serve "as a laboratory because the states largely determined their own policies in the 1920s and 1930s" (Amenta and Carruthers 1988, 662). In terms of testing comparative hypotheses, a subnational comparative design has the double advantage of not only controlling for a wide range of potentially confounding factors but also relying on more comparable data. Especially in terms of historical evidence, data are very likely to be more comparable across US states than across countries.

### 7.1.1 Determinants of Unemployment Insurance Adoption in US States

In the following, the timing of the adoption of UI by the American states is the *explanandum*. The Social Security Act of 1935 provided strong incentives for states to adopt unemployment compensation schemes but it left much leeway to the states (Baicker, Goldin, and Katz 1998). States adopted UI systems in the time range of January 1932 to June 1937 (Amenta et al. 1987, 145; Stewart et al. 1938, 28). Why were some states faster than others in adopting unemployment compensation?[3] We can draw on several broad theoretical perspectives to analyze the development of American social policy (Amenta and Carruthers 1988; Domhoff and Webber 2011; Manza 1993, 2000): economic approaches, political struggles approaches, statist approaches, and business-centered approaches. Many arguments from these different perspectives stem from cross-national or over-time considerations, but they often have clear implications for an analysis of US states at a given period.

*Economic (or functionalist) approaches* expect a close link between changing economic conditions and social policy development. Socioeconomic and technological changes generate societal needs that must be addressed by the government. Reasoning along the lines of economic approaches would make us expect that higher levels of industrialization

---

[3] The timing of unemployment legislation in US states is one of the dependent variables in Amenta and Carruthers (1988), and I closely follow their setup and data collection.

and urbanization lead to faster social policy adoption (Flora and Alber 1981; Wilensky 1975). Likewise, one may expect that states that suffered more during the Great Depression would adopt UI more quickly.

Perhaps the most prominent *political struggles (or antagonistic) approach* is the Power Resources Theory, which posits a link between the strength of the left (social-democratic parties and unions) and social policy development (Castles 1982; Huber and Stephens 2001; Korpi 1983; Stephens 1979). Other electoral factors discussed include the level of political participation, as well as the closeness of elections. Non-electoral versions focus on the role of social movements and protests.

*Statist approaches* have particularly strong supporters in the American political development literature. They consider institutional arrangements to be important and rightly point out that bureaucracies often play a crucial role in shaping policy outcomes. The work of Theda Skocpol, Edwin Amenta, and their coauthors is exemplary for the statist approach (Amenta et al. 1987; Amenta and Carruthers 1988; Orloff and Skocpol 1984; Skocpol 1980). Some scholars have argued that the New Deal legislation was decisively shaped by business groups and corporate leaders. These *business-centered approaches* posit that social policy adoption happened with the support of (some segments) of business, not resistance to it. G. William Domhoff's "superiority of class dominance theory" (Domhoff and Webber 2011) is one representative example of this approach.

To explore the determinants of the sequence of UI adoptions by US states (the dependent variable later) Amenta and Carruthers (1988) have derived specific hypotheses based on some of these approaches, and I take their empirical account as a starting point for my own empirical exploration. Before assessing the empirical merits of each of these existing approaches, as well as the plausibility of my own, I will discuss issues related to data and measurement.

### 7.1.2 Data

I seek to explain the timing of passage of state unemployment compensation legislation. The earliest state to pass unemployment compensation legislation was Wisconsin on January 29 in 1932 (Stewart et al. 1938, 28). The last state was Illinois on June 30 in 1937. All other 46 states fall somewhere between these extremes (Alaska and Hawaii became US states only in 1959). Table 7.1 lists the 48 states along with the dates of the passage of unemployment compensation legislation. The dependent

TABLE 7.1: *Date of passage of unemployment compensation legislation by state legislature*

| State | Date of passage | State | Date of passage |
|---|---|---|---|
| Wisconsin | Jan. 29, 1932 | West Virginia | Dec. 17, 1936 |
| New York | Apr. 25, 1935 | Maine | Dec. 18, 1936 |
| New Hampshire | May 29, 1935 | Tennessee | Dec. 18, 1936 |
| California | June 25, 1935 | Virginia | Dec. 18, 1936 |
| Massachusetts | Aug. 12, 1935 | New Jersey | Dec. 22, 1936 |
| Alabama | Sept. 14, 1935 | Vermont | Dec. 22, 1936 |
| Oregon | Nov. 15, 1935 | Iowa | Dec. 24, 1936 |
| Indiana | Mar. 18, 1936 | Michigan | Dec. 24, 1936 |
| Mississippi | Mar. 23, 1936 | Minnesota | Dec. 24, 1936 |
| Rhode Island | May 5, 1936 | South Dakota | Dec. 24, 1936 |
| South Carolina | June 6, 1936 | Kentucky | Dec. 29, 1936 |
| Louisiana | June 29, 1936 | Arkansas | Feb. 26, 1937 |
| Idaho | Aug. 6, 1936 | Wyoming | Feb. 26, 1937 |
| Utah | Aug. 29, 1936 | Montana | Mar. 16, 1937 |
| Texas | Oct. 27, 1936 | North Dakota | Mar. 16, 1937 |
| Colorado | Nov. 20, 1936 | Washington | Mar. 16, 1937 |
| Connecticut | Nov. 30, 1936 | Nevada | Mar. 24, 1937 |
| Arizona | Dec. 2, 1936 | Kansas | Mar. 26, 1937 |
| Pennsylvania | Dec. 5, 1936 | Georgia | Mar. 29, 1937 |
| Oklahoma | Dec. 12, 1936 | Delaware | Apr. 30, 1937 |
| New Mexico | Dec. 16, 1936 | Nebraska | Apr. 30, 1937 |
| North Carolina | Dec. 16, 1936 | Florida | June 9, 1937 |
| Maryland | Dec. 17, 1936 | Missouri | June 17, 1937 |
| Ohio | Dec. 17, 1936 | Illinois | June 30, 1937 |

*Source*: Amenta et al. 1987, table 3; Stewart et al. 1938, 28.

variable in the analysis that follows is the rank order of unemployment compensation enactment, starting with rank 1 for Wisconsin as the earliest adoption. Equal observations are assigned the average rank.[4]

My theoretical framework makes two related predictions. First, the lower risk inequality is (i.e., the more homogeneous the distribution of unemployment is), the earlier does UI adoption occur. Second, the more "flipped" (or negatively skewed) the risk distribution is, that is, the larger the difference between median and mean unemployment is, the earlier

---

[4] The dependent variable in Amenta and Carruthers (1988: 667) is 1 for Wisconsin, and the number of months a state passed its law after Wisconsin for the other states. This makes Wisconsin a clear outlier in the data set. However, the substantive results reported later are the same regardless of whether rank of adoption or number of months after Wisconsin is the dependent variable.

does unemployment adoption occur. The measures to explore these hypotheses empirically are derived from the 1910 and 1930 Censuses of Population (Ruggles et al. 2010).[5] Unfortunately, the measurement of unemployment as we define it today was not developed until the late 1930s (Card 2011). But unlike the 1920 Census, both the 1910 and 1930 Censuses contain information on unemployment and (previous) occupation that allow me to derive measures of the distribution of unemployment (and, therefore, the homogeneity of risk pools and their skew). While the resulting unemployment rates are not comparable with today's definitions, they are comparable across US states, because they are derived from the same census data.

The 1910 and 1930 Censuses contain occupational information that has been coded at the 1950 occupational classification with the goal of comparability across different censuses. That classification is available at different levels of detail. There is a trade-off between detail and reliability in the measurement of unemployment distributions. Since it is essential to derive state-specific unemployment distributions, the occupational classification has to be relatively coarse. I therefore calculate occupational unemployment at the (roughly) one digit level of the 1950 classification.[6]

Social policy adoption is a dynamic process. But most data are not available as time series, including the key explanatory variables. Therefore, the analysis that follows will rely on cross-sectional information (as in Amenta and Carruthers 1988). The 1930 Census was administered in April 1930, a few months after the Wall Street crash of October 1929 sent economies worldwide into the Great Depression. Output fell massively, and unemployment was rising rapidly. For the purposes of this analysis, these dramatic events are a blessing and a curse. On the one hand, they are likely to trigger consequential changes in risk distributions (risk flips). On the other hand, the extraordinary dynamics may provide little information about the historical distribution of risk. I will therefore employ data on risk distributions based on 1910 and 1930 Census data. The 1910 Census is used to calculate the risk inequality (the Gini coefficient of occupational unemployment rates), with higher values indicating more

---

[5] I employ the 1 percent samples made available by IPUMS (Ruggles et al. 2010).

[6] The occupational groups are professional, technical, and kindred workers; managers, officials, and proprietors, except farm; clerical and kindred workers; sales workers; craftsmen, foremen, and kindred workers; operatives and kindred workers; private household workers; service workers, except private household; laborers, except farm and mine. Excluded from the sample are "farmers and farm managers" and "farm laborers and foremen" because agricultural jobs were excluded from unemployment insurance.

unequal distribution of risk; consequently, we expect a positive correlation between this variable and the rank order of adoption.[7] The 1930 Census is used to calculate median and mean levels of unemployment in order to get a sense of their "flippedness" – values above 1 indicate that the risk distribution is flipped; consequently, we expect a negative correlation between this variable and the rank order of adoption. Figure 7.1 displays both risk pool related explanatory variables. The figure shows that there is substantial variance across states in risk pool homogeneity and the median/mean level of unemployment. It also shows that the two variables are somewhat correlated.

With respect to control variables, the preceding brief discussion on existing explanations of social policy adoption suggests that certain economic, political, and statist factors may be influential (Amenta and Carruthers 1988). Regarding economic variables, I explore the impact of unemployment and the depth of the recession as well as the level of industrialization and urbanization in different states. Partisanship is proxied by the average Democratic Vote Percentage for the Governor, Senate, and House, 1918–1934 (David and Claggett 1998).[8] Amenta and Carruthers (1988) suggest capturing elements of the statist approach with two different variables. The first is a dummy variable equaling 1 if the state labor commissioner had by 1929 rule-making authority in the administration of safety laws, and 0 otherwise. The second is a state's "fiscal capacity," proxied by total per capita tax receipts in 1932. Table 7.2 provides details on each of the variables used in the following regression analyses, while Table 7.3 shows the correlation of all variables.

### 7.1.3 Results

The bivariate correlations in Table 7.3 show that three explanatory variables are significantly correlated with the speed of UI adoption: risk inequality, "risk flippedness" (the median/mean unemployment ratio), and an indicator of industrialization (the share of the labor force in manufacturing). These three variables are also somewhat correlated with each other. Particularly noteworthy is the negative correlation between risk inequality and industrialization, indicating that more industrialized

---

[7] Results hold if all relevant measures are based on 1930 data.
[8] Various measures of partisanship can be employed, with similar substantive results. One issue may be that parties in the South were quite different, but interacting partisanship and a dummy variable for southern states do not yield different results either.

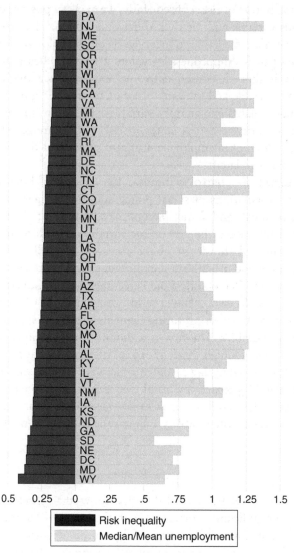

FIGURE 7.1: Risk pools in US states.

states have a more equal distribution of unemployment risk. Quite possibly, this relationship between the degree of industrialization and the equality of unemployment risk is a general pattern. This might suggest that the reason that social policy development and industrialization went hand in hand was that risk inequality decreased as industrialization

TABLE 7.2: *Description of variables*

| Variable | Operationalization | Source |
|---|---|---|
| Adoption of unemployment insurance | Rank order of adoption (earliest adoption = 1, last adoption = 48) | Amenta et al. 1987, table 3; Stewart et al. 1938, 28 |
| Risk inequality | Gini coefficient of occupational unemployment rates; higher values indicate more risk inequality | Calculated from 1910 Census |
| "Flippedness" of risk distribution | Median/mean occupational unemployment rate; values above 1 indicate a flipped risk distribution | Calculated from 1930 Census |
| Unemployment rate | Unemployment rate in 1930 | Calculated from 1930 Census |
| Recession | Manufacturing depression = wage earners in manufacturing in 1933 divided by the same measure in 1929 | US Census Bureau 1937, 765–69 |
| Industrialization | Share of labor force employed in manufacturing sector | Calculated from 1930 Census |
| Urbanization | Percentage of population in cities of 50,000 or larger in 1930 | Calculated from 1930 Census |
| Partisanship | Average vote share for Democratic candidates across three offices (governor, Senate, US House; variable dcompb), averaged for 1918–34 | David and Claggett 1998 |
| Bureaucratic capacity | Dummy equals 1 if state labor commissioner had by 1929 rule-making authority in the administration of safety laws, and 0 otherwise | Brandeis 1935, 654 |
| Fiscal capacity | Total tax receipts, per capita, 1932 | Social Security Board 1937, 367, Table 80 |

increased – unfortunately, there are no data to explore this possibility over time (and across countries).

Of particular interest in Table 7.3, of course, is the correlation between risk inequality and the order of unemployment adoption. Figure 7.2 displays that correlation. As can be seen, there is a clear positive (and

TABLE 7.3: *Correlation matrix*

| | Rank order of adoption | (2) | (3) | (4) | (5) | (6) | (7) | (8) | (9) |
|---|---|---|---|---|---|---|---|---|---|
| (2) Risk inequality (1910) | 0.4514 | 1 | | | | | | | |
| (3) Median/mean unemployment | -0.3831 | -0.5440 | 1 | | | | | | |
| (4) Unemployment rate | -0.0739 | -0.3818 | 0.357 | 1 | | | | | |
| (5) Manufacturing depression | 0.0191 | -0.1468 | 0.1756 | -0.2215 | 1 | | | | |
| (6) Industrialization | -0.3074 | -0.5186 | 0.5347 | 0.5679 | 0.1799 | 1 | | | |
| (7) Urbanization | -0.1850 | -0.3871 | 0.2034 | 0.4288 | 0.0557 | 0.6873 | 1 | | |
| (8) Democratic vote percentage | -0.0535 | 0.0649 | 0.1851 | -0.2332 | 0.1926 | -0.2496 | -0.2572 | 1 | |
| (9) Strong bureaucracy | -0.2647 | -0.2049 | -0.0711 | 0.0767 | -0.2696 | 0.0353 | 0.1498 | -0.3331 | 1 |
| (10) Total per capita tax receipts | -0.1014 | -0.2734 | -0.1098 | 0.3654 | -0.3205 | 0.4290 | 0.4502 | -0.6546 | 0.4085 |

*Notes:* Bivariate correlations; boldface entries: $p < 0.05$.

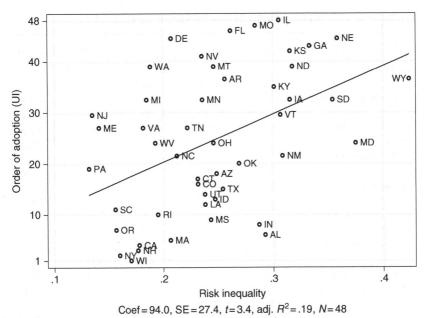

FIGURE 7.2: Risk inequality and unemployment insurance adoptions in US states.
*Note*: Risk inequality = Gini coefficient of unemployment risk (Census 1910 data)

statistically significant) correlation. US states with more homogenous risk pools (low risk inequality) adopted UI earlier than states with more heterogeneous risk pools (high risk inequality).

Which other factors are correlated with the order of unemployment policy adoption in the 1930s? The bivariate correlations in Table 7.3 already offer some answers, but the following regression analysis allows for multivariate exploration. In particular, the following two tables explore whether my risk-pool argument finds empirical support and how the economic, political, and statist approaches fare. Each table contains five models. The first regresses the order of social policy adoption on risk inequality as well as the level of risk (Table 7.4), and the "flippedness" of the risk distirbution as well as the level of risk (Table 7.5), respectively. The second through fourth models add variables related to the economic (Model 2), the political (Model 3), and the statist approaches (Model 4). The fifth model includes all variables from the previous models. While the dependent variable is ordinal, it is sufficiently fine-grained that estimation with OLS is justified.

The results suggest a robust and substantively meaningful correlation between the order of UI adoption and characteristics of unemployment risk

TABLE 7.4: *Adoption of unemployment insurance in US states I*

|  | (1) | (2) | (3) | (4) | (5) |
|---|---|---|---|---|---|
| Risk inequality | 103.2** | 94.6** | 102.8** | 96.8** | 80.3* |
|  | (29.8) | (32.6) | (30.0) | (30.4) | (34.1) |
| Unemployment rate | 0.9 | 2.2# | 0.7 | 0.7 | 2.0 |
|  | (1.1) | (1.3) | (1.1) | (1.1) | (1.3) |
| Manufacturing | | 28.3 | | | 29.2 |
| depression | | (20.0) | | | (22.3) |
| Industrialization | | −44.2 | | | −57.5# |
|  | | (28.8) | | | (29.8) |
| Urbanization | | 0.1 | | | 0.0 |
|  | | (0.1) | | | (0.1) |
| Democratic vote | | | −0.0 | | −0.1 |
| (percentage) | | | (0.1) | | (0.1) |
| Strong bureaucracy | | | | −5.9 | −7.0 |
|  | | | | (4.2) | (4.3) |
| Total per capita | | | | 0.1 | 0.1 |
| tax receipts | | | | (0.1) | (0.2) |
| Constant | −8.2 | −30.8 | −4.9 | −6.0 | −21.4 |
|  | (13.9) | (22.8) | (15.9) | (14.6) | (30.7) |
| No. of cases | 48 | 48 | 48 | 48 | 48 |
| Adj. $R^2$ | 0.180 | 0.189 | 0.166 | 0.181 | 0.202 |

Notes: #$p < 0.1$, *$p < 0.05$, **$p < 0.01$.
Coefficients above standard errors in parentheses.

pools – whether measured in terms of risk inequality (Table 7.4) or median/ mean unemployment risk (Table 7.5). The positive coefficient of the risk inequality measure (Gini coefficient of unemployment risk) in Table 7.4 suggests that the more unequally risk was distributed in a state, the later it adopted unemployment legislation. The negative coefficient of the median/ mean unemployment measure in Table 7.5 suggests that the more risk exposed the median citizen was relative to the mean citizen (the more the distribution was "flipped"), the earlier the unemployment legislation was enacted. These results are in line with expectations. In substantive terms, Model 1 in Table 7.4 suggests that a one-standard-deviation increase in risk inequality[9] would lead to a later adoption by seven or eight ranks.

[9] Here are some summary statistics for the risk inequality variable: Min: 0.13, Mean: 0.25, Max: 0.42, SD: 0.07.

TABLE 7.5: *Adoption of unemployment insurance in US states II*

|  | (1) | (2) | (3) | (4) | (5) |
|---|---|---|---|---|---|
| Median/mean | −24.8** | −22.0* | −25.7** | −28.3** | −19.4# |
| unemployment | (8.9) | (10.3) | (9.4) | (8.9) | (11.5) |
| Unemployment rate | 0.5 | 2.0 | 0.6 | 1.1 | 1.8 |
|  | (1.1) | (1.4) | (1.2) | (1.2) | (1.3) |
| Manufacturing |  | 26.2 |  |  | 16.7 |
| depression |  | (20.8) |  |  | (22.5) |
| Industrialization |  | −34.6 |  |  | −41.2 |
|  |  | (32.4) |  |  | (35.8) |
| Urbanization |  | −0.0 |  |  | 0.0 |
|  |  | (0.1) |  |  | (0.1) |
| Democratic vote |  |  | 0.0 |  | −0.1 |
| (percentage) |  |  | (0.1) |  | (0.1) |
| Strong bureaucracy |  |  |  | −7.6# | −8.5# |
|  |  |  |  | (4.1) | (4.3) |
| Total per capita |  |  |  | −0.1 | −0.0 |
| tax receipts |  |  |  | (0.1) | (0.2) |
| Constant | 44.1** | 17.7 | 42.2** | 49.5** | 34.6 |
|  | (10.6) | (20.1) | (12.3) | (11.0) | (27.2) |
| No. of cases | 48 | 48 | 48 | 48 | 48 |
| Adj. $R^2$ | 0.114 | 0.120 | 0.095 | 0.179 | 0.150 |

*Notes*: #$p < 0.1$, *$p < 0.05$, **$p < 0.01$.
Coefficients above standard errors in parentheses.

Model 1 in Table 7.4 suggests that a one-standard-deviation increase in the median/mean unemployment risk exposure would lead to faster adoption, by about six ranks.[10]

None of the control variables performs consistently well across the different models. The level of unemployment is positively correlated with the rank of adoption, but the correlation is significant only once (Model 2 in Table 7.4). Likewise, the depth of the manufacturing recession is not significantly correlated with adoption. Both (null) findings are further evidence that the depth of a crisis alone does not suffice to predict social policy development. It is not (primarily) the level, but the distribution of risk that matters. The level of industrialization – measured by the share

[10] Here are some summary statistics for the median/mean risk exposure variable: Min: 0.57, Mean: 0.97, Max: 1.37, SD: 0.23

of the labor force in manufacturing – is not consistently but occasionally significantly correlated with the speed of social policy adoption: more industrialized states tend to adopt earlier. The measure of partisanship included in the regressions does not significantly correlate with the sequence of adoptions. This finding is consistent with Amenta's and Carruther's analysis, which also does not find meaningful partisan differences. The statist approach fares better. One of the variables – the existence of strong administrative authority – is statistically significant in some of the models (and performs well in various robustness checks). All else equal, states with stronger bureaucracies adopted unemployment compensation legislation earlier. In contrast, the fiscal capacity indicator is not significantly related to the order of adoption.

Overall, then, the results suggest that the shape of the risk pool was an important determinant for the sequence of unemployment legislation adoption during the New Deal. The more equally risk was distributed, the quicker the states ratified unemployment legislation. Likewise, the more "flipped" the distribution of risk was (i.e., the higher the median to mean unemployment risk was), the faster the states introduced UI. These correlations survive the inclusion of various control variables. They also do not suffer from the problem of endogeneity prominent in the cross-country analysis on the determinants of unemployment benefit generosity. Because they did not exist before the 1930s, UI programs could not possibly have influenced the distribution of unemployment risk.[11]

## 7.2 RECENT CASES OF SOCIAL INSURANCE ADOPTION

About 64 countries worldwide have contributory UI schemes of some kind (International Labour Office 2010, 59). According to my theoretical framework we would expect that the adoption of UI schemes becomes more likely as unemployment risk inequality decreases, that is, as risk pools become more homogeneous. The previous section has shown that this prediction has considerable support when tested against the sequence of adoption in US states in the 1930s. Unfortunately, we do not have (comparable) historical longitudinal data to explore whether the timing of UI adoption in rich democracies coincided with times of low risk inequality (or even risk flips). Instead, we have to turn to

---

[11] Of course, some privately run schemes were in existence – but they were very limited in scope. For an overview of these schemes, see (Hanna 1931).

more recent experiences to trace the development of risk pools *before* UI adoption.

Five countries have adopted UI since the 1990s or so (Scholz, Bonnet, and Ehmke 2011; Vroman 2004, FN 4): South Korea in 1995 (M.-J. Kim 2010; Kwan 2000; Yi and Lee 2005), Taiwan in 1999/2003 (Chen 2005; V. Lee 2000a), Turkey in 1999/2000 (Tunali 2003), Thailand in 2004 (Asami 2010), and Vietnam in 2009 (Scholz, Bonnet, and Ehmke 2011, 358).[12] My analysis of these cases requires reasonably long time series data on unemployment risk inequality, which are not available for Vietnam. Vietnam is also the only country in this group that was not democratic before and during the adoption of UI, and I therefore do not incorporate the Vietnamese case.[13]

In the following sections I first briefly describe the genesis of UI systems in South Korea, Thailand, Taiwan, and Turkey. As just mentioned, these countries were democratic before and during the adoption of UI: according to the common definition that polity scores of 6–10 indicate democratic polities, South Korea has been democratic since 1992 (UI adoption in 1993), Taiwan since 1988 (UI adoption in 1999/2003), Thailand between 1992 and 2005 (UI adoption in 2004), and Turkey since 1983 (UI adoption in 1999).[14] I rely on existing scholarship to reconstruct the main factors that plausibly explain the motivations for and timing of UI insurance. While each case is obviously

---

[12] On the challenges of introducing unemployment insurance to developing countries, see Vodopivec (Vodopivec 2013). There are various more general accounts on recent unemployment insurance adoptions (Asami 2010; Betcherman and Islam 2001b; Chen 2005; Haggard and Kaufman 2008; Kamimura 2010; M.-J. Kim 2010; Kwon 2005; Lan and Chou 2010; E. Lee 1998; McGuire 2010; Mitani 2010; Scholz, Bonnet, and Ehmke 2011; Vandenberg 2010; Vroman 2004, FN 5; Yap 2002; Yi and Lee 2005).

[13] Being democratic is arguably a scope condition of my theoretical framework, although social insurance adoption should be easier in the presence of more homogeneous/more flipped risk distributions in all polities.

[14] The polity scale ranges from -10 (full autocracy) to +10 (full democracy); countries scored as +6 or higher are conventionally considered to be "democracies." Polity scores over time:

Taiwan: 1970–86: -8 and -7; 1987–91: -1; 1992–96: +7 and +8; 1997–2012: +9 and +10.

South Korea: 1970–71: +3; 1972–80: -9 and -8; 1981–86: -5; 1988–97: +6; 1998–2012: +8

Turkey: 1983–2012: between +7 and +9.

Thailand: 1978–90: +2 and +3; 1991: -1; 1992–2005: +9; 2006: -5; 2007: -1; 2008–10: +4; 2011–12: +7

Vietnam: 1976–2012: -7

highly specific, certain common themes emerge: democratization typically played an important role, as parties were incentivized to take voter preferences into account and engaged in "credit claiming" (Pierson 1996); oftentimes, economic and societal crises are of critical importance for the emergence and expansion of UI systems (see also Chapter 8); the adoption of UI typically enjoyed broad popular support; and the opposition to the adoption of UI was typically not directed against UI in principle, but motivated by discontent about particular aspects of the proposed system.

After briefly outlining the genesis of UI in the four recent cases of South Korea, Thailand, Taiwan, and Turkey, I trace the development of unemployment risk inequality before UI adoption in these countries. As expected from my theoretical perspective, risk pools became markedly more homogeneous before the adoption of UI in these cases. This stands in contrast to the development of similar countries that did not adopt UI, as I will show.

### 7.2.1 Country Vignettes

#### 7.2.1.1 South Korea

South Korea was one of the few economies in the region that already had a UI system established when the 1997/98 Asian financial crisis hit.[15] Its so-called Employment Insurance (EI) system was adopted in 1993 and implemented in 1995, at a time when "no one had anticipated the eruption of mass unemployment looming on the horizon" (Hwang 2013a, 7).[16] Scholars have identified the process of democratization (H. K. Lee 1999, 30; Shin 2000) coupled with a change in public support for UI as an important reason for the adoption of UI: previous attempts to introduce it – considered in the early 1980s, a time of high unemployment – were unsuccessful because "most Koreans were opposed" (M.-J. Kim 2010, 245; Yoo 1999, 1). Yet, a few years later, "social consensus was reached to adopt" UI (Kang et al. 2001, 110) and, in democracies, "public perceptions about appropriate forms of social protection will be reflected in the process of policymaking" since "the government can be expected to be sensitive to public preferences" (Shin 2000, 103). In 1990,

---

[15] A detailed account of the Korean UI is due to Yoo (Yoo 1999).
[16] Significant changes (collection of premiums) were adopted in 2003 and implemented in 2005.

the government sought the input of the Korea Labor Institute, which recommended the introduction of the EI System. "The Government reviewed the proposal from the Korea Labor Institute and held several public hearings. It later confirmed that most people supported the proposal. On August 23, 1991, the Korean government finally decided to introduce the Employment Insurance System during the mid-1990s" (M.-J. Kim 2010, 246). To this end, the government formed the EI Research Commission (May 18, 1992) (Kwan 2000, 2), consisting of scholars and observers from the government, employers, and employees. After public hearings on the committee's proposal, the National Assembly "passed the [Employment Insurance] bill unanimously on December 1, 1993, promulgating it on December 27, 1993. The Employment Insurance Law was put into effect on July 1, 1995, and the unemployment benefits, which require at least a year's contribution by the insured, became operational from July 1, 1996" (M.-J. Kim 2010, 247).

While the adoption of UI in South Korean was not the direct result of a crisis (as in other cases in the region), its rapid expansion was clearly spurred by one. During the Asian financial crisis that started at the end of 1997, the unemployment rate in South Korea increased sharply within a short period and demand for social welfare grew rapidly (Shin 2000, 103). In fact, the Asian economic crisis of 1997 profoundly affected "the value orientations of Koreans regarding the provision of social welfare" (Shin 2000, 103). In May 1997 – before the financial crisis – 51 percent of Koreans indicated that "individuals should be responsible for their own welfare" and 49 percent indicated that "the state should be responsible for everyone's economic security." In October 1998, after the economic crisis, these percentages changed to 17 percent (individuals responsible) and 83 percent (state responsible), respectively (Shin 2000, 104). In other words, the percentage of respondents who favored government provided economic security increased from 49 to 83 percentage points within less than 1.5 years. Since the economic crisis of 1997 "social demands for social rights have been largely acknowledged among the public," likely because the crisis led to "sharp declines in middle-class standards of living" (Shin 2000, 104).

The widespread demand for a more prominent role of government-provided economic security did not remain unanswered. As a way of dealing with the crisis, the Tripartite Commission – composed of representatives from the government, employees, and employer's organizations – was formed (January 15, 1998). On the basis of the commission's recommendations, UI coverage was significantly extended several times in 1998 (Hwang 2013a, 13), as was the length of time workers could benefit (Betcherman and Islam 2001a, 11, 29; Kang et al. 2001, 111; Kwan 2000, 5).[17] Further changes in the UI regulations have been implemented recently, "to tackle the effects of the global financial crisis" (Hwang 2013a, 24).

### 7.2.1.2 Thailand

Thailand adopted its UI scheme under the Thaksin government in 2003 (implementation started in January 2004).[18] The adoption of UI followed tripartite negotiations (Asami 2013, 43) and was generally well received by all the main players. Employers saw UI "as a necessary cost of further opening up the Thai economy" (Asami 2013, 42–43) and business had exerted pressure to establish an effective social safety net to prop up the economy after the 1997 crisis (Jirakiattikul 2013, 175). Likewise, "trade union leaders in Thailand had repeatedly demanded the introduction of unemployment insurance and celebrated when it was finally introduced in 2004" (Asami 2013, 40). The reaction of workers and union members was mixed: while they welcomed the protection provided by the UI, workers knew "that, for many of them, the amount of money they will pay in contributions to the unemployment insurance scheme is very likely to exceed the amount of money they will receive as unemployment benefits" (Asami 2013, 40).

Existing accounts point to two reasons for the timing of the adoption: the experience with the Asian financial crisis of 1997/98 and electoral considerations of the incumbent government (Asami 2010; Carter, Bédard, and Bista 2013; Chandoevwit 2012). First, the adoption of UI can be seen as a political legacy of the Asian financial crisis (Scholz, Bonnet, and Ehmke 2011, 358), even though the government enacted UI when the economy was in a good state (GDP growth was 7.1 percent in 2003). The crisis "created problems for all groups of workers" (Jirakiattikul 2013, 186), with consequences:

The economic crisis in 1997 changed the public perception of unemployment considerably. It was not only low-educated factory workers but also a large number of high-educated white-collar workers in the banking and financial

---

[17] Note also that industrial relations in South Korea were significantly changed toward more cooperation by the Act Concerning the Promotion of Worker Participation and Cooperation, promulgated in March 1997 (Campell 2001, 454–62; Kang et al. 2001, 105).

[18] The Thai cabinet approved a UI system on April 28, 2003. Royal Decree No. 120 Section 80 A on August 26, 2003, formed the legal basis of the system's implementation.

sectors who lost their job suddenly. Many people came to view unemployment not as a consequence of lack of diligence and ability but as a consequence of macro-economic turbulence often caused by the volatile global economy. Widely shared awareness of the necessity of a social safety net facilitates the introduction of UI. (Asami 2010, 191–92)

The crisis experience also shaped the position of employers: "through lessons learned from the financial crisis in 1997 and the unprecedented economic slump, many employers in Thailand came to realize the value of a social safety net for workers" (Jirakiattikul 2013, 198). UI was not adopted immediately because it was unfeasible

to start collecting contributions when many businesses [were] struggling just to stay afloat. In hindsight, the year 2004 happened to be the best timing for Thailand to introduce UI. The Thai economy was in a good shape, but people's memory about social pain caused by economic turmoil in 1997/98 was still vivid. The Thai economy was hit hard again by the turbulences in the global economy in the last quarter of 2008, and the number of lay-offs increased in 2009. But social pain was at least partially alleviated by UI this time. (Asami 2010, 191–92)

Second, electoral pressure provided further fertile ground for UI adoption in Thailand. Before UI adoption, the Thaksin government had already introduced a health plan, which allowed universal access to health care in 2002 after a landslide victory in 2001. Thaksin fought that election on the promise of universal care (Cook and Kwon 2007, 226; Kwon 2009, 19) – UI was introduced close to another election as well. Unemployment benefits were first paid out 7 months before the general election; in this election, the incumbent government won an unprecedented landslide victory (Asami 2010, 192; Brown and Hewison 2005).

### 7.2.1.3 Taiwan

In Taiwan, UI was provided under the Labor Insurance Act of 1958, but it was not implemented since "unemployment problems did not become problems and social concerns in the society at that time" (Lan and Chou 2010, 219). Two factors that also played an important role in the case of Thailand motivated the government to implement UI in 1999/2003. First, unemployment became recognized as a social problem (Ku and Chang 2013, 94, 102). The export-oriented development strategy exposed Taiwan to the rise and fall of world markets and to global competition, and full employment became a thing of the past. In fact, "the fear of unemployment and the poverty cycle" became common in Taiwan.

"A survey in 2002 showed that the people who regarded themselves as impoverished rose to 67%, two times higher than those who did not feel the same previously" (Ku and Chang 2013, 99–100). Second, electoral concerns played a role in the timing of UI adoption: the government recognized the "aggressive challenge of legitimacy in the upcoming presidential election in 2000" (Ku and Chang 2013, 104).

In light of that challenge and "in the wake of the massive unemployment resulting from the international economic downturn and the Asian financial turmoil, the Executive Yuan drew up the Rules for the Implementation of Unemployment Benefits under the Labor Insurance Program under the Labor Insurance Act [December 28, 1998]. The Rules came into effect on 1 January 1999 and were amended on 30 July 1999" (V. Lee 2000a, 5, 9). Unemployment continued to rise, inducing the enactment of the EI Act in 2003 (Lan and Chou 2010, 211); the law aimed at providing "better designed unemployment benefits" (Lan and Chou 2010, 221). The EI, in turn, was further amended: "The high record of the unemployment rate during the financial crisis induced amendment of the EI Act in May 2009 to extend [unemployment benefits] and provide an employment stabilization clause" (Lan and Chou 2010, 211).

### 7.2.1.4 Turkey
Introducing a UI system was attempted many times in Turkey, starting in 1976. Since then, "22 draft UI laws were prepared until 1992, but none of them has passed in the Parliament" (Malherbet and Ulus 2003, 13). While adopting a UI program had been debated since the 1960s (Ozkan 2013, 246), neither employers nor employees were strong supporters of the idea. Capital feared the increase of labor costs, while labor preferred an extension of severance payment and pension benefits (Ozkan 2013, 247). But on August 25, 1999, Law 4447, which established UI, was finally passed in the parliament – a development that was "extremely surprising, even for Turkish observers" (Hänlein 2001, 284 [my translation]). Scholars have stressed two factors that may explain the timing of UI adoption in Turkey.

First, Turkey experienced a series of political, economic, financial, and societal crises in the dismal decade of the 1990s,

the first of which occurred in the early 1990s due to the adverse effects of the Gulf War. The second crisis, in 1994, was due to financial mismanagement. The economy contracted by about 6 percent, the inflation rate soared to 90 percent and the Turkish Lira was devalued against the U.S. dollar by approximately 70 percent. The third crisis occurred in 1999 and was due to the delayed effect of the Russian crisis and two major earthquakes that occurred in the industrial heartland of the country killing thousands and destroying businesses. (Tansel and Tasci 2010, 7)

The Izmit earthquake from August 17, 1999 killed between 17,000 and 45,000 people. In light of the tragedy of the earthquake, the expected parliamentary clash about the social insurance reform – including the adoption of UI – did not occur (Hänlein 2001, 285).

Second, international organizations were quite influential in Turkey in the 1990s, and they pushed for social policy reforms, including the adoption of UI. International organizations' considerable influence was due to Turkey's political instability:

Between 1991 and 1999, eight short-lived governments were installed. In such an environment, a vacuum existed in which bureaucrats, academic experts, as well as the broader advocacy coalitions of which they formed a part, could greatly shape social and economic policy reforms. Political and economic instability also opened up space for IOs, such as the World Bank and the IMF, to exert control over the reforms (especially the social security reform which included the introduction of UI) starting from the mid-1990s. (Ozkan 2013, 240)

Therefore, unlike what is typical in other cases, "neither class-based organizations nor political parties were the main actors involved in the introduction of the UI scheme. The employer and labour confederations did not actively take part in the process of establishing UI. ... Political parties did not play a critical role in the establishment of the UI scheme either, due to great political and economic turbulence and the consequential fluidity in the sphere of partisan competition that existed at the time of the scheme's inception" (Ozkan 2013, 240).

In this setting, international organizations with a promarket position (World Bank, OECD) and a prolabor stand (ILO) proposed a UI scheme that was appealing to both sides. UI appealed to the probusiness players because it not only promised to increase labor market mobility (relative to severance payments) but also would accelerate the privatization of state economic enterprises via softening resistance to privatization (Ozkan 2013, 249). UI appealed to the prolabor actors because it promised to increase income and job security (Ozkan 2013, 251), and in 1992 the Ministry of Labor appointed an expert team to draft UI legislation (somewhat surprisingly, the committee was largely stacked with probusiness economists [Ozkan 2013, 252–53]). The economic crisis of 1994 strengthened the promarket forces and put social security reforms high on the agenda – this became even more obvious "when Turkey was facing the adverse impact of the 1999 economic crisis" (Aybars and

Tsarouhas 2010, 753; Ozkan 2013, 252). The introduction of UI was part of a large and unpopular reform of the social security system, which was a component of a stabilization program that also included decreasing inflation and accelerating privatization. The most contentious part of the reform package was an increase in pension age eligibility from 38 (women) and 43 (men) years to 58 and 60 years, respectively, and the introduction of UI can be seen as a sweetener of that deal (Hänlein 2001, 285).

### 7.2.2 Risk Inequality and Recent Cases of Unemployment Insurance

The country vignettes reveal some commonalities in the process of UI adoption, as mentioned earlier: democratization, electoral competition, and "credit claiming" (Pierson 1996) seem to have motivated politicians to establish social insurance systems; economic and societal crises were important for the birth or extension of UI; and often UI adoption enjoyed very broad support. These commonalities are notable because the four countries are quite diverse in terms of their economic structure.[19] For example, they were quite different, at the time of UI adoption, in terms of GDP, unemployment rate, and share of workers in the agricultural sector (Hwang 2013b; Kamimura 2010).[20]

From my theoretical framework, however, we would expect one structural commonality: relatively homogeneous risk pools. Did unemployment risk inequality decrease before the adoption of UI in South Korea, Thailand, Taiwan, and Turkey? To explore this question empirically, I assembled a data set containing my usual measure of risk inequality (Gini coefficient of the distribution of occupational unemployment rates) for these countries, for as far back in time as possible. I primarily relied on LABORSTA, an International Labour Office database on labor statistics),

[19] For a good comparison, see the chapters in Hwang (Hwang 2013b).
[20] One of the few comparisons of recently adopted unemployment insurance systems is due to Yasuhiro Kamimura (for details on the Republic of Korea, Thailand, and Viet Nam, see [Carter, Bédard, and Bista 2013]). After exploring structural indicators – GDP per capita, unemployment rate, size of agricultural sector – of countries with unemployment insurance system (Japan, Chinese Taipei, Korea, Thailand, China, and Vietnam) and without (Hong Kong, Singapore, Malaysia, the Philippines, and Indonesia), he concludes that "whether or not unemployment insurance is feasible depends upon an economy's philosophy and political leadership, rather than its structural conditions" (Kamimura 2010, 161). In contrast, my theoretical framework suggests that structural conditions play an important role in the adoption of social insurance.

which provides occupation-level data on employment and unemployment that are, in turn, derived from national labor force surveys. Formidable problems of data comparability and quality needed to be addressed. The level of occupational detail varies, as do the underlying classifications, which can lead to breaks in the time series. However, data for some countries are not available from LABORSTA, and I therefore relied on national sources to estimate unemployment distributions. In piecing together the data set, therefore, I could not achieve cross-national comparability; instead, I focused on comparability within countries over time, which is high.[21]

The upper part of Figure 7.3 shows the development of risk inequality over time for the four recent adopters with available long time series data (10 years or more before UI adoption). The solid triangles in the time series of risk inequality over time indicate in which year UI was adopted. The panels of the figure reveal that in each of these four countries, risk inequality markedly decreased. This pattern is particularly crisp in the cases of South Korea and Taiwan, but also shows up in Thailand and Turkey.

One concern with this evidence may be that risk inequality simply universally decreased over time in the region. To address this point, I also collected time series data on unemployment risk inequality in "comparable" countries, based on national sources: Hong Kong (V. Lee 2000b), Singapore (Wai-lam 2000), and the Philippines (A. Weber 2010).[22] Did unemployment risk inequality decrease over time in these countries? The lower part of Figure 7.3 reveals that, as far as the limited data availability allows any conclusion here, the processes of risk pool compression characteristic of the countries that adopted UI are absent in the countries that did not adopt such insurance.

The evidence in Figure 7.3 may not seem particularly striking because the levels of risk inequality differ quite a bit across countries. However, it is worth emphasizing that the data are not comparable across countries but only over time within countries. Statistical tests reveal that risk inequality is statistically significantly trending downward before adoption

---

[21] There are breaks in the series due to changes in the occupational classification (typically from ISCO68 to ISCO88) of South Korea (1993), Thailand (2002), and Singapore (1985), but the discrepancies are small. Therefore, in the figures that follow, I simply shift the series after the breakpoints to match the prebreak levels.

[22] I tried to add Malaysia (Liu and Kwong 2000) to this list, but there are no data available to analyze the case.

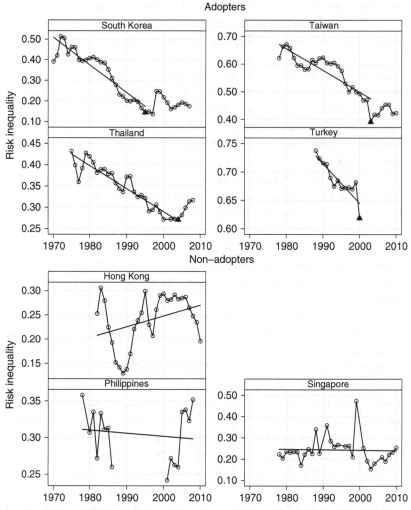

FIGURE 7.3: Risk inequality and unemployment insurance adoption/non-adoption.

*Notes*: Risk inequality measures are not comparable across countries, but over time. Solid triangles indicate year of UI adoption (in the four countries in the upper part of the figure)

in each of the four adopting countries (South Korea, Taiwan, Thailand, Turkey), while risk inequality in the non-adopting countries (Hong Kong, Philippines, Singapore) does not show such a time trend.

\* \* \*

This chapter tested a macro-level implication of my theoretical framework, namely, that social insurance adoption is more likely when risk inequality is low. I first explored the sequence of adoption of UI in the US states in 1930 and found that states with more homogeneous (and "more flipped") risk distributions introduced UI faster. I then traced the development of unemployment risk inequality several decades before UI adoption in South Korea, Taiwan, Thailand, and Turkey (the most recent cases of UI adoption, together with Vietnam, for which long time series are not available) and found that, in each of these cases, risk inequality markedly declined over time. In contrast, "comparable" countries that did not introduce UI (Philippines, Hong Kong, Singapore) did not experience a decline in risk inequality. Risk pools, it appears, played an important role in the genesis of UI programs.

In the cases under consideration, economic and societal crises played an essential role in the conception, birth, and growth of social insurance programs. In fact, crises of various kinds have been instrumental for the adoption and expansion of social policy programs throughout history. Yet, there is no systematic theoretical account for the role of crises in social policy development. The next chapter offers some ways forward in this regard, based on my theoretical framework.

# 8

# Crises and Social Policy

The stock market crash in October 1929 marked the onset of the Great Depression in the United States.[*] The Dow Jones Industrial Average lost almost 90 percent of its value, wiping out the retirement savings of many Americans. It took until November 1954 to recover these losses.[1] Between 1929 and 1933, industrial production declined by almost 50 percent and real GDP fell by almost 30 percent. Unemployment soared from 1–3 percent in 1929 to about 25 percent in 1933. Poverty and material deprivation were widespread. Suicide rates increased from 10.2 per 100,000 in 1920, to 13.9 in 1929, and to 17.4 in 1932, the highest American figure on record. Suicide rates among those aged 55–74 reached astronomic figures with 50 suicides per 100,000 elderly (Luo et al. 2011).

In 1933, President Franklin Delano Roosevelt took office and started implementing the New Deal legislation, which culminated in the Social Security Act in 1935. The law, which introduced mandatory old age and unemployment insurance (UI) in America, was passed with broad bipartisan support, winning more than 80 percent of the votes in both the House and the Senate. These social insurance programs were extended over time, are still in existence today, are at least as generous as typical European programs (Alber 2010), and generally enjoy widespread support.

It is difficult to overestimate the importance of the Great Depression for the adoption of the Social Security Act, a milestone in the history of Western welfare states. Historical counterfactuals are notoriously speculative, but many observers would agree that "absent the depression, social

---

[*] I thank Emily Lamb for competent research assistance.

[1] Comparing its peak of 381.17 points in 1929 with its trough of 41.22 points in July 1932.

security might not have been created at all" (Miron and Weil 1998, 298), and that something similar could be said about UI. Of course, history is complex, and "the New Deal was the result of a unique concatenation of forces" that led to an ideological shift "from widespread skepticism about the ability of the central government to improve the functioning of the economy to widespread faith in the competence of government" (Rockoff 1998, 125).[2] But it is simply widely understood that America's New Deal was a consequence of the Great Depression.

The United States may be the poster child for the importance of crises for social policy development – possibly the Great Recession was for the Affordable Care Act (Obamacare) what the Great Depression was for Social Security and UI. But the United States is hardly an only child. National emergencies – such as deep economic downturns, times of hyperinflation, and wars (Castles 2010) – surely have played an important role in social policy development. The Great Depression, for example, led to significant advances in social policy not only in the United States but also in New Zealand, Sweden (Castles 2010), and Norway. Cutler and Johnson (2004) identify deep recessions as the "cause of introduction" for old age pensions in New Zealand (1898), Australia (1908), Italy (1919), Spain (1920), Austria (1928), the United States (1935), and the Netherlands (1947), or almost one-third of their 20 cases, while war played an important role in Japan (1942). According to the authors, recessions also "caused" health insurance in Denmark (1933) and New Zealand (1938), and wars "caused" health insurance in the United Kingdom (1911 and 1946), Japan (1927), and Belgium (1944). In a similar vein, Hugh Hanna concludes that all but two of the UI systems that existed in 1931 were "creations of war and postwar conditions" (Hanna 1931, 177–78). More recent experiences include the Asian financial crisis of 1997/98, which spurred social policy adoption and expansion in several countries.[3]

---

[2] Besides the crisis itself, other important factors were the timing of the elections, the personalities of Hoover and Roosevelt, and the progovernment ideology of economists (Rockoff 1998, 125–26).

[3] There are various Latin American examples as well. Unemployment insurance systems were adopted in the wake of crises in Argentina (1982), Barbados (1982), and Brazil (1986) (Mazza 2000, 14, 21, 30). Some observers predict that the Great Recession "will contribute to coverage extension [in Asia]. The initiation, improvement, and further development of social security have in many countries typically been induced by crises. One option to make the 'East Asian social model' more crisis-proof is the extension of existing social security" (Scholz, Bonnet, and Ehmke 2011, 360).

It is easy to provide many examples in which national emergencies arguably had an impact on the development of welfare states, and most historical accounts mention their role in one way or another. However, the association between national emergencies and social policy development is typically ignored in quantitative historical treatments, and the relationship is not well understood theoretically.[4] Francis Castles, a prominent proponent of the parties-do-matter-for-social-policy argument, recently observed that "clear evidence" exists that unexpected national and international emergencies affect the character of welfare state interventions and welfare state development.[5] However, he laments, "the impact of emergencies is, at best, a very minor theme of welfare state analysis and one largely left to historians of the welfare state" (Castles 2010, 92). While the importance of crises for social policy development is recognized by some (Alber 1982, 58, 154; Haggard and Kaufman 2008; T. H. Marshall 1964, 270), we lack a theoretical account of how crises may or may not shape social policy. There exists, of course, some scholarship on national emergencies and the welfare state. But the well-developed literature on "warfare and welfare" is, for my purposes, too narrowly focused on wars,[6] and the small literature on economic crises

---

[4] Jens Alber's work is a partial exception. In his comprehensive quantitative historical study of welfare state development in 13 European countries, he finds little general evidence in favor of the major accounts of social policy development. He does note, however, the importance of national emergencies. Using data covering 1885–1975, he shows that the four most active five-year phases of social insurance expansion were the two post-war periods 1915–20 and 1945–50, as well as the two periods 1925–30 and 1935–40, characterized by deep economic crises. Discussing these patterns, Alber suggests that "the experience of widespread need placed social problems on top of the list of political priorities, making it almost impossible for legislators to ignore social policy reforms as soon as revenues raised with improving economic conditions" (Alber 1982, 154). Furthermore, he speculates that "the experiences of war, hyper-inflation, and the Great Depression" played a role because "they had shown that even relatively well-off classes could experience need" (Alber 1982, 58). For a good overview of the instability during the interwar period, see (Voth 2002).

[5] Castles states that "hyperinflation in Germany made that country particularly inflation averse; the Great Depression was a stimulus to welfare state development in countries such as Sweden and New Zealand; and the Second World War was a key factor in the subsequent development of the post-war British welfare state" (Castles 2010, 92).

[6] The role of war in social policy development is comparatively well understood. In my reading, the "warfare-to-welfare" literature has identified several, not necessarily competing (but largely untested) mechanisms by which wars lead to social policy expansion, including the following: (i) Wars generate demand for income maintenance of soldiers' dependents (wives, children; widows; disabled soldiers) (Titmuss 1959, 84). (ii) Wars may incentivize the government to improve the quality of current and future soldiers, for example, by providing health care (Titmuss 1959, 80). (iii) The "guns-*and*-butter"

and social policy is either ideologically charged[7] or too vague (crises sometimes put the status quo into question and they, sometimes, lead to change).[8]

In this chapter, I employ the risk pool perspective developed earlier to study the role of crises for social policy development. Why did social insurance often emerge in the aftermath of shocks? Why did some crises spur social policy development while others halted or reversed it? I suggest that crises and national emergencies can be conceptualized as shocks to risk pools. In this chapter, I will distinguish different kinds of shocks to derive a taxonomy of crises and I will argue that different types of crises have different effects on social policy development. Finally, I will test key propositions of my theoretical framework with a data set spanning 18 countries in 1870–1950 (and 1870–2000). I will show that

argument (Wilensky 1975, 72), that is, the argument that the military and government are concerned about "civilian morale" and use social policy as a "demostrategy" to win public support (Titmuss 1959, 82; and many other authors). (iv) Related, the military was in some cases concerned about domestic strikes (especially during World War I) and therefore sometimes "bought off" leftist parties and unions with (participation in) social policy. (v) The displacement effect: "people will accept, in times of crisis, methods of raising revenue formerly thought intolerable, and the acceptance of new tax levels remains when the disturbance has disappeared" (Peacock and Wiseman 1961 [2nd edition, 1967: xxxvi; see also p. 27]). (vi) Related, Jetty Klausen has argued that wartime planning can spill over to peacetime planning, potentially leading to a permanent change in the balance between state and society (Klausen 1997, 1998). (vii) The argument of "equality of sacrifice" (Wilensky 1975, 71), that is, the claim that the rich would need to pay their share of the burden as well. In a similar vein, Ken Scheve and David Stasavage have recently developed an interesting argument with respect to conscription and income taxation (Scheve and Stasavage 2010, 2012). (viii) The risk-sharing argument, that is, the claim that wars lead to a high degree of uncertainty for a majority of the population, which leads to large coalitions in favor of social insurance (Dryzek and Goodin 1986). My own take on the matter is related to this risk-sharing argument.

[7] Scholars on the left and the right interpret the correlation between national emergencies and welfare state development rather differently. Scholars on the right see crises as moments of government takeover (Higgs 1987, 2009), while scholars on the left interpret crises as moments in which capital is willing to bribe labor into submission to sustain the capitalist system (Block 1977; Skocpol 1980).

[8] While economic crises have been studied by scholars interested in social policy development, their impact on politics and policy remains vague (Kuipers 2006; Vis, Van Kersbergen, and Hylands 2011). A recent book-length treatment of crises, for example, concludes that "both economic and policy sciences offer little theoretical grip on the relationship between crisis and reform" (Kuipers 2006, 24), observing that the "window of opportunity" ("focusing events" [Kingdon 1997]) and "critical juncture" accounts common in the literature are not particularly helpful. Scholars have argued that crises potentially reshuffle existing social policy coalitions (Gourevitch 1986), undermine existing arrangements, and legitimize the unlucky (Heclo 1974; Swaan 1988). But it is often difficult or impossible to derive specific testable hypotheses from these accounts.

"social policy milestones" are significantly more likely in the four years following peaks in the suicide rate, my measure of deep societal crises in this chapter.

## 8.1 A TAXONOMY OF CRISES

Despite the importance of national emergencies for social policy change, we lack a theoretical account that can specify the role of crises in social policy development. In fact, existing literature cannot clearly answer the following basic questions: What is a crisis? What types of crises are there?[9] And why do some crises lead to social policy expansion while others lead to its retrenchment?[10] In the following, I suggest that my risk pool perspective is a productive way to understand the role of crises in social policy development. The basic idea is that a crisis is a change to the risk pool. Different types of changes to risk pools represent different crises and can be expected to lead to different social policy consequences.

As explained in Chapters 1 and 2, risk distributions have different levels (means), spreads (standard deviations), and shapes (skews), and these differences should lead to different patterns of social policy support and development. The fact that risk pools can change provides a natural interpretation of "crises": they are shocks to risk pools. In normal times, risk distributions are bottom-heavy – economic and societal crises (wars, hyperinflation, depressions, recessions) potentially lead to changes in risk pools. Four types of changes are possible:

(i)  Risk distributions remain right-skewed but become more heterogeneous: that is, risk inequality increases; compare scenario (b) with scenario (a) in Figure 2.1.

I suggest that this resembles a typical recession in which the worst-off tend to suffer first and most. For example, unemployment rises in recessions, but it increases disproportionately for low-skilled workers. Risk inequality can increase slowly, too, for example, as a result of structural change such as skill-biased technological change.

---

[9] To be sure, some classifications of crises exist. See, for example, Wibbels and Roberts (2010).
[10] Some authors seem to expect that all recessions have the same effect on public opinion (Kenworthy and Owens 2011).

(ii) Risk distributions remain right-skewed but become more homogenous: that is, risk inequality decreases; compare scenario (a) with scenario (b) in Figure 2.1.

Crises can have a homogenizing effect. An increase in risk can make risk exposure more similar. A deep recession or depression may have that effect. Historically, industrialization may have had a similar effect by shifting large parts of the workforce into similar sectors with similar risk profiles, thereby leading to a more equal distribution of risk.

(iii) Risk distributions flip from being bottom-heavy to being top-heavy; compare scenario (c) with scenario (a) in Figure 2.1.

This represents a deep crisis (or a fundamental structural transformation) and resembles catastrophic and far-reaching emergencies such as depressions or hyperinflations.

(iv) Risk is replaced by uncertainty; see scenario (d) in Figure 2.1.

Wars can be interpreted as crises so systemic that risk (where probabilities are known) is replaced by uncertainty (where probabilities are unknown).

On the basis of these types of changes, I propose to classify crises into three types.

(i) Some crises primarily affect those at the bottom (low income, high risk). As a result, risk inequality is on the rise, making social insurance more expensive for a majority of citizens. In such a scenario social policy is vulnerable to waning support, and retrenchment becomes more likely. Recessions are good examples of this sort of crisis.

(ii) Other crises affect the middle and perhaps even the top (high income, low risk) and can lead to what I call a "risk flip": the risk distribution becomes more top-heavy. In this scenario, a broad majority embraces the socialization of risk, and social policy adoption and expansion are more likely. Depressions might be a good example for this kind of crisis.

(iii) Or crises can be so extreme that a majority of citizens are uncertain about their future place in society – they know neither the distribution of bad luck, nor whether they will be lucky or unlucky. Citizens are "behind the veil of ignorance," in which risk is replaced with uncertainty. In this case, social insurance can gain very widespread support. Deep depressions or wars may resemble this scenario.

In the following, I will empirically explore the relationship between "crises" and social policy development. In particular, I will attempt to test whether deep societal crises ("risk flips") spurred the growth of the welfare state, and whether recessions slowed it down.

## 8.2 THE ROLE OF CRISES IN SOCIAL POLICY DEVELOPMENT

An empirical cross-national investigation of the role of crises in the development of welfare states faces a variety of challenges. Chief among them is the measurement of the dependent variable (welfare state development) and the key explanatory variable (crises). The next subsection discusses my measurement choices for the dependent variable(s) and explanatory variables (and controls), and the subsection following it describes my empirical strategy and discusses the results.

### 8.2.1 Data

The few existing large-N time series-cross-sectional (TSCS) quantitative studies going back to the nineteenth (or at least early twentieth) century typically pursue one of three approaches to measure welfare state development, my dependent variable in the following analysis. In the first approach, "welfare state development" is captured by how much governments spend on social policy (relative to overall government spending; relative to GDP; relative to population size) (Lindert 2004; Tanzi and Schuknecht 2000). But these data are not available in detailed historical time series and therefore are not useful for exploring the role of crises in social policy development. In the second approach, "welfare state development" is captured by "core laws," that is, social policy laws that are deemed to be crucial. Most authors simply code the first law in a given social policy domain as a (and typically the only) core law (Alber 1981, 1981, 1982; Carroll 1999; Collier and Messick 1975; Cutler and Johnson 2004; Hicks 1999; Hicks, Misra, and Ng 1995; Kangas 2012; K. Kim 2001; W. Kim 2010; Usui 1994), although some authors distinguish different types of core laws in social policy development.[11] One problem with this approach is to identify which laws should be counted as core

---

[11] For example, Hicks and co-authors differentiate among the year of initial adoption of social policy laws; the year they became binding or extensive/funded, if different; and the year they became binding and extensive/funded (Hicks 1999; Hicks, Misra, and Ng 1995).

laws – some cases are easy do decide, but often different authors draw different conclusions.[12] In the third approach, "welfare state development" is captured by social insurance coverage (Alber 1981, 1982; W. Kim 2007; Mares 2004), that is, by measures that code what percentage of the population or workforce is covered by a particular social insurance program.[13]

I combine the latter two approaches. While I am interested in the determinants of milestones in social policy development, I prefer identifying them by major expansions of social insurance coverage, not by core laws. The problem with core laws is that there is no reliable way of identifying them for a large set of countries and domains. To identify milestones, I generate dummy variables that indicate large increases in coverage in each of the four main domains (accident, old age, sickness, unemployment), on the basis of historical data from the Social Citizenship Indicator Programme (SCIP) and the Growth to Limits project (Alber 1982; Flora and Alber 1981; Korpi and Palme 2007).[14] Large increases can be identified in various ways – the results that follow define them as increases that are among the top 5 percent growth rates.[15]

---

[12] In this approach, a common estimation strategy is event history modeling (also called survival analysis, duration models, hazard models, and failure-time models), although other types of analyses exist too (e.g., qualitative comparative analysis). Here, a variety of thorny issues need to be examined. For example, few social insurance programs were created at once, and it is far from obvious how to model multiphased adoptions, especially in multiple-record data (countries) in multiple strata (social policy domains).

[13] Some studies using social insurance coverage also explore replacement rates, but the focus is typically on the former. One problem with this general approach is the distinction between social assistance and social insurance programs (which SCIP and Alber handle partially differently). One challenge is the dynamic characteristic of the data: theoretically, the data range from 0 to 100 percent of coverage, and we know that countries started out at 0 and headed toward high numbers of coverage. The data, therefore, are unlikely to be stationary, but mean and variance cannot increase indefinitely (Beck and Katz 2011). While dynamics in TSCS can, and have been, modeled – using autoregressive distributive lag (ADL) or error correction (EC) models – there are surprisingly few established best practices (De Boef and Keele 2008; Keele and Kelly 2006).

[14] These data sets are not annual, and the time series were therefore (mildly) interpolated. In some cases (country-domain-years), neither of these sources has data before 1930 (the starting year for SCIP), and coverage rates were extrapolated backward, using information on program adoption and other country-specific information.

[15] These calculations are performed separately for pre- and post-1950. For the pre-1950 years (which are employed in the main analysis that follows), this algorithm identifies the following domain-country-years as large increases: Accident: AUS: 1926, 1934; AUT: 1887, 1934, 1935, 1936; BEL: 1903, 1931, 1932; CAN: 1908, 1909, 1910; CHE: 1881, 1882, 1883, 1884; DEU: 1884, 1886, 1887, 1888; DNK: 1898, 1906, 1907; FIN: 1896, 1897, 1898; FRA: 1898, 1899, 1900; GBR: 1897, 1906, 1907; IRL: 1922, 1948; ITA:

Figure 8.1 gives a sense of the development of social insurance coverage by displaying coverage rates averaged across accident, old age, sickness, and UI. (In the main analyses that follow, the dependent variable will also be domain-specific coverage rates, which are not shown in the figure).

I now discuss the core explanatory variable in the analysis to follow. My framework suggests that social policy milestones are more likely in the event of a "risk flip" (and also when risk inequality is low). It also distinguishes different kinds of crises, namely, those that are expected to spur social policy development (depressions) and those that are expected to curb it (recessions). Applying these propositions to historical data is difficult because it is unclear how to measure risk inequality for historical time series, or how to identify risk flips. In the analyses in previous chapters, I derived measures of risk inequality from occupational unemployment rates, but this is not an option for a historical TSCS analysis, simply because there are no useful data. The constraints in terms of historical data availability are indeed severe: we do not even have unemployment rates for many countries in the late nineteenth and early twentieth centuries, let alone information on the distribution of unemployment. While it is in principle possible to measure risk flips directly by using either objective risk or subjective risk perception data, in practice there are no historical data on either.

Because I cannot measure risk distributions and risk flips directly, I need to proxy them. It is a formidable challenge to develop a proxy for risk flips – or widespread societal crises – that can be collected for a comparative quantitative analysis that covers almost all of today's rich democracies over the last 150 years or so. Eventually, I narrowed down

1898, 1916, 1917; JPN: 1898, 1911, 1912; NLD: 1901, 1948, 1949; NOR: 1894, 1911, 1926; NZL: 1908, 1909, 1910; SWE: 1901, 1916, 1917; USA: 1912, 1913.

Health: AUT: 1888, 1916, 1917, 1918; BEL: 1894, 1895, 1896; CHE: 1916, 1917; DEU: 1883, 1886, 1887, 1888; DNK: 1892, 1893, 1894; FRA: 1898, 1899, 1900; GBR: 1911, 1934; IRL: 1922, 1934; ITA: 1886, 1940, 1941, 1942; JPN: 1922, 1923; NLD: 1929, 1931; NOR: 1911, 1916; SWE: 1891, 1892, 1893.

Pension: AUT: 1906, 1907, 1934; BEL: 1900, 1901, 1902; CHE: 1948, 1949; DEU: 1891, 1921, 1922; FIN: 1934, 1935; FRA: 1895, 1896, 1897; GBR: 1908, 1928, 1934; ITA: 1901, 1902, 1916; JPN: 1940, 1941; NLD: 1920, 1934; NOR: 1934, 1935; NZL: 1940, 1941; SWE: 1914, 1948; USA: 1936.

Unemployment: AUT: 1920, 1948, 1949; BEL: 1920, 1931; CAN: 1940, 1941; CHE: 1924, 1926; DEU: 1927, 1934; DNK: 1907, 1908, 1909; FIN: 1917, 1940; FRA: 1921, 1922; GBR: 1911, 1921; IRL: 1922, 1931; ITA: 1919, 1921; JPN: 1948, 1949; NLD: 1916, 1917; NOR: 1906, 1907, 1940; SWE: 1934, 1935; USA: 1936.

Robustness checks revealed that different plausible ways to identify "large increases" lead to comparable results.

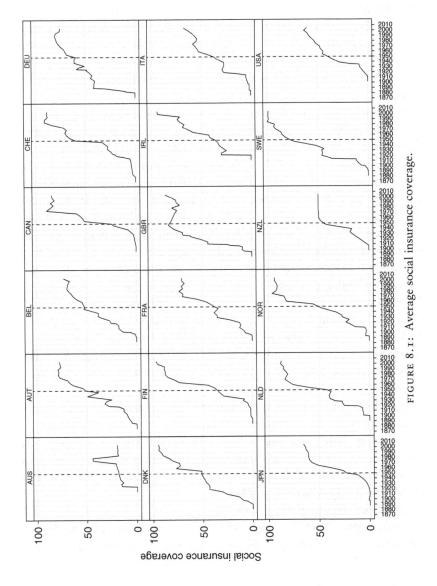

FIGURE 8.1: Average social insurance coverage.

my search to two plausible proxies of widespread societal crises: data on (stock) market volatilities (Gerlach, Ramaswamy, and Scatigna 2006; Ineichen 2000) and data on suicide rates. In this chapter, I will rely on the latter data – suicide rates – rather than the former to measure widespread social stress. I do not use stock market volatility measures because there are at least two main issues with these data as a proxy of widespread social stress. First, stock market developments reflect the views of a highly select subgroup, not societies at large. Second, the very concept of stock market volatility is quite contested in the relevant literature.

In the following, I will therefore rely on suicide rates. In particular, I will use peaks in suicide rates to identify widespread societal crises (in which risk flips are likely, at least in terms of perceptions). Suicide is not a topic that has received much attention in political science (with the partial exception of suicide terrorism), but there is a rich literature in sociology, psychology, medicine, and other disciplines (Horwitz 1984; Wanberg 2012; Wray, Colen, and Pescosolido 2011). Durhkeim's classic work on suicide – published in 1897 (Durkheim 2006) – built on an even older literature (Quetelet; Morselli) that suggested that "modernity" was to blame for rising suicide rates. Going beyond these attempts, Durkheim "sought to understand how negative meanings and emotions were pro-duced in individuals and groups during times of dramatic social change" (Wray, Colen, and Pescosolido 2011, 507). For him, suicide was more likely in cases of extreme values on integration and regulation: egoistic suicide occurs when integration is too low – individuals experience a sense of meaninglessness; altruistic suicide occurs when integration is too high; anomic suicide occurs when there is too little regulation – people feel they have nothing left to lose, or no reason to live; and fatalistic suicide occurs when there is too much regulation. Major crises can affect both integra-tion and regulation, increasing both anomic and egoistic suicides. Or, put differently, during crises, "the terrors of life [more frequently] come to outweigh the terrors of death," in which case "a man will put an end to his life" (Schopenhauer 1973, 78).

Durkheim could already state that "it is a well-known fact that economic crises have an aggravating effect on the suicidal tendency" (Durkheim 2006, chap. 5).[16] Since then, literally hundreds of empirical

---

[16] Scholarship investigating the relationship between crises and suicide goes at least as far back as 1822, when Falret (1822) "contended that suicide rates tend to rise during periods of rapid change and in times of economic depression" (Platt 1984, 93).

studies on the relationship between unemployment and suicide have been published.[17] In terms of quantitative and qualitative studies with various empirical strategies one can "confidently state that there is an association between unemployment and suicide but [one] cannot specify with the same degree of confidence the nature of this association" (Platt 1984, 108). Various causal mechanisms are plausible: unemployment can directly affect suicide risk of the unemployed (or their family members) "through eroding the incomes, economic welfare, self-esteem, and other suicidogenic factors"; unemployment can also affect suicide risk of the employed (Brenner 1987) "through a higher level of anxiety among the employed who fear losing their jobs" or lowered real wages and job opportunities (Stack 2000, 156).[18]

Whatever ultimately leads to the correlation between unemployment and suicide rates, it seems plausible to assume – as I will in the following – that unusually high suicide rates indicate unusually deep societal or economic crises. These crises – or national emergencies – may be triggered by economic factors (such as a depression), but they may also be of a different nature. For example, it has been shown "that suicide rates increase after severe earthquakes, floods, and hurricanes" (Krug et al. 1998). It seems particularly plausible to assume that high suicide rates are indicative of deep societal crises in the absence of established welfare states. After all, welfare states should have an ameliorative effect on suicide (Farber 1965, 373).[19]

In summary, a rich and rigorous literature has established a close – possibly causal – relationship between high unemployment (and other crises) and suicide rates. While acknowledging the complexity of that association, I will in the following empirical analysis rely on (peaks in) suicide rates as an indicator of (deep) societal crises in order to explore

[17] Stephen Platt reviews empirical contributions from the 1920s through about 1980 (Platt 1984), and 165 empirical studies from the period 1984–99 (Platt and Hawton 2000; Stack 2000); Wanberg provides an update through the 2000s (Wanberg 2012). There is also a large qualitative literature on suicide and unemployment.

[18] It is also possible that the correlation between unemployment and suicide is spurious – both variables could be caused by a third variable, for example, "psychiatric illness."

[19] Bizarrely enough, the opposite assertion – that welfare states increase suicide – enjoyed some popularity in the 1960s. Unsurprisingly, this belief has no empirical support. For example, it has been shown that suicide rates among the elderly dropped sharply in the United States after the introduction of Social Security (Cutler and Meara 2001). Or, as Farber puts it, "I have never, incidentally, encountered a man who attempted suicide because he had just received a social security check" (Farber 1965, 373).

the relationship between crises and social policy milestones.[20] Because a strong safety net can be expected to ameliorate the effect of crises on suicide rates, my proposed indicator arguably is more useful in circumstances when social policy programs do not yet exist, or are not yet fully developed. This is why I will restrict the main analysis to the years before 1950.

In the following empirical exploration of the link between crises (measured by suicide rates) and social policy development (measured by milestones or coverage rates) my preferred approach will employ "peaks" in suicide rates, a variable that indicates high local maxima in suicide rates. Identifying peaks by eyeballing a time series is relatively straightforward; identifying them statistically is not. I have decided to define peaks as local maxima (i.e., the suicide rate in the previous and following years are lower) that are among the highest 5 percent (analogous to the definition of social policy milestones, which are defined as increases that are among the top 5 percent).[21] Figure 8.2 displays suicide rates in 1870–2012, or all available years, and indicates peaks as defined previously; the figure also displays all available unemployment rates (on the right axis), but the country-year coverage is rather limited.

Several aspects of Figure 8.2 are noteworthy. First, levels in suicide rates vary tremendously across countries. Because the figure has country-specific vertical axes, this may not be immediately obvious. But compare, for example, the suicide rates of the neighboring countries Austria (AUT) and Italy: while the highest value of the Italian suicide rate is 10.6 (suicides per 100,000 citizens) in 1927, the lowest value in Austria/ Austria-Hungary has been below that number only once (at 9, in 1873);

---

[20] The case narratives in Chapter 7 revealed the importance of the Asian financial crisis in 1997–98 for social policy development in various East/Southeast Asian countries. Several of these countries also saw a marked increase in suicide rates, likely due to the crisis (Chang et al. 2009).

[21] This algorithm classifies the following country-years as years with peak suicide rates (these calculations are preformed separately for before and after 1950): AUS 1903, 1912, 1915, 1930, 1963, 1965, 1967; AUT 1932, 1938, 1945, 1982, 1986; BEL 1933, 1938, 1940, 1984; CAN 1930, 1932, 1937, 1978, 1983, 1986; CHE 1932, 1936, 1945, 1980, 1983, 1985; DEU 1932, 1977; DNK 1878, 1886, 1980; FIN 1931, 1939, 1990; FRA 1892, 1894, 1898, 1985; GBR 1903, 1932, 1956, 1963; IRL 1912, 1929, 1998, 2001; ITA 1927, 1931, 1985, 1993, 1997; JPN 1932, 1936, 1958, 1998, 2003; NLD 1932, 1940, 1942, 1945, 1984; NOR 1875, 1945, 1988, 1991; NZL 1929, 1932, 1995, 1998; SWE 1910, 1912, 1932, 1967, 1970; USA 1908, 1915, 1932, 1977, 1986. Note that most analysis that follows will be restricted to the period before 1950. I experimented with a variety of different ways of identifying peaks with similar results.

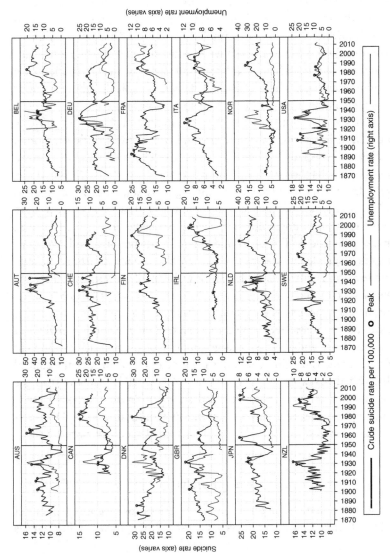

FIGURE 8.2: Suicide rates and unemployment rates.

193

the highest suicide rate from Austria is 45 (in 1945).[22] The differences in levels of suicide rates across countries are not well understood – for example, the four Scandinavian countries in the sample (Finland, Sweden, Norway, and Denmark) have many commonalities, yet their suicide rates differ greatly (Norway's highest suicide rate is roughly as high as Denmark's lowest). As another example, some of the "happiest" countries (in terms of subjective indicators of well-being) also post the highest suicide rates (Switzerland and Denmark).[23] Second, there is much variation over time within countries. The highest suicide rate is typically about 2 (or 3) times as high as the lowest, although in some countries the maximum is 5 (Austria) or even 10 times greater than the minimum (Finland). Third, in various countries, suicide rates and unemployment rates track each other fairly closely, especially before 1950 (see the United States, the United Kingdom, the Netherlands, Belgium, France, Austria [AUT], Italy, Australia [AUS], and New Zealand, but arguably some other countries as well). Fourth, the suicide rates in some countries follow trends that seem to have little relation to unemployment levels, especially after 1950 (see, e.g., Denmark or Sweden). Trying to understand cross-national and over-time differences in suicide rates seems to be a topic that is ripe for further research.

With respect to control variables, I follow the small set of statistical investigations of social policy development before 1950 or so, referenced earlier. One of the many problems that these studies face is a dearth of comparable historical (annual) data. As a result, most studies only include a small set of control variables, and there is a large amount of overlap across different studies. My study is no different in this respect, and I will include the control variables listed in Table 8.1 (the table lists all variables employed in the analysis, as well as their definitions and sources). Broadly speaking, these variables capture socioeconomic (urbanization, industrialization, GDP, recessions, imports, and exports) and political factors (democracy, partisanship).

### 8.2.2 Results

With the given data structure – a time series-cross-sectional data set spanning 18 countries and 140 years or so, although the main analysis

---

[22] Suicide rates are also available by gender, but for fewer years. Male suicide rates are almost always (much) higher than female suicide rates. The highest suicide rate in the entire data set is for males in Austria in 1938 (60.7 per 100,000).

[23] Tara Parker-Pope (2011): Happiest places post highest suicide rates. well.blogs.nytimes.com/2011/04/22/happiest-places-post-highest-suicide-rates/?_php=true&_type=blogs&_r=0

TABLE 8.1: *Variables for analysis on crises and social policy development*

| Variable | Definition | Source |
| --- | --- | --- |
| Dependent variable: social insurance coverage | Social insurance coverage, by domains (accident, sickness, old age, unemployment) (or averaged across these domains) | Based on SCIP (Korpi and Palme 2007), Alber (1982), and country-specific sources |
| Dependent variable: social policy milestones | Major expansion in coverage, defined as top 5 percent increase | Calculated from coverage |
| Suicide rates | Crude suicide rate (men and women), per 100,000 | Agerbo, Stack, and Petersen 2011; Carter 2006; Cavan 1928; Chesnais 1976; Felber and Winiecki 2008; Halbwachs 1978; Krose 1906; Lester and Yang 1998; Sonneck, Stein, and Voracek 2003; Thomas and Gunnell 2010; World Health Organization 1956, 2014 |
| Peak in suicide rates | Peaks in suicide rates, as defined in text | |
| Period | Ordinal variable distinguishing year 1870–1918, 1919–49, 1950/1975, and 1976+ | |
| Democracy | Dummy variable for democracy, that is, polity score$\geq 6$ | Polity IV Project (Marshall, Gurr, and Jaggers 2012) |
| Left head of government | Head of government (HoG) from left party (left: Communist, Socialist, Social Democratic, or having an otherwise strongly redistributive platform) | Brambor and Lindvall 2013; Brambor, Lindvall, and Stjernquist 2013 www.reformcapacity .org/data.html (hog_ dataset_country_year_ v1.2.dta; March 9, 2015) |
| Religious head of government | Head of government with explicitly Christian platform | As above |
| Growth rate | Growth in GDP per capita, 2006 = 100 | Barro-Ursúa MacroeconomicData (2010) (http://rbarro .com/data-sets/) (Barro and Ursúa 2012) |

(*continued*)

TABLE 8.1: (*continued*)

| Variable | Definition | Source |
|---|---|---|
| Recession | Number of years in the last decade with negative growth (GDP) | Calculated from variable GDP; see Cutler and Johnson 2004 |
| Imports | Imports per capita (US$) (slightly interpolated) | Banks and Wilson 2012 |
| Exports | Exports per capita (US$) (slightly interpolated) | As above |
| Industrialization | Share of population not in agriculture or services (slightly interpolated) | Mitchell 2013 |
| Urbanization | Population, cities of 100,000 and more per capita (slightly interpolated) | As above |

*Note*: Suicide rates for the United Kingdom (= England and Wales) are age-adjusted.

will be restricted to about 75 years – there are various plausible empirical strategies. In the following, I report results from fixed effects (i.e., conditional) logit estimates in which the dependent variable is a dummy variable equaling 1 for a social policy "milestone" (measured by an increase in social insurance coverage that is among the top 5 percent increases).[24] The level of analysis is the country-domain-year level because the four domains of accident, old age, sickness, and unemployment are "stacked." This approach allows for the possibility that a crisis may have influenced the development in more than one social policy domain; for example, the Social Security Act in the United States introduced social insurance coverage for both old age and unemployment.[25] A country-domain enters the analysis nine years before coverage exceeds 0 percent – because Germany's sickness insurance from 1883 is the first social insurance program in the data set, the earliest observation is from 1874.[26] Also, it is worth

[24] I explored two alternative estimation strategies. First, I estimated autoregressive distributive lag (ADL)/error correction (EC) models, with (continuous) coverage rates as the dependent variable and (continuous) suicide rates as key explanatory variable. Second, I estimated various types of survival analysis with "social policy milestones" as the dependent variable. The substantive findings are roughly comparable across these different estimation strategies.

[25] Robustness checks at the country-year level with large increases in coverage averaged across the four domains yield similar results.

[26] This is an arbitrary choice, but alternative ways to set the starting point for a country-domain's being "at risk" of a social policy milestone yield similar results.

noting that some country domains are essentially dropped from the fixed effects analysis because the dependent variable consists entirely of 0s.[27] The reported analysis is restricted to the years before 1950, but the results are comparable if the period is extended to 2010.

Table 8.2 displays the results of this analysis. The table reports six models, all of which share a minimal set of explanatory variables. This baseline estimation is reported in Model 1, which includes four dummy variables indicating peaks in suicide rates in years $t - 1$ to $t - 4$, an indicator variable for democracy, and an indicator variable that divides the period under investigation (1874–1949) into years before and after 1919.[28] The substantive reason for including the explanatory variable of main interest – peaks in suicide rates – as lags for years $t - 1$ to $t - 4$ is simple: historical accounts of social policy suggest that there are often intervals between causes (such as crises) and their effects (such as social policy milestones). Four years of lags is a somewhat arbitrary choice, except that it roughly coincides with the length of electoral cycles. Consistent with my theoretical framework's predictions, the results suggest that "social policy milestones" were more common two, three, and four years after peaks in suicide rates. The results also suggest that milestones were more frequent in the period 1919–49, compared to 1874–1918, while the dummy for democracy is not significant.

Models 2, 3, 5, and 6 in Table 8.2 add various sets of control variables. Model 2 controls for the partisanship of the head of government at $t$ and $t - 1$ with dummy variables for left and religious heads of government. None of the coefficients on these partisanship variables is significant, a non-result that reinforces previous findings of the limited systematic impact of left governments in statistical historical analysis (Scheve and Stasavage 2009). This does not mean that partisanship is irrelevant for understanding welfare state politics – there is no question that it was, in some cases, a crucial ingredient for social policy development. Furthermore, the employed variable capturing the power resource logic is fairly crude. But the absence of a significant correlation between left (or religious) heads of governments and social policy milestones suggests that the role of partisanship may be best observed under specific historical

---

[27] Following the coding rules of the SCIP project, there was no social insurance against sickness in Australia, New Zealand, and the United States and no social insurance against unemployment in Australia and New Zealand during the period under investigation.

[28] This follows a plausible periodization (Schustereder 2010, 41): 1870–1918 (genesis of social policy), 1919–49 (interwar consolidation), 1951–75 (golden age expansion), and 1976+.

TABLE 8.2: *Crises and social policy development*

| | (1) | (2) | (3) | (4) | (5) | (6) |
|---|---|---|---|---|---|---|
| | Dependent variable: social policy milestones (Dummy = 1 if social insurance coverage increase is among top 5 percent) | | | | | |
| Peak in suicide rate ($t - 1$) | −0.246 | −0.136 | −0.227 | | −0.277 | −0.086 |
| | (0.528) | (0.533) | (0.540) | | (0.536) | (0.548) |
| Peak in suicide rate ($t - 2$) | 0.782* | 0.928** | 0.739* | | 0.784* | 0.952* |
| | (0.339) | (0.345) | (0.359) | | (0.350) | (0.374) |
| Peak in suicide rate ($t - 3$) | 0.828* | 0.913* | 0.932* | | 0.906* | 1.121** |
| | (0.358) | (0.362) | (0.366) | | (0.366) | (0.379) |
| Peak in suicide rate ($t - 4$) | 1.161** | 1.404** | 1.351** | | 1.272** | 1.556** |
| | (0.293) | (0.303) | (0.305) | | (0.303) | (0.324) |
| Democracy | 0.411 | −0.208 | 0.230 | 0.069 | 0.399 | −0.032 |
| | (0.302) | (0.404) | (0.323) | (0.302) | (0.338) | (0.463) |
| Years 1919–49 | −1.539** | −1.341** | −1.553** | −1.295** | −0.990** | −0.651# |
| | (0.234) | (0.267) | (0.249) | (0.226) | (0.324) | (0.360) |
| Left head of government ($t$) | | 0.027 | | | | −0.015 |
| | | (0.557) | | | | (0.561) |
| Left head of government ($t - 1$) | | −0.818 | | | | −0.587 |
| | | (0.591) | | | | (0.593) |
| Religious head of government ($t$) | | 0.610 | | | | 0.067 |
| | | (0.698) | | | | (0.812) |
| Religious head of government ($t - 1$) | | 0.309 | | | | 0.669 |
| | | (0.724) | | | | (0.827) |

| | (1) | (2) | (3) | (4) | (5) | (6) |
|---|---|---|---|---|---|---|
| Change in GDP | | | 0.042 | 0.118 | | 0.027 |
| | | | (0.081) | (0.076) | | (0.103) |
| Recession | | | -0.074 | -0.055 | | -0.123 |
| | | | (0.071) | (0.064) | | (0.081) |
| Imports | | | | | -0.005 | -0.005 |
| | | | | | (0.006) | (0.006) |
| Exports | | | | | -0.000 | -0.001 |
| | | | | | (0.008) | (0.008) |
| Industrialization | | | | | -2.860 | -3.411 |
| | | | | | (3.669) | (3.900) |
| Urbanization | | | | | -4.076 | -4.320 |
| | | | | | (2.658) | (2.947) |
| N. of cases | 2474 | 2229 | 2367 | 2752 | 2295 | 2062 |
| Countries | 18 | 18 | 17^ | 17^ | 18 | 17^ |
| Pseudo $R^2$ | 0.069 | 0.080 | 0.078 | 0.047 | 0.085 | 0.101 |
| Log likelihood | -434 | -396 | -412 | -476 | -392 | -358 |

*Notes*: Coefficients (from logit fixed effects estimates (= conditional logit)) above standard errors. Years covered in analysis: 1874–1949.
^No data on GDP for Ireland
#$p < 0.10$, *$p < 0.05$, **$p < 0.01$

circumstances. Moreover, parties other than left parties also sometimes strongly supported welfare state expansion (Van Kersbergen 1995). Model 3 adds to the baseline model (i.e., Model 1) two variables related to GDP. The first variable simply captures the change in GDP, but the variable is not statistically significant. The second variable counts the number of years with negative growth rates in the previous decade and therefore indicates a country's recent experience with recessions (Cutler and Johnson 2004). Recessions are negatively (though in these models not significantly) correlated with social policy milestones.[29] Model 4 removes the suicide variables from Model 3, to explore whether GDP-related variables perform differently when not controlling for peaks in suicide rates (they do not), while Model 5 adds to the baseline model a set of variables that capture to which degree a country is exposed to international trade (imports; exports), how industrialized, and how urbanized it is. None of these variables reaches statistical significance.

Finally, Model 6 includes all right-hand-side variables. The patterns are similar: the only statistically significant correlates of social policy milestones are peaks in suicide rates (lagged two, three, or four years) and the period dummy. Neither partisanship, nor trade exposure (imports/exports), nor urbanization is significantly correlated with social policy milestones in Model 6. These findings are consistent with my theoretical framework, which suggests that risk flips or deep societal crises (here measured by peaks in suicide rates) induce social policy development, while increasing risk inequality (here measured by the variable "recession") slows it.

Of course, statistical significance does not guarantee substantive importance. What is the (estimated) substantive effect of peaks in suicide rates on social policy milestones? It is possible to convert the estimated coefficients into odds ratios, which have a rather intuitive interpretation (though they are not particularly popular in political science). The estimated coefficients in Model 6 in Table 8.2 suggest that a peak in suicide rates at $t - 1$ decreases the odds of a social policy milestone from 1 to 0.91, but increases the odds in the following three years. In particular, a peak in suicide rates increases the likelihood of social policy milestones two years later by 2.6, three years later by 3.1, and four years later

---

[29] An ADL(1, 4) model with average social policy coverage as the (continuous) dependent variable and suicide rates as a (continuous) explanatory leads to similar results, except that the two GDP variables are statistically significant (positive changes in GDP are positively correlated with increases in social insurance; recessions are negatively correlated with them).

by a staggering 4.7. Adding and subtracting these odds ratios suggest that social policy milestones are 11 times more likely to happen in close proximity to peaks in suicide rates! The odds ratio for the recession coefficient is 0.88, suggesting that social policy milestones are less likely to occur in the aftermath of recessions (though, as mentioned, this is not a statistically significant coefficient in this model). Put differently, some crises spur social policy development, while others slow it down.

# 9

# Conclusion

Why did citizens increasingly rely on the state to cope with the adversities of life? Why did every one of today's rich democracies set up "nationwide collective and state-controlled arrangements" (Swaan 1988, 222) covering the risks of accident, sickness, unemployment, and old age? Different accounts emphasize different aspects of the remarkable transition of night-watchman states into welfare states, such as morality, the class struggle, and bureaucracies. Building on and extending existing scholarship, my account stresses the role of risk exposure, which motivates individual behavior and sets the stage for the politics of social solidarity. Welfare state preferences and politics are decisively shaped by risk and the distribution of risk within a society.

The basic ingredients of my theoretical framework are simple: at the micro-level, someone's relative position in the risk distribution (co-)determines whether he or she will gain or lose from a social insurance program, a factor that influences someone's attitudes toward that program. At the macro-level, a risk distribution's mean, standard deviation, and skew influence social policy making: only fairly common risks become social questions (mean); more commonly shared risks (lower risk inequality) enable broader coalitions in support of welfare state programs (standard deviation); and whether a risk distribution is bottom- or top-heavy influences whether a majority will lose or win from risk pooling (skew).

This simple framework, which is developed in Chapter 2, makes predictions regarding individual level social policy attitudes (Chapter 3), risk perceptions (Chapter 4), aggregate popular support for social policy (Chapter 5), the timing of social policy milestones (Chapters 7 and 8), the differing degrees of welfare state generosity (Chapter 5), and the occurrence of welfare state retrenchment (Chapter 6). Some of these predictions are intuitive, others less so; some are variations of existing accounts; some are reinterpretations; and others are novel. All of them are derived from the same underlying framework developed in Chapter 2, and the various tests throughout the book lend considerable empirical support to many of these predictions.

What determines social policy attitudes? My framework suggests that individual-level support for social insurance is proportional to one's relative risk exposure: the higher risk exposure is, the stronger is social policy support, *ceteris paribus*. This intuitive insight has very strong support in the data, with both objective as well as subjective risk exposure measures (Chapter 3). This finding raises the intriguing questions of how individuals know their objective risk exposure, how they form their subjective risk perceptions, and how accurate these perceptions are. Chapter 4 explores this novel agenda. The evidence reveals that citizens are quite well informed about their risk exposure, in terms of both their objective relative position in the risk pool as well as their absolute level of risk exposure (at least in some risk domains). In light of much survey literature, which portrays citizens as uninformed and uninterested, this surprising finding begs the question how individuals know about their position in risk distributions. The chapter shows that social policy risks have certain characteristics that motivate and enable people to learn about them: social policy risks are common and people care about them. Social policy risks are also correlated over time, correlated across domains, and correlated within social networks, providing opportunities for individuals to learn about them. And, indeed, subjective risk perceptions are shaped by past experiences, present experiences in other domains, and the experiences of one's social networks.

Chapters 5 through 8 deal with different macro-level implications of my theoretical framework. Why does the popularity of social policy differ across countries and domains? And why are welfare states more generous in some countries? Chapter 5 explores two related predictions on these topics. First, risk inequality and social policy popularity should be negatively correlated (higher risk inequality is associated with lower support for social policy) because more commonly shared risk exposure leads to less opposition to social insurance. Second, risk inequality and social policy generosity should also be negatively correlated (higher risk inequality is associated with lower social policy generosity) because we can expect social policy making and public opinion to be roughly in sync in democracies. Various empirical tests – using various types of data and empirical strategies – lend considerable support to these predictions: more homogeneous risk distributions are, indeed, associated with higher support for, and generosity of, social policy.

When is social policy retrenched? This is a question that also has received considerable attention in the comparative political economy literature, and I address it in Chapter 6. My framework predicts that retrenchment occurs when risk inequality increases sufficiently. One case in which this occurred, I argue, was Germany after reunification. The merging of the East and West German risk pools sharply increased risk inequality, and that, I argue, considerably weakened support for generous benefits and gave the red-green government a mandate to retrench, resulting in harsh labor market retrenchment (the Hartz Reforms).

When is social policy born or significantly extended? What explains the timing of social policy milestones? Chapters 7 and 8 give answers to these questions, based on my risk pool framework. Chapter 7 deals with the adoption of new social policy programs, in two quite different settings. The first part of the chapter explains the order in which unemployment insurance (UI) legislation was passed in the US states during the New Deal. The empirical analysis reveals that certain characteristics of a state's risk distribution are strong predictors of the speed by which it implemented UI. In particular, both the homogeneity of risk distributions as well as their "flippedness" predict the order of adoption. The second part of Chapter 7 turns to a very different set of cases, namely, countries that adopted UI programs recently (South Korea, Thailand, Taiwan, and Turkey). Country "vignettes" describe the genesis of UI programs in these countries, and evidence on risk distributions reveals that one common development in these countries was the decreasing risk inequality before adoption. This trend is noticeably absent in "comparable" countries in the region that did not adopt UI programs.

Social policy making is a dynamic process. Many qualitative accounts of social policy development highlight the importance of crises – such as recessions, depressions, or wars – yet there is little theoretical or empirical work that connects crises and social policy making systematically. How do crises influence social policy making? My theoretical framework offers a way to think about crises and social policy development, as elaborated in Chapter 8. I distinguish different types of crises and derive predictions regarding their impact on social policy. A quantitative historical analysis of the determinants of social policy milestones reveals considerable empirical support for key predictions derived from my framework. In particular, I find that social policy milestones between 1870 and 1950 were much more likely in the aftermath of peaks in suicide rates, my measure of deep societal crises in that chapter.

My theoretical framework is fairly simple, and it brackets several important topics. Four simplifications are particularly stark. First, I have, by and large, treated risk distributions as exogenously given. To be sure, several of the empirical tests earlier address the possibility that risk distributions are being shaped by social policy. And quite often, changes in risk pools *are* exogenous, because they are caused by either exogenous technological developments or exogenous shocks. But I have not offered a model that explains variation in risk distributions across countries, domains, or time. Developing such a model may not be feasible, although thinking about technological change and labor market developments as determinants of unemployment risk distributions seems a promising step in the right direction. Today's advanced economies have gone through profound shifts in terms of output and employment in different sectors. Simply put, they started out as agricultural societies, developed dominant manufacturing sectors (industrialization), transitioned to service sector economies (deindustrialization), and are arguably heading toward knowledge-based economies. I find it plausible that risk exposure and risk inequality differ systematically at these different stages of economic development. To speculate, unemployment risk became only common enough to pose a social question during industrialization. Eventually, the employment shift from the primary to the secondary sector likely led to low unemployment risk inequality. In industrial societies, the fates of low- and high-skilled workers were connected to a certain degree, since they were complements in production (Wallerstein 1990), leading to the golden age of social solidarity (due to low risk inequality). While deindustrialization may have increased demand for social protection (Iversen 2001; Iversen and Cusack 2000) it probably also increased risk inequality, thereby eventually undermining social solidarity. The observable pattern of job polarization likely increased and continues to increase risk inequality (Rehm 2011a) and has the potential to bifurcate labor markets into high- and low-risk workers, with little mobility between them. According to my theoretical framework, those developments would seriously undermine support for generous social policies in the future (more on this point later).

A second topic my framework pays little attention to is the role of income: income and income inequality are mostly treated as control variables. There are good theoretical and empirical reasons to prioritize risk over income: theoretically, a focus on risk aligns the core explanatory variable with the core task of welfare states, which is the management and mitigation of risk. It also takes into consideration that most individuals are risk averse and seek security. Moreover, risk is domain-specific and therefore allows for a more nuanced analysis of individuals' economic insecurity. Empirically, the explanatory power of income with respect to social policy preferences and outcomes is often underwhelming. Income correlates with some social policy attitudes, but not with others. More importantly, the key macro-level prediction of income-based perspectives – that inequality and redistribution are positively correlated – has little support in the data. But this does not mean that income or the joint distribution of income and risk does not influence social policy making. In fact, the joint distribution of income and risk can play an important role in the politics of social solidarity (Rehm 2011a; Rehm, Hacker, and Schlesinger 2012).

A third topic that I have largely omitted is the role of institutions. Political outcomes are a function of preferences, institutions, and context – the present work prioritizes the first and the last. This does not deny the relevance of institutions: surely political institutions have an important role to play in the politics of social solidarity (a major theme in existing scholarship). For example, different political institutions aggregate preferences differently, and different wage bargaining systems influence labor markets differently (arguably including their level and possibly distribution of unemployment risk). And other government policies – such as active labor market policies, minimum wages, or labor market regulations more generally – potentially influence (risk and income) inequality, at least at the margin. But political institutions have been extensively studied and their impact on policy making is comparatively well understood and I have therefore focused on the much less studied and less understood roles of preferences and risk inequality.

A fourth and related simplification is my political model: the majority rules, either because the median voter is decisive, or because policy follows majority public opinion. This (somewhat functional) political model is quite common in the literature, but the aggregation of preferences into policies is clearly more complex. This topic, which has received considerable attention in the American politics literature (Erikson, MacKuen, and Stimson 2002), seems worth studying from a comparative perspective in the future.

Besides its parsimony and limitations, I believe that the risk perspective I have developed not only offers novel, empirically supported observable implications (as shown throughout the analysis) but also sheds new light on some well-established theories. My claim is not that these various theories are wrong, or that my reinterpretations – outlined later – are right. I have not tested any of them. But I believe that my risk pool framework provides a fresh perspective on these established theories. At least two types of arguments in the welfare state literature can be reinterpreted from a risk inequality perspective, at least in principle: heterogeneity theories and risk-level theories. I discuss these in turn.

Various prominent theories link *heterogeneity* to social policy outcomes. It has been argued that heterogeneity in traits such as race, ethnicity, or religion (Alesina and Glaeser 2004; Alesina, Glaeser, and Sacerdote 2001); heterogeneity due to immigration (Eger 2010);[1] hetero-geneity due to labor market status (Rueda 2007); or heterogeneity due to geography (Beramendi 2012; Carroll 1999, 20; Korpi 2008, 21) is asso-ciated with smaller welfare states. From my risk pool perspective, this is to be expected: heterogeneity within populations is almost always associated with higher risk inequality, either in reality or in perceptions, which lowers support for (and supply of) risk pooling. In populations that are divided into readily identifiable groups – defined by skin color, ethnicity, country of origin, region, and so on – it is often the case that risk is not randomly distributed across these groups, but concentrated in particular subpopulations, which are often minorities. Examples abound.

For instance, it is easy to single out low-skilled immigrants as high-risk types, which emphasizes or magnifies (actual or perceived) risk inequality. In such a scenario, the (non-immigrant) majority often wishes either to exclude immigrants from risk pooling, or to lower benefit generosity. (Sweden seems to be going through this experience at the moment.) A second example is the role of race in the American social policy dis-course, which exaggerates the degree to which African Americans benefit from social policy programs ("black welfare queen") and downplays the risks that high-risk whites face. As a consequence, the (white) majority is very sensitive to risk inequality, and quite possibly overestimates it, leading to comparatively lower support for, and provision of, social benefits. The dynamics in federal countries are another example. Federal countries typically have clearly identifiable disadvantaged regions (East Germany, the South in Italy, and so on). Once again, risk inequality is easily identified – and often magnified by particular parties – leading to anemic support for social policy, or demands to limit risk pooling.

The other type of argument in the welfare state literature that can be reexamined from a risk inequality perspective is about *risk levels*. Several influential theories link risk levels to social policy outcomes. First, it has been shown that small open economies have more generous social policies (Cameron 1978; Katzenstein 1985; Rodrik 1998). The details differ

---

[1] For a critical view on the topic, see Brady and Finnigan (2014).

among scholars, but the gist of existing explanations suggests that higher levels of risk exposure lead to more demand for, and hence supply of, social insurance mainly because workers demand compensation for the higher risks they face. According to my theoretical framework, however, higher levels of risk are not nearly as important as the inequality of the risk pool. The association between small open economies and large welfare states, therefore, may be the result of a more equal distribution of risk in small open economies (not their higher levels of risk exposure). It certainly seems plausible that small economies that are well integrated into world markets specialize in their comparative advantage, which should lead to concentration of industrial production and very similar risk profiles for workers in these countries. This situation also provides fertile ground for successful collective action (Cameron 1978). According to my risk perspective, what may be special about small open economies is not (only) that risk is common but (also) that it is commonly shared. And common fate enables solidarity.

Second, it has been argued that economic insecurity increased in the last few decades because of either globalization (Garrett 1998) or deindustrialization (Iversen and Cusack 2000). This, various scholars argue, has increased citizens' demands for government protection. But according to my theoretical framework, once again, levels are less relevant than distributions. In principle, it is conceivable that globalization and/or deindustrialization had a homogenizing effect on risk distributions, at least initially (as mentioned previously, it is likely that service sector and knowledge economies are or will eventually be characterized by higher levels of risk inequality, compared to industrialized economies).

The third argument that could be seen in a different light from a risk inequality perspective pertains to skill specificity at the individual level and vocational training intensity at the country level as drivers of generous welfare spending (Estevez-Abé, Iversen, and Soskice 2001; Iversen 2005; Iversen and Soskice 2001). Such a reinterpretation would explore whether countries with higher prevalence of specific skills also have more equal risk distributions, which would explain why they tend to have more generous social insurance systems. This interpretation has some plausibility, I believe, because vocational training targets lower-skilled workers and lifts them into better, safer jobs, thereby potentially decreasing risk inequality.

My account of social policy preferences and outcomes is quite upbeat: social policy is popular, solidarity is widespread, and deep crises give birth to social policy milestones. Unfortunately, I think that the future of the welfare state is bleaker than its past. Despite their remarkable resilience (Pierson 1994), I believe existing welfare state arrangements will come under intense pressure and their broad support will erode. Various developments will transform welfare state contestation from being a matter of degree ("more or less") to being a matter of kind ("whether or not"). In a nutshell, I believe that various developments – spelled out later – will put pressure on existing social policy arrangements from below and from above. At the bottom of the risk pool, an increasingly visible and sizable group of "permanent bad risks" (mainly low-skilled workers) with little upward mobility will emerge. At the other end of the risk distribution, it will be increasingly unattractive for the well-to-do to pool risks with the rest of society, making it increasingly difficult to maintain broad support for mandatory social insurance programs that are so typical of rich democracies. This would significantly and qualitatively alter the politics of social solidarity.

In this book, I have argued that social policy support is widespread if risk (and income/wealth) inequality is low, if risk is less easily predictable, and if income and risk are cross-cutting rather than reinforcing traits. Simply put, welfare states thrive behind a veil of ignorance, where (net benefit) winners and losers of social insurance programs are not easily identifiable ex ante (before a risk event, such as unemployment, occurs), and where they are not very far apart from each other. Several developments suggest that rich democracies are moving from conditions under which welfare states can thrive to those under which they will be under intense pressure, at least with respect to the domains of work and old age (but not necessarily health). In these domains, ongoing technological and social changes will likely increase risk inequality, increase the predictability of risk, increase income and wealth inequality, and increase the overlap between income and risk.

Perhaps the most important *labor market* development in advanced industrial societies is polarized job growth (Autor, Katz, and Kearney 2006; Goos and Manning 2007; Goos, Manning, and Salomons 2009; Oesch 2013; Rehm 2011a; E. O. Wright and Dwyer 2003), that is, the phenomenon that only high-skilled and low-skilled jobs grow (if any), while medium-skilled jobs disappear.[2] As a result, risk inequality, the predictability of risk, and the overlap of income and risk will increase over time. These developments squarely benefit high-skilled (low-risk)

---

[2] This trend is likely due to our increasing ability to replace "routine" tasks with computers or robots and it is worsened by our increasing ability to trade services, including low-skilled services (Wren 2013).

labor, while low-skilled (high-risk) labor will primarily suffer from them.[3] If the (skill) gap between the bottom and the top increases, it will be more difficult to climb up the social ladder. Most of the low-skilled jobs that are still growing have little room for productivity and hence wage increases (Baumwol's disease). The fates of low- and high-skilled labor will be increasingly different and divorced.[4] As a result of these developments, we can expect the emergence of a sizable and visible group of citizens who are "bad risks" with little prospect for improvement. If winners and losers are clearly identifiable ex ante, social insurance does not fare well. A sizable group of low-skilled workers with no attractive job opportunities and very little upward mobility would be very visible ("precariat"), and it would require hammock-style social policy (permanent social assistance), which is unpopular. This would put pressure on existing social policy programs from below.

Welfare states will also experience pressure from above, mainly due to increasing income and wealth inequalities that are related to developments in terms of *retirement arrangements*: the wider the gap between the rich and the poor is, the less attractive is it for the rich to be part of a mandatory risk pool, especially if they have sufficient resources to self-insure even significant bad events. There are many developments that are likely to increase income inequality. They include the trend of job polarization already mentioned, which directly increases income inequality and indirectly decreases social mobility. Increasing assortative mating (especially in combination with smaller families) reinforces that trend, especially since human capital investment in children from well-off families tends to be a lot more aggressive. Wealth inequality is also likely to increase, for various reasons. Piketty (2014) has argued that $r > g$ (meaning that return on capital is generally higher than economic growth, a trend that increases wealth inequality). Assortative mating and small families mean that wealth holding patterns are reinforced over time (larger bequests are concentrated on fewer offspring).

I believe that another trend stealthily contributes to wealth inequality: the privatization of social policy risks, a phenomenon that Jacob Hacker

---

[3] David Autor, a leading scholar on this topic, correctly points out that low-skilled labor benefits from automatization/routinization to a certain degree because low-skilled labor is not always substitutable but sometimes is a complement in production processes affected by these developments (Autor 2014).

[4] This contrasts with Fordist production schemes, in which low-skilled labor had hold-up power vis-à-vis high-skilled labor and could therefore negotiate wage increases (Wallerstein 1990).

has called "the great risk shift" (Hacker 2008). This shift is especially strong with respect to pensions. All rich democracies have public (or mandatory private) pension programs of sorts, often complemented by (voluntary or mandatory, industrywide or personal) alternative "pillars." Over the last three decades or so, pension reforms have generally been in the direction of less generous replacements rates and a shift from defined benefits (pay-as-you-go) to defined contribution (funded)[5] pension systems (Börsch 2009; OECD 2013, 2014; Perotti and Schwienbacher 2009). This quiet development, I believe, puts pressure on existing social policy programs from above and has the potential to undermine social solidarity seriously. The reason is simple: the more privatized pension risks are (i.e., the lower public pension replacement rates, and/or the higher the share of defined contributions), the more private savings are necessary to maintain a reasonably high standard of living in old age. In order to retire comfortably and safely, massive private wealth accumulation is necessary in privatized systems. With some exceptions (such as survivor pensions), public pension entitlements expire with the death of the recipient. In contrast, private savings are transferred to the next generation – in essence, the aggressive savings of one generation are equivalent to deferred consumption opportunities for the next generation. Put differently: if one wants to retire comfortably, one accidentally will make one's offspring rich in the process.[6] The inherited wealth may well be significant enough for the offspring to pay itself a private and fairly generous monthly stipend ("private basic income") to sustain a middle-class level of living, without participating in the labor market.

---

[5] Defined benefits and pay-as-you go systems, on the one hand, and defined contribution and funded systems are not the same, although they typically go hand in hand.

[6] Here is a back-of-the-envelope example. Let us say there are two working parents making a combined \$10,000 (10k) (net) per month, for about 30 years (totaling 10k\*12\*30=3,600,000). They want to retire at 5k (though most people would define "comfortable" at about 70 percent of their earnings, i.e., 7k), and they anticipate being in retirement for 30 years. Depending on a variety of uncertain parameters (return on investment, life expectancy, and so on), the parents will need to save up about 1–2 million, or about roughly half of their income. Typically, one would buy an annuity for about half of the savings and leave the other half as principal (so that is 500k -1 mio). The (typically) only child will inherit that principal (plus, in the preceding scenario, likely also a house), and this bequest is at best mildly taxed. If s/he decides to, the offspring can essentially decide not to participate in the labor market (depending on assumptions, s/he could pay herself about 3–4k/month, forever (largely tax-free, and certainly contribution free) – not bad, especially if you do not pay rent. All of this will only happen if private pension savings are not wiped out, as historically happened occasionally via stock market crashes, wars, inflation, nationalization, etc.

In this scenario, support for social insurance can be expected to erode because citizens who can rely on a private basic income could self-insure labor market, education, and pension risks, taking away most incentives to support risk pooling in these social policy domains (health insurance may be the exception here, since self-insurance requires enormous private resources – see later discussion).[7] Furthermore, the remaining citizens – the ones who cannot self-insure – are likely to be worse risks (lower education, lower income, etc.), making social insurance more expensive and less attractive. In this case, welfare states are heading toward a (social) insurance death spiral.

The inequality and predictability of risks may also change in the domain of *health*. At the moment, health risks are still relatively unpredictable and relatively randomly distributed - fertile ground for widespread support for risk pooling. But with advances in medical technology (such as genome-based prediction of diseases), this could change. In the not very distant future, it may well be possible to predict medical futures/histories, in which case people would know, ex ante, whether they are good or bad medical risks. In such a scenario, good health risks would have little incentives to pool with bad risks, especially since they would have attractive private insurance options (this scenario would be particularly bad if bad health risks and low income overlap).[8] What the (anticipated) increased predictability and inequality of health risk will mean for social solidarity is difficult to predict: much depends on whether health risks will highly correlate with socioeconomic characteristics or not. But it may well be easier to maintain social solidarity in the health domain, as opposed to the work or old age domain.

Ultimately, the developments described may well break future societies into three separate risk groups ("trialization"): permanent bad risks (those who have to participate in labor markets but without good jobs or prospects of upward mobility – call them low-skilled labor; the

---

[7] There are already examples of how the rich can opt out of risk pooling. In the United States, for example, "only" the first 117k is taxed with Social Security contributions (the so-called wage base) – clearly a way for the rich and wealthy to opt out of the old age risk pool; most funding problems of Social Security would be solved without that restricted wage base.

[8] Furthermore, it may well be that these types of advances also increase the predictability of longevity, with potential consequences for pension politics: being part of a mandatory public pension system is a lot more attractive for those with high longevity. If longevity and health risks were positively correlated (e.g., because medical risks increase in age), one could envision some logrolling between bad health risk with low longevity and good health risks with high longevity: I pool my health risks with you if you pool your longevity risk (pensions) with me.

working poor; the precariat; or permanent outsiders); medium to good risks (those who have to participate in labor markets with good job and mobility prospects – call them insiders or high-skilled labor); and those who can self-insure most risks because they have a choice to participate in labor markets or not (those with private basic incomes – call them voluntary labor market outsiders).

This scenario seems undesirable from a normative point of view, as it would in no sense resemble equality of opportunity or meritocracy. It would also put enormous pressure on existing social insurance arrangements. What, if anything, could be done to deal with this scenario? Most of the developments sketched are structural in nature – policy interventions may slow the speed of change, but they are unlikely to stop the trends. This is not to say that nothing can be done. In my opinion, a "basic income" (Parijs 1997) – an unconditional, reasonably generous, flat-rate benefit paid to all citizens – is a social policy tool that deserves serious consideration.

Replacing (most) social policy programs with an unconditional, reasonably generous, flat-rate "basic income" for all citizens is by no means an uncontested proposal (Fitzpatrick and Campling 1999), but the basic income idea has some attractive features that seem able to address some of the problems discussed here. Perhaps most importantly, it would level the playing field in terms of labor supply: participating in the labor market would become optional for everybody, not just those who can afford a private basic income. There would still be large inequalities in income and wealth, but a basic income would allow even citizens without resources and with lower skill levels to take risks that could pay off and make them upwardly mobile. A basic income, which is unconditional and paid to every citizen, would also offer a livelihood for the "permanent outsiders" identified earlier, without the stigma (and discourses of deservingness) typical of means-tested programs. The positive effects of a basic income would be reinforced if aggressive inheritance taxation would curb the increasing inequality in financial resources.

A basic income could replace many existing social policy programs, but we cannot do without a comprehensive health insurance system that pools the risks of all citizens. One of the attractions of the basic income is its simplicity: it replaces all other social policy efforts, therefore hugely decluttering welfare states and the bureaucracies they entail. One of its problems is that a basic income cannot really insure against health risks: disability and chronic or expensive diseases cannot be shouldered with an unconditional, flat-rate monthly stipend. Therefore, the basic income needs to be coupled with mandatory health insurance in which premiums are not linked to risks. Fortunately, health is a domain in which risk pooling could remain attractive for a vast majority of citizens, making it easier to sustain or build a broad coalition in support of mandatory health insurance systems. This would be particularly true if "pulling the veil of ignorance" regarding health risks were tightly regulated (no scaling of premiums based on DNA, etc.).

\* \* \*

The history of the welfare state is a remarkable success story. Within a relatively short period, all of today's rich democracies changed from being night-watchman states into being insurance states by setting up myriad social policy programs that cover all main risks, often from the cradle to the grave. The commonality of this development is as striking as are observable cross-national and time-varying differences when it comes to social policy: while all of today's rich democracies cover all main risks, the degree to which citizens are "in care of the state" varies quite dramatically over time and space.

According to my theoretical framework, this more or less outright triumph of social solidarity is not so much the result of citizens becoming more altruistic, or progressive bureaucrats becoming more decisive, or left parties becoming more influential, or vocational training systems becoming more prevalent, or to other factors nominated by main explanations of welfare state development (and preferences). Rather, I have argued that both the commonality of the experience and the differences across space and time can be explained with a focus on risk. At the micro-level, risk exposure shapes social policy preferences. At the macro-level, the distribution of risk within societies – risk inequality – shapes social policy popularity and generosity. According to my theoretical framework, we should expect widespread support for, and supply of, social policy when risk pooling is an attractive proposition for a large majority of citizens, that is, when risk inequality is low, especially when private insurance is not viable.

The attractiveness of mandatory risk pooling, and the viability of private insurance alternatives, vary across time and space. There are good reasons to believe that the conditions in the last 150 years or so enabled widespread social policy support. Because nothing is certain except death, I have quipped, there are taxes. However, the focus on risk also suggests that the various economic and societal developments discussed above are decreasing the attractiveness of social insurance and increasing the viability of private insurance alternatives for many citizens. As a result, welfare state politics is about to change radically.

# References

Abou-Chadi, Tarik, and Ellen Immergut. 2014. "Public Opinion, Political Institutions and Welfare State Change." *Paper prepared for Presentation at the 110th Annual Meeting of the American Political Science Association*, Washington, DC, August 28–31, 2014.

Agerbo, Esben, Steven Stack, and Liselotte Petersen. 2011. "Social Integration and Suicide: Denmark, 1906–2006." *Social Science Journal* 48(4): 630–40.

Alber, Jens. 1981. "Government Responses to the Challenge of Unemployment: The Development of Unemployment Insurance in Western Europe." In *The Development of Welfare States in Europe and America*, eds. Peter Flora and Arnold J. Heidenheimer. Herndon, VA: Transaction, 151–83.

  1982. *Vom Armenhaus Zum Wohlfahrtsstaat: Analysen Zur Entwicklung Der Sozialversicherung in Westeuropa*. Frankfurt a.M.: Campus.

  2010. "What the European and American Welfare States Have in Common and Where They Differ: Facts and Fiction in Comparisons of the European Social Model and the United States." *Journal of European Social Policy* 20(2): 102–25.

Alesina, Alberto, and Edward Glaeser. 2004. *Fighting Poverty in the US and Europe: A World of Difference*. Oxford: Oxford University Press.

Alesina, Alberto, and Eliana La Ferrara. 2005. "Preferences for Redistribution in the Land of Opportunities." *Journal of Public Economics* 89(5–6): 897–931.

Alesina, Alberto, and George-Marios Angeletos. 2005. "Fairness and Redistribution." *American Economic Review* 95(4): 960–80.

Alesina, Alberto, and Paola Giuliano. 2011. "Preferences for Redistribution." In *Handbook of Social Economics*, eds. Jess Benhabib, Alberto Bisin, and Matthew O. Jackson. Amsterdam: North-Holland, 93–131.

Alesina, Alberto, Edward Glaeser, and Bruce Sacerdote. 2001. "Why Doesn't the United States Have a European-Style Welfare State?" *Brookings Papers on Economic Activity* 2001(2): 187–254.

Allan, James, and Lyle Scruggs. 2004. "Political Partisanship and Welfare State Reform in Advanced Industrial Societies." *American Journal of Political Science* 48(3): 496–512.

Amenta, Edwin et al. 1987. "The Political Origins of Unemployment Insurance in Five American States." *Studies in American Political Development* 2(Spring): 137–82.

Amenta, Edwin, and Bruce G. Carruthers. 1988. "The Formative Years of U.S. Social Spending Policies: Theories of the Welfare State and the American States during the Great Depression." *American Sociological Review* 53(5): 661–78.

Anderson, Christopher J., and Jonas Pontusson. 2007. "Workers, Worries and Welfare States: Social Protection and Job Insecurity in 15 OECD Countries." *European Journal of Political Research* 46(2): 211–35.

Andersson, Walter. 1938. "The Swedish State Unemployment Insurance and the Reinsurance Problem of the Funds." *Scandinavian Actuarial Journal* 1938 (3–4): 157–207.

Ansell, Ben. 2014. *The Political Economy of Ownership: Housing Markets and the Welfare State. American Political Science Review* 108(2): 383–402.

Armingeon, Klaus, and Giuliano Bonoli. 2006. *The Politics of Post-Industrial Welfare States: Adapting Post-War Social Policies to New Social Risks.* London: Routledge.

Armingeon, Klaus, Panajotis Potolidis, Marlène Gerber, and Philipp Leimgruber. 2009. *Comparative Political Data Set 1960–2007.* Berne, Switzerland: Institute of Political Science, University of Berne.

Arts, Wil, and John Gelissen. 2001. "Welfare States, Solidarity and Justice Principles: Does the Type Really Matter?" *Acta Sociologica* 44(4): 283–99.

Asami, Yasuhito. 2010. "Unemployment Insurance in Thailand: Rationales for the Early Introduction in a Second-Tier Newly Industrializing Economy." In *Towards a More Resilient Society: Lessons from Economic Crises Report of the Social Resilience Project*, ed. Japan Institute of International Affairs. Tokyo: Japan National Committee for Pacific Economic Cooperation, 171–96.

2013. *Unemployment Insurance in Thailand: Rationales for the Early Introduction in a Second-Tier Newly Industrializing Economy.* Geneva: ILO.

Atkinson, Anthony B. 1990. "Income Maintenance for the Unemployed in Britain and the Response to High Unemployment." *Ethics* 100(3): 569–85.

Autor, David. 2014. *Polanyi's Paradox and the Shape of Employment Growth.* National Bureau of Economic Research. Working Paper 20485.

Autor, David, Lawrence F. Katz, and Melissa S. Kearney. 2006. *The Polarization of the US Labor Market.* National Bureau of Economic Research. Working Paper 11986.

Aven, Terje, and Ortwin Renn. 2010. *Risk Management and Governance: Concepts, Guidelines and Applications.* Berlin: Springer.

Aybars, Ayse Idil, and Dimitris Tsarouhas. 2010. "Straddling Two Continents: Social Policy and Welfare Politics in Turkey." *Social Policy & Administration* 44(6): 746–63.

Baicker, Katherine, Claudia Goldin, and Lawrence F. Katz. 1998. "A Distinctive System: Origins and Impact of U.S. Unemployment Compensation." In *The Defining Moment: The Great Depression and the American Economy in the Twentieth Century*, eds. Michael D. Bordo, Claudia Goldin, and Eugene White. Chicago: Chicago University Press, 227–64. www.nber.org/chapters/c6895.

Baldwin, Peter. 1990. *The Politics of Social Solidarity: Class Bases of the European Welfare State, 1875–1975*. Cambridge: Cambridge University Press.

Banks, Arthur S., and Kenneth A. Wilson. 2012. *Cross-National Time-Series Data Archive*. Jerusalem, Israel: Databanks International. www.databanksinternational.com.

Barber, Benjamin, Pablo Beramendi, and Erik Wibbels. 2013. "The Behavioral Foundations of Social Politics: Evidence from Surveys and a Laboratory Democracy." *Comparative Political Studies* 46(10): 1155–89.

Barr, Nicholas. 2001. *The Welfare State as Piggy Bank: Information, Risk, Uncertainty, and the Role of the State*. Oxford: Oxford University Press.

2004. *The Economics of the Welfare State*, 4th ed. Oxford: Oxford University Press.

Barro, Robert J., and José F. Ursúa. 2012. "Rare Macroeconomic Disasters." *Annual Review of Economics* 4(1): 83–109.

Baslevent, Cem, and Hasan Kirmanoglu. 2011. "Discerning Self-Interested Behaviour in Attitudes towards Welfare State Responsibilities across Europe." *International Journal of Social Welfare* 20(4): 344–52.

Beck, Nathaniel, and Jonathan N. Katz. 2011. "Modeling Dynamics in Time-Series–Cross-Section Political Economy Data." *Annual Review of Political Science* 14(1): 331–52.

Bénabou, Roland, and Efe A. Ok. 2001. "Social Mobility and the Demand for Redistribution: The POUM Hypothesis." *Quarterly Journal of Economics* 116(2): 447–87.

Bénabou, Roland, and Jean Tirole. 2006. "Belief in a Just World and Redistributive Politics." *Quarterly Journal of Economics* 121(2): 699–746.

Beramendi, Pablo. 2012. *The Political Geography of Inequality*. Cambridge: Cambridge University Press.

Beramendi, Pablo, and Philipp Rehm. 2016. "Who Gives, Who Gains? Redistribution and Preference Formation." *Comparative Political Studies*.

Bertaut, Jules. 1916. *Napoleon in His Own Words: From the French of Jules Bertaut*. Chicago: A. C. McClurg.

Betcherman, Gordon, and Rizwanul Islam. 2001a. "East Asian Labor Markets and the Economic Crisis: An Overview." In *East Asian Labor Markets and the Economic Crisis: Impacts, Responses and Lessons*, eds. Gordon Betcherman and Rizwanul Islam. Washington, DC: World Bank, 3–37.

2001b. *East Asian Labor Markets and the Economic Crisis: Impacts, Responses & Lessons*. Washington, DC: World Bank.

Black, Carmel. 1991. "The Origins of Unemployment Insurance in Queensland 1919–1922." *Labour History* 60(May): 34–50.

Block, Fred. 1977. "The Ruling Class Does Not Rule: Notes on the Marxist Theory of the State." *Socialist Revolution* 7(3): 6–28.

Boadway, Robin, and Andrew Oswald. 1983. "Unemployment Insurance and Redistributive Taxation." *Journal of Public Economics* 20(2): 193–210.

Boholm, Åsa. 1996. "Risk Perception and Social Anthropology: Critique of Cultural Theory." *Ethnos* 61(1–2): 64–84.

 1998. "Comparative Studies of Risk Perception: A Review of Twenty Years of Research." *Journal of Risk Research* 1(2): 135–63.

Boix, Carles. 1998. *Political Parties, Growth and Equality: Conservative and Social Democratic Economic Strategies in the World Economy.* Cambridge: Cambridge University Press.

Börsch, Alexander. 2009. "Many Roads to Rome: Varieties of Funded Pensions in Europe and Asia." *Pensions: An International Journal* 14(3): 172–80.

Brady, David, and Ryan Finnigan. 2014. "Does Immigration Undermine Public Support for Social Policy?" *American Sociological Review* 79(1): 17–42.

Brambor, Thomas, and Johannes Lindvall. 2013. *Democratic Breakdowns in Economic Crises: The Role of Political Ideology.* Lund, Sweden: Lund University, Department of Political Science.

Brambor, Thomas, Johannes Lindvall, and Annika Stjernquist. 2013. *The Ideology of Heads of Government, 1870–2012 (Version 1.0).* Lund, Sweden: Lund University, Department of Political Science.

Brandeis, Elizabeth. 1935. "Labor Legislation." In *History of Labor in the United States, 1896–1932,* ed. John R. Commons. New York: Macmillan.

Brenner, M. Harvey. 1987. "Economic Instability, Unemployment Rates, Behavioral Risks, and Mortality Rates in Scotland, 1952–1983." *International Journal of Health Services* 17(3): 475–87.

Briggs, Asa. 1961. "The Welfare State in Historical Perspective." *European Journal of Sociology* 2(02): 221–58.

Brooks, Clem, and Jeff Manza. 2006a. "Social Policy Responsiveness in Developed Democracies." *American Sociological Review* 71(3): 474–94.

 2006b. "Why Do Welfare States Persist?" *Journal of Politics* 68(4): 816–27.

 2007. *Why Welfare States Persist: The Importance of Public Opinion in Democracies.* Chicago: University of Chicago Press.

Brooks, Sarah M. 2009. *Social Protection and the Market in Latin America: The Transformation of Social Security Institutions.* Cambridge: Cambridge University Press.

Brown, Andrew, and Kevin Hewison. 2005. "'Economics Is the Deciding Factor': Labour Politics in Thaksin's Thailand." *Pacific Affairs* 78(3): 353–75.

Buchanan, James M. 1983. "Social Security Survival: A Public-Choice Perspective." *Cato Journal* 3(2): 339–53.

Bundesanstalt für Arbeit. 1996. *Amtliche Nachrichten der Bundesanstalt für Arbeit, Arbeitsstatistik 1996.* Nürnberg: Bundesanstalt für Arbeit.

Bundesministerium für Arbeit und Soziales. 2011. *Statistisches Taschenbuch 2011.* Bonn: Bundesministerium für Arbeit und Soziales.

Bundesverband deutscher Banken. 2002. "Inter/esse. Informationen, Daten, Hintergründe." 11: 1–8.

 2004a. "Inter/esse. Informationen, Daten, Hintergründe." 8: 1–8.

2004b. "Inter/esse. Informationen, Daten, Hintergründe." 11: 1–8.

2005. "Inter/esse. Informationen, Daten, Hintergründe." 11: 1–8.

Burstein, Paul. 1998. "Bringing the Public Back In: Should Sociologists Consider the Impact of Public Opinion on Public Policy?" *Social Forces* 77(1): 27–62.

2003. "The Impact of Public Opinion on Public Policy: A Review and an Agenda." *Political Research Quarterly* 56(1): 29–40.

Cameron, David R. 1978. "The Expansion of the Public Economy: A Comparative Analysis." *American Political Science Review* 72(4): 1243–61.

Campell, Duncan. 2001. "Social Dialogue and Labor Market Adjustment in East Asia after the Crisis." In *East Asian Labor Markets and the Economic Crisis: Impacts, Responses and Lessons*, eds. Gordon Betcherman and Rizwanul Islam. Washington, DC: World Bank, 423–66.

Card, David. 2011. "Origins of the Unemployment Rate: The Lasting Legacy of Measurement without Theory." *American Economic Review* 101(3): 552–57.

Carroll, Eero. 1999. "Emergence and Structuring of Social Insurance Institutions: Comparative Studies on Social Policy and Unemployment Insurance." Dissertation (*Swedish Institute for Social Research*).

Carter, John, Michel Bédard, and Céline Peyron Bista. 2013. *Comparative Review of Unemployment and Employment Insurance Experiences in Asia and Worldwide*. Geneva: ILO.

Carter, Susan B. 2006. *Historical Statistics of the United States: Earliest Times to the Present*. Cambridge: Cambridge University Press.

Casey, Bernard H. 2004. "The OECD Jobs Strategy and the European Employment Strategy: Two Views of the Labour Market and the Welfare State." *European Journal of Industrial Relations* 10(3): 329–52.

Castles, Francis G. 1982. *The Impact of Parties: Politics and Policies in Democratic Capitalist States*. Beverly Hills, CA: Sage.

2010. "Black Swans and Elephants on the Move: The Impact of Emergencies on the Welfare State." *Journal of European Social Policy* 20(2): 91–101.

Cavan, Ruth Shonle. 1928. *Suicide*. Chicago: University of Chicago Press.

Cebulla, Andreas. 2004. "Risk Events and Learning from Error: When Are Assessments of the Risk of Unemployment Revised?" *Risk, Decision, and Policy* 9(4): 297–336.

Chandoevwit, Worawan. 2012. "A Review of Unemployment Insurance in Thailand after Nine Years of Implementation." *TDRI Quarterly Review* 27(4): 3–12.

Chang, Shu-Sen et al. 2009. "Was the Economic Crisis 1997–1998 Responsible for Rising Suicide Rates in East/Southeast Asia? A Time-Trend Analysis for Japan, Hong Kong, South Korea, Taiwan, Singapore and Thailand." *Social Science & Medicine* 68(7): 1322–31.

Chen, Fen-ling. 2005. "Unemployment and Policy Responses in Taiwan: Gender and Family Implications." In *Transforming the Developmental Welfare State in East Asia*, ed. Huck-ju Kwon. London: Palgrave Macmillan, 170–90.

Chesnais, Jean-Claude. 1976. *Les Morts violentes en France depuis 1826: Comparaisons internationales*. Paris: INED.

Chong, Dennis, Jack Citrin, and Patricia Conley. 2001. "When Self-Interest Matters." *Political Psychology* 22(3): 541–70.

Citrin, Jack, and Donald P. Green. 1990. "The Self-Interest Motive in American Public Opinion." *Research in Micropolitics* 3(1): 1–28.

Clasen, Jochen. 2000. "Motives, Means and Opportunities: Reforming Unemployment Compensation in the 1990s." *West European Politics* 23(2): 89–112.

2007. *Reforming European Welfare States: Germany and the United Kingdom Compared*. Oxford: Oxford University Press.

Clasen, Jochen, and Daniel Clegg. 2011. *Regulating the Risk of Unemployment: National Adaptations to Post-Industrial Labour Markets in Europe*. Oxford: Oxford University Press.

Collier, David, and Richard E. Messick. 1975. "Prerequisites versus Diffusion: Testing Alternative Explanations of Social Security Adoption." *American Political Science Review* 69(4): 1299–1315.

Cook, Sarah, and Huck-ju Kwon. 2007. "Social Protection in East Asia." *Global Social Policy* 7(2): 223–29.

Corneo, Giacomo, and Hans Peter Gruner. 2000. "Social Limits to Redistribution." *American Economic Review* 90(5): 1491–1507.

Coughlin, Richard M. 1980. *Ideology, Public Opinion and Welfare Policy: Attitudes toward Taxes and Spending in the Industrialized Societies*. Berkeley: University of California Press.

1990. "The Economic Person in Sociological Context: Case Studies in the Mediation of Self-Interest." *Journal of Behavioral Economics* 19(2): 181–207.

Cousins, Mel. 2005. *European Welfare States: Comparative Perspectives*. Beverly Hills, CA: Sage.

Cusack, Thomas, Torben Iversen, and Philipp Rehm. 2006. "Risks at Work: The Demand and Supply Sides of Government Redistribution." *Oxford Review Economic Policy* 22(3): 365–89.

Cutler, David, and Ellen Meara. 2001. *Changes in the Age Distribution of Mortality over the 20th Century*. National Bureau of Economic Research. Working Paper 8556.

Cutler, David, and Richard Johnson. 2004. "The Birth and Growth of the Social Insurance State: Explaining Old Age and Medical Insurance across Countries." *Public Choice* 120(1–2): 87–121.

David, Paul T., and William Claggett. 1998. *Party Strength in the United States: 1872–1996* [Computer File]. University of Virginia and Florida State University, ICPSR, 06895-v1.

Davidsson, Johan Bo, and Paul Marx. 2013. "Losing the Issue, Losing the Vote: Issue Competition and the Reform of Unemployment Insurance in Germany and Sweden." *Political Studies* 61(3): 505–22.

De Boef, Suzanna, and Luke Keele. 2008. "Taking Time Seriously." *American Journal of Political Science* 52(1): 184–200.

De Witte, Hans. 1999. "Job Insecurity and Psychological Well-Being: Review of the Literature and Exploration of Some Unresolved Issues." *European Journal of Work and Organizational Psychology* 8(2): 155–77.

2005. "Job Insecurity: Review of the International Literature on Definitions, Prevalence, Antecedents and Consequences." *SA Journal of Industrial Psychology* 31(4): 1–6.

Deutsche Bundestag. 2006. "Antwort Der Parlamentarischen Staatssekretärin Dr. Barbara Hendricks Vom 28. März 2006." *Drucksache* 16(1111): 7.

Dickerson, Andy, and Francis Green. 2012. "Fears and Realisations of Employment Insecurity." *Labour Economics* 19(2): 198–210.

Dingeldey, Irene. 2011. "Germany: Moving towards Integration whilst Maintaining Segmentation." In *Regulating the Risk of Unemployment: National Adaptations to Post-Industrial Labour Markets in Europe*, eds. Jochen Clasen and Daniel Clegg. Oxford: Oxford University Press, 55–74.

Di Tella, Rafael, and Robert J. MacCulloch. 2002. "The Determination of Unemployment Benefits." *Journal of Labor Economics* 20(2): 404–434.

Domhoff, G. William, and Michael Webber. 2011. *Class and Power in the New Deal: Corporate Moderates, Southern Democrats, and the Liberal-Labor Coalition.* Stanford, CA: Stanford University Press.

Douglas, Mary, and Aaron Wildavsky. 1982. *Risk and Culture: An Essay on the Selection of Technical and Environmental Dangers.* Berkeley: University of California Press.

Dryzek, John, and Robert E. Goodin. 1986. "Risk-Sharing and Social Justice: The Motivational Foundations of the Post-War Welfare State." *British Journal of Political Science* 16(1): 1–34.

Duell, Nicola, and Tim Vetter. 2012. *EEO Review: Long-Term Unemployment, 2012: Germany.* Luxembourg: European Employment Observatory.

Durkheim, Emile. 2006 [1897]. *On Suicide.* Harmondsworth, UK: Penguin.

Dyson, Kenneth. 2005. "Binding Hands as a Strategy for Economic Reform: Government by Commission." *German Politics* 14(2): 224–47.

Eger, Maureen A. 2010. "Even in Sweden: The Effect of Immigration on Support for Welfare State Spending." *European Sociological Review* 26(2): 203–17.

Engels, Dietrich. 2001. "Abstand zwischen Sozialhilfe und anderem Arbeitseinkommen: Neue Ergebnisse zu einer alten Kontroverse." *Sozialer Fortschritt* 50(3): 56–62.

Erikson, Robert, and Laura Stoker. 2011. "Caught in the Draft: The Effects of Vietnam Draft Lottery Status on Political Attitudes." *American Political Science Review* 105(2): 221–37.

Erikson, Robert, Michael B. MacKuen, and James A. Stimson. 2002. *The Macro Polity.* Cambridge: Cambridge University Press.

Esping-Andersen, Gosta. 1985. *Politics against Markets: The Social Democratic Road to Power.* Princeton, NJ: Princeton University Press.

———. 1990. *The Three Worlds of Welfare Capitalism.* Princeton, NJ: Princeton University Press.

Estevez-Abé, Margarita, Torben Iversen, and David Soskice. 2001. "Social Protection and the Formation of Skills: A Reinterpretation of the Welfare State." In *Varieties of Capitalism: The Institutional Foundations of Comparative Advantage*, eds. Peter A. Hall and David Soskice. Oxford: Oxford University Press, 145–83.

Ewald, François. 1991. "Insurance and Risk." In *The Foucault Effect: Studies in Governmentality*, eds. Graham Burchell, Colin Gordon, and Peter Miller. Chicago: University of Chicago Press, 197–210.

———. 1993. *Der Vorsorgestaat [L'état providence].* Frankfurt a.M.: Suhrkamp Verlag.

Falret, Jean-Pierre. 1822. *De l'hypochondrie et du suicide considérations sur les causes, sur le siége et le traitement de ces maladies, sur les moyens d'en arrêter les progrès et d'en prévenir le développement.* Paris: Croullebois.

Farber, Maurice L. 1965. "Suicide and the Welfare State." *Mental Hygiene* 49(3): 371–73.

Felber, Werner, and Peter Winiecki. 2008. *Suizid-Statistik - Aktuelle Ausgewählte Statistisch-Epidemiologische Daten zu Deutschland und Osteuropa mit Kommentaren.* Dresden: TU Dresden. www.suizidprophylaxe.de.

Finkel, Steven E. 1995. *Causal Analysis with Panel Data.* Beverly Hills, CA: Sage.

Fitzpatrick, Tony, and Jo Campling. 1999. *Freedom and Security: An Introduction to the Basic Income Debate.* London: Palgrave Macmillan.

Flavin, Patrick. 2012. "Income Inequality and Policy Representation in the American States." *American Politics Research* 40(1): 29–59.

Fleckenstein, Timo. 2008. "Restructuring Welfare for the Unemployed: The Hartz Legislation in Germany." *Journal of European Social Policy* 18(2): 177–88.

Flora, Peter, and Arnold J. Heidenheimer. 1981. "The Historical Core and Changing Boundaries of the Welfare State." In *The Development of Welfare States in Europe and America*, eds. Peter Flora and Arnold J. Heidenheimer. Herndon, VA: Transaction, 17–34.

Flora, Peter, and Jens Alber. 1981. "Modernization, Democratization, and the Development of Welfare States in Western Europe." In *The Development of Welfare States in Europe and America*, eds. Peter Flora and Arnold J. Heidenheimer. Herndon, VA: Transaction, 37–80.

Fong, Christina. 2001. "Social Preferences, Self-Interest, and the Demand for Redistribution." *Journal of Public Economics* 82(2): 225–46.

Forschungsgruppe Wahlen. 2006. *Blitzumfrage Zuer Bundestagswahl 2005 (ZA4397).* Köln: GESIS Datenarchiv.

2012. *Partial Cumulation of Politbarometers West 1977–2007 (ZA2391).* Mannheim: GESIS Data Archive, Cologne. Data file Version 2.0.0, doi:10.4232/1.11369.

Friedman, Milton. 1962. *Capitalism and Freedom.* Chicago: University of Chicago Press.

Gallup. 2013. *State of the American Workplace 2010–2012.* www.gallup.com/services/178514/state-american-workplace.aspx.

Garrett, Geoffrey. 1998. *Partisan Politics in the Global Economy.* Cambridge: Cambridge University Press.

Garside, William R. 2002. *British Unemployment 1919–1939: A Study in Public Policy.* Cambridge: Cambridge University Press.

Gelissen, John. 2002. *Worlds of Welfare, Worlds of Consent?: Public Opinion on the Welfare State.* Leiden, Netherlands: Brill.

Gerlach, Stefan, Srichander Ramaswamy, and Michela Scatigna. 2006. "150 Years of Financial Market Volatility." *BIS Quarterly Review* (September): 77–91.

GESIS - Leibniz-Institut für Sozialwissenschaften. 2012. *Allgemeine Bevölkerungsumfrage Der Sozialwissenschaften ALLBUS - Kumulation 1980–2010*

*(ZA4574 Datenfile Version 1.0.1).* Köln: GESIS Datenarchiv. doi:10.4232/ 1.11486.

Gilens, Martin. 2005. "Inequality and Democratic Responsiveness." *Public Opinion Quarterly* 69(5): 778–96.

2009. "Preference Gaps and Inequality in Representation." *PS: Political Science & Politics* 42(2): 335–41.

Gingrich, Jane R., and Ben Ansell. 2012. "Preferences in Context: Micro Preferences, Macro-Contexts and the Demand for Social Policy." *Comparative Political Studies* 45(12): 1624–54.

Giuliano, Paola, and Antonio Spilimbergo. 2009. *Growing Up in a Recession: Beliefs and the Macroeconomy.* National Bureau of Economic Research. Working Paper 15321.

Goodin, Robert E. 1988. *Reasons for Welfare: The Political Theory of the Welfare State.* Princeton, NJ: Princeton University Press.

1990. "Stabilizing Expectations: The Role of Earnings-Related Benefits in Social Welfare Policy." *Ethics* 100(3): 530–53.

Goodin, Robert E., and John Dryzek. 1987. "Risk-Sharing and Social Justice: The Motivational Foundations of the Post-War Welfare State." In *Not Only the Poor*, eds. Robert E. Goodin and Julian Le Grand. London: Allen & Unwin, 37–73.

Goos, Maarten, and Alan Manning. 2007. "Lousy and Lovely Jobs: The Rising Polarization of Work in Britain." *Review of Economics and Statistics* 89(1): 118–33.

Goos, Maarten, Alan Manning, and Anna Salomons. 2009. "Job Polarization in Europe." *American Economic Review Papers and Proceedings* 99(2): 58–63.

Gourevitch, Peter Alexis. 1986. *Politics in Hard Times: Comparative Responses to International Economic Crises.* Ithaca, NY: Cornell University Press.

Graham, John David, and Jonathan Baert Wiener. 1997. *Risk versus Risk: Trade-offs in Protecting Health and the Environment.* Cambridge, MA: Harvard University Press.

Hacker, Jacob S. 2004. "Privatizing Risk without Privatizing the Welfare State: The Hidden Politics of Social Policy Retrenchment in the United States." *American Political Science Review* 98(2): 243–60.

2008. *The Great Risk Shift: The New Economic Insecurity and the Decline of the American Dream.* 2nd ed. Oxford: Oxford University Press.

Hacker, Jacob S., Philipp Rehm, and Mark Schlesinger. 2010. *Standing on Shaky Ground: Americans' Experiences with Economic Insecurity.* www.economic securityindex.org.

2013. "The Insecure American: Economic Experiences and Policy Attitudes amid the Great Recession." *Perspectives on Politics* 11(1): 23–49.

Haggard, Stephan, and Robert R. Kaufman. 2008. *Development, Democracy, and Welfare States: Latin America, East Asia, and Eastern Europe.* Princeton, NJ: Princeton University Press.

Halbwachs, Maurice. 1978. *The Causes of Suicide.* London: Routledge & Kegan Paul.

Hamermesh, Daniel S. 1989. "Why Do Individual-Effect Models Performs so Poorly?" *Southern Economic Journal* 56(1): 39–45.

2004. "Subjective Outcomes in Economics." *Southern Economic Journal* 71(1): 2–11.

Hänlein, Andreas. 2001. "Neue Arbeitslosenversicherung in der Türkei oder: Experimentelle Gesetzgebung als Aufgabe für die Praxis." *Recht der internationalen Wirtschaft* 47(4): 284–87.

Hanna, Hugh S. 1931. *Unemployment-Benefit Plans in the United States and Unemployment Insurance in Foreign Countries*. Washington, DC: U.S. Government Printing Office.

Hassel, Anke. 2010. "Twenty Years after German Unification: The Restructuring of the German Welfare and Employment Regime." *German Politics & Society* 28(2): 102–15.

Hayes, John, and Peter Nutman. 1981. *Understanding the Unemployed: The Psychological Effects of Unemployment*. London: Tavistock.

Heclo, Hugh. 1974. *Modern Social Policies in Britain and Sweden*. New Haven, CT: Yale University Press.

Hegelich, Simon. 2011. *Agenda 2010: Strategien, Entscheidungen, Konsequenzen*. Wiesbaden: VS Verlag für Sozialwissenschaften.

Hellwig, Timothy T. 2005. "The Origins of Unemployment Insurance in Britain: A Cross-Class Alliance Approach." *Social Science History* 29(1): 107–36.

Hicks, Alexander. 1999. *Social Democracy and Welfare Capitalism*. Ithaca, NY: Cornell University Press.

Hicks, Alexander, Joya Misra, and Tang Nah Ng. 1995. "The Programmatic Emergence of the Social Security State." *American Sociological Review* 60(3): 329–49.

Higgs, Robert. 1987. *Crisis and Leviathan: Critical Episodes in the Growth of American Government*. Oxford: Oxford University Press.

2009. *The Political Economy of Crisis Opportunism*. Mercatus Policy Series.

Hinrichs, Karl. 2010. "A Social Insurance State Withers Away: Welfare State Reforms in Germany – Or: Attempts to Turn Around in a Cul-de-Sac." In *A Long Goodbye to Bismarck?: The Politics of Welfare Reform in Continental Europe*, ed. Bruno Palier. Amsterdam: Amsterdam University Press, 45–72.

Horwitz, Allan V. 1984. "The Economy and Social Pathology." *Annual Review of Sociology* 10(1): 95–119.

Howell, David R., and Miriam Rehm. 2009. "Unemployment Compensation and High European Unemployment: A Reassessment with New Benefit Indicators." *Oxford Review of Economic Policy* 25(1): 60–93.

Huber, Evelyn, and John D. Stephens. 2001. *Development and Crisis of the Welfare State: Parties and Policies in Global Markets*. Chicago: University of Chicago Press.

Hudson, John, and Philip Jones. 1994. "Testing for Self-Interest: 'The Economic Person in Sociological Context' Revisited." *Journal of Socio-Economics* 23(1–2): 101–12.

Hwang, Deok Soon. 2013a. "Unemployment Benefits in Korea." In *Unemployment Insurance in Asia*, ed. Deok Soon Hwang. Seoul: Korea Labor Institute, 7–48.

2013b. *Unemployment Insurance in Asia*. Seoul: Korea Labor Institute.

Ince, Godfrey Herbert. 1937. *Report on Unemployment Insurance in Australia.* Canberra: L. F. Johnston, Commonwealth Government Printer.

Ineichen, Alexander M. 2000. "Twentieth Century Volatility." *Journal of Portfolio Management* 27(1): 93–101.

International Labour Office. 2010. *World Social Security Report 2010/11. Providing Coverage in Times of Crisis and Beyond.* Geneva: ILO.

ISSP Research Group. 2005. *International Social Survey Programme (ISSP): Work Orientation III.* Distributor: GESIS Cologne Germany ZA4350, Data Version 2.0.0 doi:10.4232/1.11648.

———. 2006. *International Social Survey Programme (ISSP): Role of Government IV.* Distributor: GESIS Cologne Germany ZA4700, Data Version 1.0.

Iversen, Torben. 2001. "The Dynamics of Welfare State Expansion: Trade Openness, Deindustrialization and Partisan Politics." In *The New Politics of the Welfare State*, ed. Paul Pierson. Oxford: Oxford University Press, 45–79.

———. 2005. *Capitalism, Democracy, and Welfare.* Cambridge: Cambridge University Press.

Iversen, Torben, and David Soskice. 2001. "An Asset Theory of Social Policy Preferences." *American Political Science Review* 95(4): 875–95.

Iversen, Torben, and Thomas Cusack. 2000. "The Causes of Welfare State Expansion. Deindustrialization or Globalization?" *World Politics* 52(April): 313–49.

Jacobi, Lena, and Jochen Kluve. 2006. "Before and after the Hartz Reforms: The Performance of Active Labour Market Policy in Germany." *IZA Discussion Paper* 2100.

Jirakiattikul, Sopin. 2013. "Unemployment Insurance in Thailand." In *Unemployment Insurance in Asia*, ed. Deok Soon Hwang. Seoul: Korea Labor Institute, 137–74.

Jung, Matthias, and Dieter Roth. 1998. "Wer zu späht geht, den bestraft der Wähler: Eine Analyse der Bundestagswahl 1998." *Aus Politik und Zeitgeschichte* 52: 3–19.

———. 2002. "Ablösung Der Regierung vertagt: Eine Analyse der Bundestagswahl." *Aus Politik und Zeitgeschichte* 49–50: 3–17.

Kamimura, Yasuhiro. 2010. "Employment Structure and Unemployment Insurance in East Asia: Establishing Social Protection for Inclusive and Sustainable Growth." In *Towards a More Resilient Society: Lessons from Economic Crises Report of the Social Resilience Project*, ed. Japan Institute of International Affairs. Tokyo: Japan National Committee for Pacific Economic Cooperation, 153–70.

Kang, Soon-Hie, Jaeho Keum, Dong-Heon Kim, and Donggyun Shin. 2001. "Korea: Labor Market Outcomes and Policy Responses after the Crisis." In *East Asian Labor Markets and the Economic Crisis: Impacts, Responses and Lessons*, eds. Gordon Betcherman and Rizwanul Islam. Washington, DC: World Bank, 97–140.

Kangas, Olli E. 1997. "Self-Interest and the Common Good: The Impact of Norms, Selfishness and Context on Social Policy Opinions." *Journal of Socio-Economics* 26(5): 475–94.

2003. "The Grasshopper and the Ants: Popular Opinions of Just Distribution in Australia and Finland." *Journal of Socio-Economics* 31(6): 721–43.

2012. "Testing Old Theories in New Surroundings: The Timing of First Social Security Laws in Africa." *International Social Security Review* 65(1): 73–97.

Katzenstein, Peter J. 1985. *Small States in World Markets. Industrial Policy in Europe.* Ithaca, NY: Cornell University Press.

Keele, Luke, and Nathan J. Kelly. 2006. "Dynamic Models for Dynamic Theories: The Ins and Outs of Lagged Dependent Variables." *Political Analysis* 14(2): 186–205.

Kemmerling, Achim. 2009. *Taxing the Working Poor: The Political Origins and Economic Consequences of Taxing Low Wages.* Cheltenham, UK: Edward Elgar.

Kemmerling, Achim, and Oliver Bruttel. 2006. "'New Politics' in German Labour Market Policy? The Implications of the Recent Hartz Reforms for the German Welfare State." *West European Politics* 29(1): 90–112.

Kenworthy, Lane. 2009. "The Effect of Public Opinion on Social Policy Generosity." *Socio-Economic Review* 7(4): 727–40.

Kenworthy, Lane, and Leslie McCall. 2008. "Inequality, Public Opinion and Redistribution." *Socio-Economic Review* 6(1): 35–68.

Kenworthy, Lane, and Lindsay A. Owens. 2011. "The Surprisingly Weak Effects of Recessions on Public Opinion." In *The Great Recession*, eds. David B. Grusky, Bruce Western, and Christopher Wimer. New York: Russell Sage Foundation, 196–219.

Kim, Kyo-seong. 2001. "Determinants of the Timing of Social Insurance Legislation among 18 OECD Countries." *International Journal of Social Welfare* 10 (1): 2–13.

Kim, Myoung-Jung. 2010. "Employment Insurance System in Korea and Recent Revision." In *Towards a More Resilient Society: Lessons from Economic Crises Report of the Social Resilience Project,* ed. Japan Institute of International Affairs. Tokyo: Japan National Committee for Pacific Economic Cooperation, 245–82.

Kim, Wonik. 2007. "Social Insurance Expansion and Political Regime Dynamics in Europe, 1880–1945." *Social Science Quarterly* 88(2): 494–514.

2010. "Unemployment Risks and the Origins of Unemployment Compensation." *Studies in Comparative International Development (SCID)* 45(1): 57–82.

King, Desmond. 1995. *Actively Seeking Work? The Politics of Unemployment and Welfare Policy in the United States and Great Britain.* Chicago: University of Chicago Press.

King, Miriam et al. 2009. *Integrated Public Use Microdata Series, Current Population Survey: Version 2.0. [Machine-Readable Database].* Minneapolis: Minnesota Population Center [producer and distributor].

Kingdon, John W. 1997. *Agendas, Alternatives, and Public Policies,* 2nd ed. New York: Pearson Education.

Kitschelt, Herbert. 2001. "Partisan Competition and Welfare State Retrenchment. When Do Politicians Choose Unpopular Policies?" In *The New Politics of the Welfare State*, ed. Paul Pierson. Oxford: Oxford University Press, 265–302.

Kitschelt, Herbert, and Philipp Rehm. 2014. "Occupations as a Site of Political Preference Formation." *Comparative Political Studies* 47(2): 1670–1706.

Kitschelt, Herbert, and Wolfgang Streeck. 2003. "From Stability to Stagnation: Germany at the Beginning of the Twenty-First Century." *West European Politics* 26(4): 1–34.

Klausen, Jytte. 1997. "From the Warfare State to the Welfare State: Postwar Reconstruction and National Incorporation." In *European Integration in Social and Historical Perspective: 1850 to the Present*, eds. Jytte Klausen and Louise Tilly. Lanham, MD: Rowman & Littlefield, 147–70.

1998. *War and Welfare: Europe and the United States, 1945 to the Present*. London: Palgrave Macmillan.

Knight, Frank H. 1921. *Risk, Uncertainty and Profit*. New York: Hart, Schaffner and Marx.

Knuth, Daniela, Doris Kehl, Lynn Hulse, and Silke Schmidt. 2014. "Risk Perception, Experience, and Objective Risk: A Cross-National Study with European Emergency Survivors." *Risk Analysis*: 34(7): 1286–98.

Korpi, Walter. 1983. *The Democratic Class Struggle*. London: Routledge.

2004. "Changing Class Structures and the Origins of Welfare States: The Breakthrough of Social Insurance 1860–1940." Manuscript.

2008. "Origins of Welfare States: Changing Class Structures, Social Democracy, and Christian Democracy." Manuscript.

Korpi, Walter, and Joakim Palme. 1998. "The Paradox of Redistribution and Strategies of Equality: Welfare State Institutions, Inequality, and Poverty in the Western Countries." *American Sociological Review* 63(5): 661–87.

2003. "New Politics and Class Politics in the Context of Austerity and Globalization: Welfare State Regress in 18 Countries, 1975–95." *American Political Science Review* 97(3): 425–46.

2007. *The Social Citizenship Indicator Program (SCIP)*. Stockholm: Swedish Institute for Social Research, Stockholm University.

Krose, Hermann Anton. 1906. *Der Selbstmord im 19. Jahrhundert nach seiner Verteilung auf Staaten und Verwaltungsbezirk: mit einer Karte*. Freiburg: Herder.

Krug, Etienne G. et al. 1998. "Suicide after Natural Disasters." *New England Journal of Medicine* 338(6): 373–78.

Ku, Yeun-wn, and Yu-fang Chang. 2013. "Unemployment Insurance in Taiwan." In *Unemployment Insurance in Asia*, ed. Deok Soon Hwang. Seoul: Korea Labor Institute, 89–136.

Kuipers, Sanneke. 2006. *The Crisis Imperative: Crisis Rhetoric and Welfare State Reform in Belgium and the Netherlands in the Early 1990s*. Amsterdam: Amsterdam University Press.

Kwan, Chau Pak. 2000. *Unemployment-Related Benefit Systems in South Korea*. Research and Libary Services Division, Legislative Council Secretariat. www.legco.gov.hk/yr99-00/english/sec/library/e21.pdf.

Kwon, Huck-ju, ed. 2005. *Transforming the Developmental Welfare State in East Asia*. London: Palgrave Macmillan.

2009. "The Reform of the Developmental Welfare State in East Asia." *International Journal of Social Welfare* 18(1): S12–21.

Lan, Ke-Jeng, and Wen-Chi Chou. 2010. "Employment Insurance and Active Labor Market Policies in Chinese Taipei." In *Towards a More Resilient Society: Lessons from Economic Crises Report of the Social Resilience Project*, ed. Japan Institute of International Affairs. Tokyo: Japan National Committee for Pacific Economic Cooperation, 197–244.

Lau, Richard R, and Caroline Heldman. 2009. "Self-Interest, Symbolic Attitudes, and Support for Public Policy: A Multilevel Analysis." *Political Psychology* 30(4): 513–37.

Lee, Eddy. 1998. *The Asian Financial Crisis: The Challenge for Social Policy*. Geneva: International Labour Organization.

Lee, H. K. 1999. "Globalization and the Emerging Welfare State — the Experience of South Korea." *International Journal of Social Welfare* 8(1): 23–37.

Lee, Vicky. 2000a. *Unemployment Insurance and Assistance Systems in Taiwan*. Research and Libary Services Division, Legislative Council Secretariat. www.legco.gov.hk/yr99-oo/english/sec/library/e20.pdf.

2000b. *Unemployment-Related Assistance System of Hong Kong*. Research and Libary Services Division, Legislative Council Secretariat. www.legco.gov.hk/yr99-oo/english/sec/library/e19.pdf.

Lester, David, and Bijou Yang. 1998. *Suicide and Homicide in the Twentieth Century: Changes over Time*. Hauppauge, NY: Nova Science Publishers.

Lind, Jo Thori. 2005. "Why Is There So Little Redistribution?" *Nordic Journal of Political Economy* 31: 111–25.

Lindbeck, Assar, and Dennis J. Snower. 1989. *The Insider-Outsider Theory of Employment and Unemployment*. Cambridge, MA: MIT Press.

Lindert, Peter H. 2004. *Growing Public: Social Spending and Economic Growth since the Eighteenth Century*. Cambridge: Cambridge University Press.

Liu, Eva, and Walter Kwong. 2000. *Unemployment-Related Benefits Systems in Malaysia*. Research and Libary Services Division, Legislative Council Secretariat. www.legco.gov.hk/yr99-oo/english/sec/library/e22.pdf.

Luo, Feijun et al. 2011. "Impact of Business Cycles on US Suicide Rates, 1928–2007." *American Journal of Public Health* 101(6): 1139–46.

Lupu, Noam, and Jonas Pontusson. 2011. "The Structure of Inequality and the Politics of Redistribution." *American Political Science Review* 105(2): 316–36.

Luttmer, Erzo F. P. 2001. "Group Loyalty and the Taste for Redistribution." *Journal of Political Economy* 109(3): 500–528.

Malherbet, Franck, and Mustafa Ulus. 2003. *Unemployment Insurance and Labor Reallocation*. Centre de Recherche en Economie et Statistique. Working Paper.

Manza, Jeff. 1993. "Four Theories of Political Change and the Origins of the New Deal Labor Legislation." *Research in Political Sociology* 6: 71–115.

2000. "Political Sociological Models of the U.S. New Deal." *Annual Review of Sociology* 26: 297–322.

Mares, Isabela. 2003. *The Politics of Social Risk: Business and Welfare State Development*. Cambridge: Cambridge University Press.

2004. "Economic Insecurity and Social Policy Expansion: Evidence from Interwar Europe." *International Organization* 58(4): 745–74.

Marshall, Monty G., Ted Robert Gurr, and Keith Jaggers. 2012. *Polity IV Project: Political Regime Characteristics and Transitions, 1800–2012.*

Marshall, T. H. 1964. *Class, Citizenship, and Social Development.* Garden City, NY: Doubleday.

Martin, Cathie Jo, and Duane Swank. 2004. "Does the Organization of Capital Matter? Employers and Active Labor Market Policy at the National and Firm Levels." *American Political Science Review* 98(4): 593–611.

Mayda, Anna Maria, and Dani Rodrik. 2005. "Why Are Some People (and Countries) More Protectionist than Others?" *European Economic Review* 49(6): 1393–1430.

Mazza, Jacqueline. 2000. *Unemployment Insurance: Case Studies and Lessons for Latin America and the Caribbean.* Washington, DC: InterAmerican Development Bank, Working Paper No. 411.

McCarty, Nolan, Keith T. Poole, and Howard Rosenthal. 2006. *Polarized America: The Dance of Ideology and Unequal Riches.* Cambridge, MA: MIT Press.

McGuire, James W. 2010. *Wealth, Health, and Democracy in East Asia and Latin America.* Cambridge: Cambridge University Press.

McPherson, Miller, Lynn Smith-Lovin, and James M Cook. 2001. "Birds of a Feather: Homophily in Social Networks." *Annual Review of Sociology* 27(1): 415–44.

Meltzer, Allan H., and Scott F. Richard. 1981. "A Rational Theory of the Size of Government." *Journal of Political Economy* 89(5): 914–27.

Meyer, Peter B., and Anastasiya M. Osborne. 2005. "Proposed Category System for 1960–2000 Census Occupations." *BLS Working Paper* (383).

Miller, D. T., and R. K. Ratner. 1996. "The Power of the Myth of Self-Interest." In *Current Societal Issues about Justice*, eds. Leo Montada and Melvin J. Lerner. New York: Plenum Press, 25–48.

Miron, Jeffrey A., and David N. Weil. 1998. "The Genesis and Evolution of Social Security." In *The Defining Moment: The Great Depression and the American Economy in the Twentieth Century*, eds. Michael D. Bordo, Claudia Goldin, and Eugene White. Chicago: University of Chicago Press, 297–322. www.nber.org/chapters/c6891.

Mitani, Naoki. 2010. "Employment Insurance and Active Labor Market Programs in Japan." In *Towards a More Resilient Society: Lessons from Economic Crises Report of the Social Resilience Project*, ed. Japan Institute of International Affairs. Tokyo: Japan National Committee for Pacific Economic Cooperation, 283–308.

Mitchell, Brian. 2013. *International Historical Statistics.* Basingstoke, UK: Palgrave/Macmillan.

Moene, Karl O., and Michael Wallerstein. 2001. "Inequality, Social Insurance, and Redistribution." *American Political Science Review* 95(4): 859–74.

2003. "Earnings Inequality and Welfare Spending: A Disaggregated Analysis." *World Politics* 55(July): 485–516.

Mughan, Anthony. 2007. "Economic Insecurity and Welfare Preferences: A Micro-Level Analysis." *Comparative Politics* 39(3): 293–310.

Mughan, Anthony, and Dean Lacy. 2002. "Economic Performance, Job Insecurity and Electoral Choice." *British Journal of Political Science* 32(3): 513–33.

Mughan, Anthony, C. Bean, and I. McAllister. 2003. "Economic Globalization, Job Insecurity and the Populist Reaction." *Electoral Studies* 22(4): 617–33.

Mutz, Diana C. 1993. "Direct and Indirect Routes to Politicizing Personal Experience: Does Knowledge Make a Difference?" *Public Opinion Quarterly* 57(4): 483–502.

1998. *Impersonal Influence: How Perceptions of Mass Collectives Affect Political Attitudes*. Cambridge: Cambridge University Press.

Mutz, Diana C., and Jeffery J. Mondak. 1997. "Dimensions of Sociotropic Behavior: Group-Based Judgements of Fairness and Well-Being." *American Journal of Political Science* 41(1): 284–308.

Myles, John, and Jill Quadagno. 2002. "Political Theories of the Welfare State." *Social Service Review* 76(1): 34–57.

Neugart, Michael. 2005a. "Unemployment Insurance: The Role of Electoral Systems and Regional Labour Markets." *European Journal of Political Economy* 21(4): 815–29.

2005b. "Why German Labour Market Reform Has Begun." *Economic Affairs* 25(3): 11–16.

OECD. 2008. *Growing Unequal? Income Distribution and Poverty in OECD Countries*. Paris: OECD.

2011. *Government at a Glance 2011*. Paris: OECD.

2013. *Pensions at a Glance 2013*. Paris: OECD.

2014. *Pension Markets in Focus 2014*. Paris: OECD.

Oesch, Daniel. 2013. *Occupational Change in Europe: How Technology and Education Transform the Job Structure*. Oxford: Oxford University Press.

Olofsson, Anna, and Saman Rashid. 2011. "The White (Male) Effect and Risk Perception: Can Equality Make a Difference?" *Risk Analysis* 31(6): 1016–32.

Orloff, Ann Shola, and Theda Skocpol. 1984. "Why Not Equal Protection? Explaining the Politics of Public Social Spending in Britain, 1900–1911, and the United States, 1880s–1920." *American Sociological Review* 49(6): 726–50.

Overbye, Einar. 1995. "Explaining Welfare Spending." *Public Choice* 83(3–4): 313–35.

Ozkan, Umut Riza. 2013. "Translating Travelling Ideas: The Introduction of Unemployment Insurance in Turkey." *Global Social Policy* 13(3): 239–60.

Pallage, Stéphane, and Christian Zimmermann. 2005. "Heterogeneous Labor Markets and Generosity towards the Unemployed: An International Perspective." *Journal of Comparative Economics* 33(1): 88–106.

2006. "On Voters' Attitudes towards Unemployment Insurance Subsidies across Regions: A Canadian Simulation." *Journal of Population Economics* 19(2): 391–410.

Parijs, Philippe van. 1997. *Real Freedom for All: What (If Anything) Can Justify Capitalism?* Oxford, UK: Clarendon Press.

Peacock, Alan T., and Jack Wiseman. 1961. *The Growth of Public Expenditure in the United Kingdom*. Princeton, NJ: Princeton University Press.

Pecoraro, Brandon. 2014. "Inequality in Democracies: Testing the Classic Democratic Theory of Redistribution." *Economics Letters* 123(3): 398–401.

Perotti, Enrico, and Armin Schwienbacher. 2009. "The Political Origin of Pension Funding." *Journal of Financial Intermediation* 18(3): 384–404.

Picot, Georg. 2012. *Politics of Segmentation: Party Competition and Social Protection in Europe.* London: Routledge.

Pierson, Paul. 1994. *Dismantling the Welfare State? Reagan, Thatcher, and the Politics of Retrenchment.* Cambridge: Cambridge University Press.

———. 1996. "The New Politics of the Welfare State." *World Politics* 48(2): 143–79.

Piketty, Thomas. 1995. "Social Mobility and Redistributive Politics." *Quarterly Journal of Economics* 110(3): 551–84.

———. 2014. *Capital in the Twenty-First Century.* Cambridge, MA: Harvard University Press.

Pitlik, Hans, Gerhard Schwarz, Barbara Bechter, and Bernd Brandl. 2011. "Near Is My Shirt but Nearer Is My Skin: Ideology or Self-Interest as Determinants of Public Opinion on Fiscal Policy Issues." *Kyklos* 64(2): 271–90.

Platt, Stephen. 1984. "Unemployment and Suicidal Behaviour: A Review of the Literature." *Social Science & Medicine* 19(2): 93–115.

Platt, Stephen, and Keith Hawton. 2000. "Suicidal Behaviour and the Labour Market." In *The International Handbook of Suicide and Attempted Suicide,* eds. Keith Hawton and Kees van Heeringen. West Sussex, UK: John Wiley & Sons, 309–84.

Polavieja, Javier G., and Lucinda Platt. 2014. "Nurse or Mechanic? The Role of Parental Socialization and Children's Personality in the Formation of Sex-Typed Occupational Aspirations." *Social Forces* 93(1): 31–61.

Pollak, Andreas. 2007. "Optimal Unemployment Insurance with Heterogeneous Agents." *European Economic Review* 51(8): 2029–53.

Pontusson, Jonas. 1990. "Conditions of Labor-Party Dominance: Sweden and Britain Compared." In *Uncommon Democracies: The One-Party Dominant Regimes,* ed. T. J. Pempel. Ithaca, NY: Cornell University Press, 58–82.

Pryor, Frederic L. 1968. *Public Expenditures in Communist and Capitalist Nations.* London: Unwin.

Quadagno, Jill. 1987. "Theories of the Welfare State." *Annual Review of Sociology* 13(1): 109–28.

Quirk, Victor. 2010. *The Queensland Unemployed Workers Bill of 1919.* Newcastle, UK: Centre of Full Employment and Equity, University of Newcastle: Working Paper No. 10-01.

Rawls, John. 1971. *A Theory of Justice.* Cambridge: Cambridge University Press.

Rehm, Philipp. 2005. "Citizen Support for the Welfare State: Determinants of Preferences for Income Redistribution." *Discussion Paper SP II 2005-02, Wissenschaftszentrum Berlin* [dx.doi.org/10.2139/ssrn.670761].

———. 2008. "Risk Inequality: Social Policy and Polarization by Popular Demand." Dissertation (*Duke University*).

———. 2009. "Risks and Redistribution: An Individual-Level Analysis." *Comparative Political Studies* 42(7): 855–81.

———. 2011a. "Risk Inequality and the Polarized American Electorate." *British Journal of Political Science* 41(2): 363–87.

2011b. "Social Policy by Popular Demand." *World Politics* 63(2): 271–99.

Rehm, Philipp, Jacob S. Hacker, and Mark Schlesinger. 2012. "Insecure Alliances: Risk, Inequality, and Support for the Welfare State." *American Political Science Review* 106(2): 386–406.

Rimlinger, Gaston V. 1971. *Welfare Policy and Industrialization in Europe, America, and Russia.* New York: Wiley.

Rockoff, Hugh. 1998. "By Way of Analogy: The Expansion of the Federal Government in the 1930s." In *The Defining Moment: The Great Depression and the American Economy in the Twentieth Century*, eds. Michael D. Bordo, Claudia Goldin, and Eugene White. Chicago: University of Chicago Press, 125–54. www.nber.org/chapters/c6891.

Rodrik, Dani. 1998. "Why Do More Open Economies Have Bigger Governments?" *Journal of Political Economy* 106(5): 997–1032.

Rueda, David. 2005. "Insider–Outsider Politics in Industrialized Democracies: The Challenge to Social Democratic Parties." *American Political Science Review* 99(1): 61–74.

2007. *Social Democracy Inside Out: Partisanship and Labor Market Policy in Advanced Industrialized Democracies.* Oxford: Oxford University Press.

2013. "Food Comes First, Then Morals? Redistribution Preferences, Altruism, and Group Heterogeneity in Western Europe." Manuscript.

Rueda, David, and Daniel Stegmueller. 2013. *Equality or Crime? Redistribution Preferences and the Externalities of Inequality in Western Europe.* Manuscript.

2014. *Preferences That Matter: Redistribution and Voting in the US.* Manuscript.

Ruggles, Steven et al. 2010. *Integrated Public Use Microdata Series: Version 5.0 [Machine-Readable Database].* Minneapolis: Minnesota Population Center [producer and distributor].

Saint-Paul, Gilles. 1996. "Exploring the Political Economy of Labour Market Institutions." *Economic Policy* 11(23): 263–315.

2000. *The Political Economy of Labour Market Institutions.* Oxford: Oxford University Press.

Schaeffer, Noel Edward. 2008. *Models of Risk Perception and Risky Choice: Theoretical Modeling and Empirical Testing in Hypothetical and Real-Life Situations.* Dissertation (*University of South Dakota*).

Scharpf, Fritz W. 1988. "The Joint-Decision Trap: Lessons from German Federalism and European Integration." *Public Administration* 66(3): 239–78.

Scheve, Kenneth, and David Stasavage. 2006. "Religion and Preferences for Social Insurance." *Quarterly Journal of Political Science* 1(3): 255–86.

2009. "Institutions, Partisanship, and Inequality in the Long Run." *World Politics* 61(2): 215–53.

2010. "The Conscription of Wealth: Mass Warfare and the Demand for Progressive Taxation." *International Organization* 64(4): 529–61.

2012. "Democracy, War, and Wealth: Lessons from Two Centuries of Inheritance Taxation." *American Political Science Review* 106(1): 81–102.

Scheve, Kenneth, and Matthew J. Slaughter. 2001. "What Determines Individual Trade-Policy Preferences?" *Journal of International Economics* 54(2): 267–92.

Schlozman, Kay Lehman, and Sidney Verba. 1979. *Injury to Insult: Unemployment, Class, and Political Response.* Cambridge, MA: Harvard University Press.

Scholz, Wolfgang, Florence Bonnet, and Ellen Ehmke. 2011. "Income Support in Times of Global Crisis: An Assessment of the Role of Unemployment Insurance and Options for Coverage Extension in Asia." In *Poverty and Sustainable Development in Asia: Impacts and Responses to the Global Economic Crisis*, eds. Armin Bauer and Myo Thant. Manila: Asian Development Bank, 341–66.

Schopenhauer, Arthur. 1973. *Essays and Aphorisms.* Reissue ed. Harmondsworth, UK: Penguin Classics.

Schustereder, Ingmar J. 2010. *Historical Phases of Welfare State Development.* Wiesbaden: Gabler.

Schwander, Hanna, and Philip Manow. 2014. "'Modernize and Die'? German Social Democracy and the Electoral Consequences of the Agenda 2010." *Paper Presented at the 21th Conference for European Studies* (Washington, DC, March 14–16, 2014).

Scruggs, Lyle. 2004. *Comparative Welfare Entitlements Dataset.* Hartford: University of Connecticut: sp.uconn.edu/~scruggs/wp.htm.

Scruggs, Lyle, and James Allan. 2006. "Welfare-State Decommodification in 18 OECD Countries: A Replication and Revision." *Journal of European Social Policy* 16(1): 55–72.

Sears, David O., and Carolyn L. Funk. 1990a. "Self-Interest in Americans' Political Opinions." In *Beyond Self-Interest*, ed. Jane J. Mansbridge. Chicago: University of Chicago Press, 147–70.

1990b. "The Limited Effect of Economic Self-Interest on the Political Attitudes of the Mass Public." *Journal of Behavioral Economics* 19(3): 247–71.

1991. "The Role of Self-Interest in Social and Political Attitudes." *Advances in Experimental Social Psychology* 24(1): 1–91.

Seeleib-Kaiser, Martin, and Timo Fleckenstein. 2007. "Discourse, Learning and Welfare State Change: The Case of German Labour Market Reforms." *Social Policy & Administration* 41(5): 427–48.

Shayo, Moses. 2009. "A Model of Social Identity with an Application to Political Economy: Nation, Class, and Redistribution." *American Political Science Review* 103(2): 147–74.

Shin, Dong-Myeon. 2000. "Financial Crisis and Social Security: The Paradox of the Republic of Korea." *International Social Security Review* 53(3): 83–107.

Sinn, Hans-Werner. 1995. "A Theory of the Welfare State." *Scandinavian Journal of Economics* 97(4): 495–526.

1996. "Social Insurance, Incentives and Risk Taking." *International Tax and Public Finance* 3(3): 259–80.

Sjöberg, Lennart. 1996. "A Discussion of the Limitations of the Psychometric and Cultural Theory Approaches to Risk Perception." *Radiation Protection Dosimetry* 68(3–4): 219–25.

1998a. "World Views, Political Attitudes and Risk Perception." *Risk: Health, Safety & Environment* 9(Spring): 137–52.

1998b. "Worry and Risk Perception." *Risk Analysis* 18(1): 85–93.

2000. "Factors in Risk Perception." *Risk Analysis* 20(1): 1–12.

2006. "Rational Risk Perception: Utopia or Dystopia?" *Journal of Risk Research* 9(6): 683–96.

Skocpol, Theda. 1980. "Political Response to Capitalist Crisis: Neo-Marxist Theories of the State and the Case of the New Deal." *Politics & Society* 10(2): 155–201.

Slovic, Paul. 1987. "Perception of Risk." *Science* 236(4799): 280–85.

Smith, Tom W., Peter V. Marsden, Michael Hout, and Jibum Kim. 2011. *General Social Surveys, 1972–2010 [machine-Readable Data File]*. Principal Investigator, Tom W. Smith; Co-Principal Investigator, Peter V. Marsden; Co-Principal Investigator, Michael Hout; Sponsored by National Science Foundation. NORC ed. Chicago: National Opinion Research Center [producer]; Storrs, CT: The Roper Center for Public Opinion Research, University of Connecticut [distributor].

Social Security Board. 1937. *Social Security in America: The Factual Background of the Social Security Act as Summarized from Staff Reports to the Committee on Economic Security*. Washington, DC: U.S. Government Printing Office. www.ssa.gov/history/reports/ces/cesbook.html.

Sonneck, Gernot, Claudius Stein, and Martin Voracek. 2003. *Suizide von Männern in Österreich*. Wien: Bundesministeriun für soziale Sicherheit, Generationen und Konsumentenschutz.

Stack, Steven. 2000. "Suicide: A 15-Year Review of the Sociological Literature. Part I: Cultural and Economic Factors." *Suicide and Life-Threatening Behavior* 30(2): 145–62.

Stephens, John D. 1979. *The Transition from Capitalism to Socialism*. New York: Macmillan.

Stewart, Bryce Morrison et al. 1938. *Planning and Administration of Unemployment Compensation in the United States: A Sampling of Beginnings*. New York: Industrial Relations Counselors.

Stiller, Sabina Johanna. 2007. *Innovative Agents versus Immovable Objects: The Role of Ideational Leadership in German Welfare State Reforms*. Nijmegen: Radboud University.

Stimson, James A., Michael B. Mackuen, and Robert S. Erikson. 1995. "Dynamic Representation." *The American Political Science Review* 89(3): 543–65.

Stone, Randall W. 2009. "Risk in International Politics." *Global Environmental Politics* 9(3): 40–60.

Streeck, Wolfgang, and Christine Trampusch. 2005. "Economic Reform and the Political Economy of the German Welfare State." *German Politics* 14(2): 174–95.

Svallfors, Stefan. 1995. *In the Eye of the Beholder. Opinions on Welfare and Justice in Comparative Perspective*. Umea: Scandbook.

Swaan, Abram de. 1988. *In Care of the State: Health Care, Education and Welfare in Europe and the USA in the Modern Era*. Oxford: Oxford University Press.

Swank, Duane, and Cathie Jo Martin. 2001. "Employers and the Welfare State: The Political Economic Organization of Firms and Social Policy in Contemporary Capitalist Democracies." *Comparative Political Studies* 34(8): 889–923.

Swenson, Peter A. 2002. *Capitalists against Markets: The Making of Labor Markets and Welfare States in the United States and Sweden*. Oxford: Oxford University Press.

Tansel, Aysit, and H. Mehmet Tasci. 2010. *Hazard Analysis of Unemployment Duration by Gender in a Developing Country: The Case of Turkey*. Rochester, NY: Social Science Research Network. SSRN Scholarly Paper.

Tanzi, Vito, and Ludger Schuknecht. 2000. *Public Spending in the 20th Century: A Global Perspective*. Cambridge: Cambridge University Press.

Taylor-Gooby, Peter. 2005. *New Risks, New Welfare: The Transformation of the European Welfare State*. Oxford: Oxford University Press.

Thelen, Kathleen. 2010. "Economic Regulation and Social Solidarity: Conceptual and Analytic Innovations in the Study of Advanced Capitalism." *Socio-Economic Review* 8(1): 187–207.

Thomas, Kyla, and David Gunnell. 2010. "Suicide in England and Wales 1861–2007: A Time-Trends Analysis." *International Journal of Epidemiology* 39(6): 1464–75.

Titmuss, Richard Morris. 1959. "War and Social Policy." In *Essays on the Welfare State*, New Haven, CT: Yale University Press, 75–87.

Tsebelis, George. 2003. *Veto Players: How Political Institutions Work*. Princeton, NJ: Princeton University Press.

Tufte, Edward R. 2003. *The Cognitive Style of PowerPoint*. Cheshire, CT: Graphics Press.

Tunali, Insan. 2003. *Background Study on Labour Market and Employment in Turkey*. Torino: European Training Foundation.

U.S. Census Bureau. 1937. *Statistical Abstract of the United States 1937*. Washington, DC: U.S. Government Printing Office.

Usui, Chikako. 1994. "Welfare State Development in a World System Context: Event History Analysis of First Social Insurance Legislation." In *The Comparative Political Economy of the Welfare State*, eds. Thomas Janoski and Alexander M. Hicks. Cambridge: Cambridge University Press, 254–77.

Vandenberg, Paul. 2010. "Is Asia Adopting Flexicurity?" *International Labour Review* 149(1): 31–58.

Van Kersbergen, Kees. 1995. *Social Capitalism: A Study of Christian Democracy and the Welfare State*. London: Routledge.

Van Kersbergen, Kees, and Philip Manow. 2008. "The Welfare State." In *Comparative Politics*, ed. Danièle Caramani. Oxford: Oxford University Press, 445–72.

Van Kersbergen, Kees, and Uwe Becker. 2002. "Comparative Politics and the Welfare State." In *Comparative Democratic Politics: A Guide to Contemporary Theory and Research*, ed. Hans Keman. Beverly Hills, CA: Sage, 185–212.

Vis, Barbara, Kees Van Kersbergen, and Tom Hylands. 2011. "To What Extent Did the Financial Crisis Intensify the Pressure to Reform the Welfare State?" *Social Policy & Administration* 45(4): 338–53.

Vliet, Olaf Van, and Koen Caminada. 2012. "Unemployment Replacement Rates Dataset among 34 Welfare States 1971–2009: An Update, Extension and Modification of the Scruggs' Welfare State Entitlements Data Set." *NEU-JOBS Special Report*, Leiden University.

Vodopivec, Milan. 2013. "Introducing Unemployment Insurance to Developing Countries." *IZA Journal of Labor Policy* 2(1): 1–23.

Voth, Hans-Joachim. 2002. "Why Was Stock Market Volatility So High during the Great Depression? Evidence from 10 Countries during the Interwar Period." *CEPR Discussion Paper* 3254.

Vroman, Wayne. 2004. *International Evidence on Unemployment Compensation Prevalence and Costs*. Manuscript, Urban Institute.

———. 2007. "Replacement Rates and UC Benefit Generosity." Manuscript, Urban Institute.

Wai-lam, Cheung. 2000. *Unemployment-Related Benefits Systems in Singapore*. Research and Libary Services Division, Legislative Council Secretariat. www.legco.gov.hk/yr99-oo/english/sec/library/e17.pdf.

Wallerstein, Michael. 1990. "Centralized Bargaining and Wage Restraint." *American Journal of Political Science* 34(4): 982–1004.

Wanberg, Connie R. 2012. "The Individual Experience of Unemployment." *Annual Review of Psychology* 63(1): 369–96.

Weber, Axel. 2010. *Social Protection in Case of Unemployment in the Philippines*. Geneva: ILO.

Weber, Elke U., and Jessica S. Ancker. 2011. "Risk Perceptions and Risk Attitudes in the United States and Europe." In *The Reality of Precaution: Comparing Risk Regulation in the United States and Europe*, eds. Jonathan Baert Wiener, Michael D. Rogers, James K. Hammitt, and Peter H. Sand. Washington, DC: RFF Press, 480–91.

Wibbels, Erik, and Kenneth Roberts. 2010. "The Politics of Economic Crisis in Latin America." *Studies in Comparative International Development* 45(4): 383–409.

Wildavsky, Aaron, and Karl Dake. 1990. "Theories of Risk Perception: Who Fears What and Why?" *Daedalus* 119(4): 41–60.

Wilensky, Harold L. 1975. *The Welfare State and Equality: Structural and Ideological Roots of Public Expenditures*. Berkeley: University of California Press.

Wilper, Andrew P. et al. 2009. "Health Insurance and Mortality in US Adults." *American Journal of Public Health* 99(12): 2289–95.

Wlezien, Christopher. 2004. "Patterns of Representation: Dynamics of Public Preferences and Policy." *Journal of Politics* 66(1): 1–24.

World Health Organization. 1956. *Epidemiological and Vital Statistics Report*. Geneva: : World Health Organization.

———. 2014. *WHO Mortality Database (25 February 2014 Update)*. Geneva: World Health Organization.

Wray, Matt, Cynthia Colen, and Bernice Pescosolido. 2011. "The Sociology of Suicide." *Annual Review of Sociology* 37(1): 505–28.

Wren, Anne. 2013. *The Political Economy of the Service Transition*. Oxford: Oxford University Press.

Wright, Erik Olin, and Rachel Dwyer. 2003. "The Patterns of Job Expansions in the United States, a Comparison of the 1960s and 1990s." *Socio-Economic Review* 1(3): 289–325.

Wright, Randall. 1986. "The Redistributive Roles of Unemployment Insurance and the Dynamics of Voting." *Journal of Public Economics* 31(3): 377–99.

Yap, Mui Teng. 2002. *Employment Insurance: A Safety Net for the Unemployed.* Institute of Policy Studies, Report Prepared for the Remaking Singapore Committee.

Yi, Ilcheong, and Byung-hee Lee. 2005. "Development Strategies and Unemployment Policies in Korea." In *Transforming the Developmental Welfare State in East Asia*, ed. Huck-ju Kwon. London: Palgrave Macmillan, 143–69.

Yoo, Kil-Sang. 1999. *The Employment Insurance System in Korea.* Seoul: Korea Labor Institute.

Ziblatt, Daniel. 2002. "Recasting German Federalism?" *Politische Vierteljahresschrift* 43(4): 624–52.

# Index

Other Books in the Series (*continued from page ii*)

James Mahoney, *Colonialism and Postcolonial Development: Spanish America in Comparative Perspective*

James Mahoney and Dietrich Rueschemeyer, eds., *Comparative Historical Analysis in the Social Sciences*

Scott Mainwaring and Matthew Soberg Shugart, eds., *Presidentialism and Democracy in Latin America*

Isabela Mares, *From Open Secrets to Secret Voting: Democratic Electoral Reforms and Voter Autonomy*

Isabela Mares, *The Politics of Social Risk: Business and Welfare State Development*

Isabela Mares, *Taxation, Wage Bargaining, and Unemployment*

Cathie Jo Martin and Duane Swank, *The Political Construction of Business Interests: Coordination, Growth, and Equality*

Anthony W. Marx, *Making Race, Making Nations: A Comparison of South Africa, the United States, and Brazil*

Bonnie M. Meguid, *Party Competition between Unequals: Strategies and Electoral Fortunes in Western Europe*

Joel S. Migdal, *State in Society: Studying How States and Societies Constitute One Another*

Joel S. Migdal, Atul Kohli, and Vivienne Shue, eds., *State Power and Social Forces: Domination and Transformation in the Third World*

Scott Morgenstern and Benito Nacif, eds., *Legislative Politics in Latin America*

Kevin M. Morrison, *Nontaxation and Representation: The Fiscal Foundations of Political Stability*

Layna Mosley, *Global Capital and National Governments*

Layna Mosley, *Labor Rights and Multinational Production*

Wolfgang C. Müller and Kaare Strøm, *Policy, Office, or Votes?*

Maria Victoria Murillo, *Political Competition, Partisanship, and Policy Making in Latin American Public Utilities*

Maria Victoria Murillo, *Labor Unions, Partisan Coalitions, and Market Reforms in Latin America*

Monika Nalepa, *Skeletons in the Closet: Transitional Justice in Post-Communist Europe*

Ton Notermans, *Money, Markets, and the State: Social Democratic Economic Policies since 1918*

Eleonora Pasotti, *Political Branding in Cities: The Decline of Machine Politics in Bogotá, Naples, and Chicago*

Aníbal Pérez-Liñán, *Presidential Impeachment and the New Political Instability in Latin America*

Roger D. Petersen, *Understanding Ethnic Violence: Fear, Hatred, and Resentment in Twentieth-Century Eastern Europe*

Roger D. Petersen, *Western Intervention in the Balkans: The Strategic Use of Emotion in Conflict*

Simona Piattoni, ed., *Clientelism, Interests, and Democratic Representation*

Paul Pierson, *Dismantling the Welfare State?: Reagan, Thatcher, and the Politics of Retrenchment*

Marino Regini, *Uncertain Boundaries: The Social and Political Construction of European Economies*

Kenneth M. Roberts, *Changing Course in Latin America: Party Systems in the Neoliberal Era*

Marc Howard Ross, *Cultural Contestation in Ethnic Conflict*

Ben Ross Schneider, *Hierarchical Capitalism in Latin America: Business, Labor, and the Challenges of Equitable Development*

Lyle Scruggs, *Sustaining Abundance: Environmental Performance in Industrial Democracies*

Jefferey M. Sellers, *Governing from Below: Urban Regions and the Global Economy*

Yossi Shain and Juan Linz, eds., *Interim Governments and Democratic Transitions*

Beverly Silver, *Forces of Labor: Workers' Movements and Globalization since 1870*

Prerna Singh, *How Solidarity Works for Welfare: Subnationalism and Social Development in India*

Theda Skocpol, *Social Revolutions in the Modern World*

Dan Slater, *Ordering Power: Contentious Politics and Authoritarian Leviathans in Southeast Asia*

Regina Smyth, *Candidate Strategies and Electoral Competition in the Russian Federation: Democracy Without Foundation*

Richard Snyder, *Politics after Neoliberalism: Reregulation in Mexico*

David Stark and László Bruszt, *Postsocialist Pathways: Transforming Politics and Property in East Central Europe*

Sven Steinmo, *The Evolution of Modern States: Sweden, Japan, and the United States*

Sven Steinmo, Kathleen Thelen, and Frank Longstreth, eds., *Structuring Politics: Historical Institutionalism in Comparative Analysis*

Susan C. Stokes, *Mandates and Democracy: Neoliberalism by Surprise in Latin America*

Susan C. Stokes, ed., *Public Support for Market Reforms in New Democracies*

Susan C. Stokes, Thad Hall, Marcelo Nazareno, and Valeria Brusco, *Brokers, Voters, and Clientelism: The Puzzle of Distributive Politics*

Duane Swank, *Global Capital, Political Institutions, and Policy Change in Developed Welfare States*

Sidney Tarrow, *Power in Movement: Social Movements and Contentious Politics, Revised and Updated 3rd Edition*

Tariq Thachil, *Elite Parties, Poor Voters: How Social Services Win Votes in India*

Kathleen Thelen, *How Institutions Evolve: The Political Economy of Skills in Germany, Britain, the United States, and Japan*

Kathleen Thelen, *Varieties of Liberalization and the New Politics of Social Solidarity*

Charles Tilly, *Trust and Rule*

Daniel Treisman, *The Architecture of Government: Rethinking Political Decentralization*

Guillermo Trejo, *Popular Movements in Autocracies: Religion, Repression, and Indigenous Collective Action in Mexico*

Lily Lee Tsai, *Accountability without Democracy: How Solidary Groups Provide Public Goods in Rural China*